THE
FISHERMAN'S
BEDSIDE BOOK

'No life, my honest scholar, no life so happy and so
pleasant as the life of a well-governed angler; for
when the lawyer is swallowed up with business,
the statesman in preventing or contriving plots,
then we sit on cowslip banks, hear the birds sing,
and possess ourselves in as much quietness as
these silent silver streams, which we now see glide
so quietly by us.'

ISAAK WALTON, *Compleat Angler*

'. . . We sit on cowslip banks'

THE FISHERMAN'S BEDSIDE BOOK

Compiled by
'BB'

Illustrated by
DENYS WATKINS-PITCHFORD
F.R.S.A., A.R.C.A.

Foreword by
IAN NIALL

White Lion Books
CAMBRIDGE

White Lion Books
an imprint of
Colt Books Ltd
9 Clarendon Road
Cambridge CB2 2BH
Tel: 01223 357047 Fax: 01223 365866

This edition first published by
White Lion Books 1993
Reprinted 1994, 1996, 1998, 2000

Compilation © 1945 and 1955 'BB'
and © 1993 The Estate of D. J. Watkins-Pitchford
Illustrations © 1945 Denys Watkins-Pitchford
and © 1993 The Estate of Denys Watkins-Pitchford
Foreword © Ian Niall 1993

ISBN 1 874762 02 3

British Library Cataloguing-in-Publication Data
A catalogue record for this book is available from the
British Library

Designed by Clare Byatt

Typeset in 10/12 Palatino by Goodfellow & Egan Ltd, Cambridge

Printed in Great Britain by Biddles Ltd, *www.biddles.co.uk*

CONTENTS

TROUT

COARSE FISH

CARP

TENCH

BARBEL

PERCH

ROACH

BREAM

PIKE

CHUB

SEA FISHING

FISHERMEN'S HAUNTS

FOREWORD

by Ian Niall

'BB''s pseudonym was adopted from the cartridge box, the shot size favoured by wildfowlers and marsh shooters, but he was much more than a man of the marsh and the fen. He was a wonderful observer of nature. He wrote evocatively of fishing and shooting. His children's books are justly famous. He trained as an artist in Paris and London, and was a fellow of the Royal Society of Art and an Associate of the Royal College of Art. For many years he taught art at Rugby School.

Most writers are compelled to accept the images supplied by illustrators chosen by their publishers. All too often the artwork is far from the writer's conception. But 'BB' had no difficulty here. He suffered no frustration, except from the occasional filling-in that might result from the use of a poor quality paper or the clogging up of old blocks. He could look at the reeds and rushes, the ancient, pollarded willow by the pool and the duck shedding water droplets from frantically beating wings as it sprang into the air. What he saw he could both describe in words and bring to life in one of his inimicable illustrations.

The Fisherman's Bedside Book is packed with angling anecdotes edited with great skill. Many of the writers whose work 'BB' selected had already gone to their long home, Francis Francis, Cholmondeley Pennel, Richard Jefferies, W.H. Hudson, Charles St John, G.E.M. Skues and Abel Chapman. Since 1945, when this Bedside Book first appeared, many more of the contributors have joined them. But their love of fishing, a bond uniting them with fishermen of today, lives on in this varied and vivid collection of fishing stories. Arthur Ransome was unstinting in his praise. He said *The Fisherman's Bedside Book* was the best fishing anthology he had ever read.

For my part 'BB''s *Confessions of a Carp Fisher* was his most enchanting book, although I was never going to be a carp-catcher. Only Negley Farson produced anything quite as magical. Like 'BB''s *Confessions, Going Fishing* was a book that prompted thousands of readers to reach for a rod or go out and buy one. Two extracts from *Going Fishing* are included in this anthology. And 'BB' has brought together a generous collection of carp fishing pieces.

I read the *Confessions of a Carp Fisher* when I moved to Wales, a long time ago. When, later on, I moved south and looked for a place to cast a fly I found one about thirty miles away and hadn't been fishing there for very long before I discovered I was walking in the footsteps of 'BB' and his disciple, Richard Walker. Both are still spoken of with reverence by the old hands in that part of the world. When 'BB''s eightieth birthday was approaching I received an invitation to a celebration put on by some of his friends, but I was unable to be there on that particular day. I greatly regret not having met him, a man with whom I had shared so many dreams. Through his writing I have sat with him on his carp fishing vigils with the heavens dotted with stars. We have both listened to the frogs croaking and the rasping voice of a mallard drake.

One of 'BB''s books that came to me a few years ago was *The Quiet Fields* and advertised on the jacket was *Ramblings of a Sportsman Naturalist* with a review quotation I had written at the time of its publication. Yet again 'BB' had written and illustrated another book that demonstrated his artistry and endorsed his reputation not only as a naturalist and a sportsman but as a man with certain poetic flair. Like *Ramblings of a Sportsman Naturalist* it is of the pure ore he has mined for years. The output of this man of the fields was prodigious. We all have our 'BB' favourites and some of mine include: *The Sportsman's Bedside Book* (1937), *Wild Lone* (1939), *Manka* (1939), *Idle Countryman* (1943), *The Wayfaring Tree* (1945), *Shooting Man's Bedside Book* (1948), *Confessions of a Carp Fisher* (1950), *Dark Estuary* (1952), *A Summer on The Nene*, (1967), *Recollections of a Longshore Gunner* (1976), *Ramblings of a Sportsman Naturalist* (1979), *The Naturalist's Bedside Book* (1980), *The Quiet Fields* (1981). He also wrote many books for children including *The Little Grey Men* (1941) for which he was awarded The Carnegie Medal.

Of them all, *Confessions of a Carp Fisher* has become the most sought after book by 'BB' since his death in 1990 and is a highly-prized item among collectors. To my chagrin the person to whom I loaned my copy didn't think to bring it back or confess that they had appropriated it. I am quite sure that his work will be recognised long after I am gone, for he must be ranked with White of Selborne as an observer of the minute – the fine detail – that makes a naturalist of the first order.

INTRODUCTION

ALL fishermen are not liars and this book sets out to prove it. In these pages will be found, scattered here and there, authentic accounts of the capture of record fish and very big fish, both game and coarse, during the last century. As far as possible I have shamelessly skimmed the cream from most of the well-written angling books I could lay my hands upon, but, owing to space, I have had to omit a great deal of excellent writing.

In addition to classic accounts by well-known authors there are stories by ordinary anglers who make no pretence at authorship. They tell, in straightforward language, their own accounts of their battles with big fish and some of these make good reading indeed. Anglers in all walks of life have contributed and this is as it should be, for all belong to the Brotherhood, whether he be salmon fisher or humble angler for roach. There are not many books for the 'poor man' fisher, which is a pity, for the latter are by far in the majority.

Sea fishing I have barely touched upon, but if ever a second edition of this volume be called for, this branch of angling might be dealt with more fully; nor have I dealt with eels, or any of the lesser fish.

Though fishermen have the reputation for telling tales of their prowess I found it by no means easy to get the actual stories for this book. I must confess that this came as a great surprise to me. Despite the fact I inserted letters in *The Field*, and the leading fishing journals asking for good stories of big fish, surprisingly few replies were received. I even circulated angling clubs, some hundreds odd, and only three replied.

I can only think that fishermen are afraid of being laughed at and accused of spinning yarns!

After some considerable trouble I managed to contact several holders of fish records and their own stories appear in these pages. But many I could not trace. What of the 39½lb. lake trout caught in Loch Awe in 1886 by Mr. Muir, or the 14lb. trout from Lough Corrib, caught by Mr. Thomas Sullivan in 1934? And that 64lb. salmon from the Tay, captured by a lady in 1922 – *what* a story that would make!

There is a 48lb. pike from Lough Corrib (1905), and that unbeliev-able trout from the Test, caught by Brigadier-General Hickman in 1922. It weighed 18lb. and came from the same pool from which Lady Mount Temple took a 14lb. fish. It is recorded that she first caught an

11lb. trout from this pool but returned it as *it was not the one she was after*, a most sporting gesture which deserves to be put on record for all time! It also shows an intentness of purpose which is lacking in the male.

As for barbel, was there not a 14lb. 8oz. fish caught in the Hampshire Avon in 1933 and an 8lb. chub from Christchurch Avon? And what of that 21lb. sea trout caught in the Frome by Mr. Hardy Corfe in 1918, a fish that rivals any from far Norway's rivers?

Perhaps one day I may get these stories, perhaps readers of this book will send me others. I hope they will. Many good writers on angling have been left out of these pages but that was unavoidable. I have tried to include the perhaps lesser-known writers on fish and fishing matters rather than the obvious classical authors and I believe that, from the point of view of the public, I am right. Isaak Walton and John Cotton are so well known (or ought to be) that most people know their works by heart.

'BB'

Woodford Lodge
Nr Kettering
1945

FISH AND FISHING

Heaven

Fish (fly-replete, in depth of June,
Dawdling away their wat'ry noon)
Ponder deep wisdom, dark or clear,
Each secret fishy hope or fear.
Fish say, they have their Stream and Pond;
But is there anything Beyond?
This life cannot be All, they swear,
For how unpleasant, if it were!
One may not doubt that, somehow, Good
Shall come of Water and of Mud;
And, sure, the reverent eye must see
A Purpose in Liquidity.
We darkly know, by Faith we cry,
The future is not Wholly Dry.
Mud unto mud! – Death eddies near –
Not here the appointed End, not here!
But somewhere, beyond, Space and Time,
Is wetter water, slimier slime!
And there (they trust) there swimmeth One
Who swam ere rivers were begun,
Immense, of fishy form and mind,

1

Squamous, omnipotent, and kind;
And under that Almighty Fin,
The littlest fish may enter in.
Oh! never fly conceals a hook,
Fish say, in the Eternal Brook,
But more than mundane weeds are there,
And mud, celestially fair;
Fat caterpillars drift around,
And Paradisal grubs are found;
Unfading moths, immortal flies,
And the worm that never dies.
And in that Heaven of all their wish,
There shall be no more land, say fish.

RUPERT BROOKE

The Anglers Take Their Ease

LEND me not to another and I will be a quiet companion in all your wanderings. Wherever thou goest there go I, through the eagle's air and over the wide seas; through heat and cold, calm and tempest, and the changing years. When thou layest thyself down upon thy bed when the weary day is over read of me a little and thy dreams shall be sweet; of camp sheathings and murmuring willows, of the weir's thunder, and the bright throats of streams. Ye shall dream of the jewelled fishes that live in those places; of waterfalls, brown burns, and the wild lilies; of the freshness of morning, the burden of noon, and that tranquil hour when cockchafers are abroad and owls and fishes wake to feed.

And so shall ye sleep sweetly for I will ever be beside thee and none shall take me away.

Pisc.
My hostess has two beds, and I know you and I may have the best; we'll rejoice with my brother Peter and his friend, tell tales, or sing ballads, or make a catch, or find some harmless sport to content us, and pass away a little time without offence to God or man.

Ven.
A match, good master, let's go to that house, for the linen looks white, and smells of lavender, and I long to lie in a pair of sheets that smell so; let's be going, good master, for I am hungry again with fishing.

ISAAK WALTON, *Compleat Angler*

2

The Fishes' Element

A S this book concerns fish something must first be said of the world in which they live, and move, and have their being. A curious world it must be, but a very beautiful one. We do not know exactly what a fish can see, whether it can distinguish colour from colour, but we do know that light and shadow affect it, and also vibration. Their range of vision is long. In my own garden I have an ornamental pool in which roach, tench, and sticklebacks live in apparent harmony. It is set in a lawn some ten feet or so from the house and when the sticklebacks are on the surface (in mild weather they are always on the top) they know at once when I appear at either an upper or a lower window. I doubt if they can feel vibration because I have walked quietly to the window. But even (in a manner of speaking) through the double glass of water and window-pane they can see me, and every fish simultaneously dives from view.

This surely shows that their sight is very keen, especially when there is any movement at a *higher level* than themselves. It is natural that this should be so. The kingfishers always have their fishing places on an upper bough, and for uncounted centuries fish have come to suspect danger from above. Even a bird flying over the pool sends every fish down, and in that case, there can be no vibrations transmitted through the earth.

How varied are the haunts and homes of fishes! What greater contrast than the flat fenland dykes – which Mr. Ransome has so aptly likened to flooded railway cuttings – and the clear and joyful mountain torrents of the North! Compare the still lily-studded pool, where the great carp lie basking in the heat of summer, to the lonely loch high up among the peat hags and mountains.

The fishes' world may be as real to them as our own. They have their thickets and trees of weed and root, their own wide sandy plains, their hills and valleys, even their flowers, grasses, and highways.

They have their favourite hiding- and resting-places, their basking and feeding localities, and they, with the rest of animate things, appear to take some sort of delight in living.

It is not very difficult to picture the fishes' world below the roaring weir. Down in those shadowed and ever uneasy depths the great trout and barbel lurk, together with the banded perch. There must be a continuous thunder below the solid sheet of falling water, with bubble chains ever boring and surging upwards, and the water weeds for ever moving on the mossy wooden weir piles. The light

The Fishes' Element

down there must be dim, even when the summer sun shines brightly.

It is not difficult to conjure up the bed of the salmon pool with its multi-coloured shingle, its boulders and smooth sand, all very clean, very bright, scoured by the race of waters over thousands of years.

Bright fish in bright waters, spotted and varnished to match their environment; always, always the sound of the waters, year in, year out.

And the deep and slumberous pool ... no sand or glistening boulders there, no painted pebbles, but deep black mud, the accumulation, perhaps, of centuries, leaf-mould from the park trees about. And no sound of moving waters but a silence and brooding peace, with here and there the circular spots made by the lily leaves above, spots of shade which form good parasols to a basking pike or carp in the dog days.

We can only see the reverse side, as it were, of these different aquatic worlds; the sedges along the margins, the play of light and shadow on the face of the pool or river, the numberless gem-like water plants that flourish with such joyous profusion in summer's high days.

So here are a few descriptions taken from the writings of great men, Thoreau, Richard Jefferies, Hudson and a few lesser stars.

There is peace and contentment to be found beside the waters and even a canal in June is far more beautiful than the dusty highway with all its bustle and noise.

The enjoyment of one's surroundings is not the least fascination about the art of fishing. Who can ever forget the evening walk among the water meadows by the Test, or the still blue massif of some Scottish mountain reflected in the smooth mirror of the loch?

Looking back at the good days and nights of one's angling career these pictures return, taking their place in true perspective, with the splashing, fighting fish as it is drawn towards the net. One of the greatest charms of angling is that fish dwell in the pleasant places, we subconsciously associate them with contentment and peace, with the beauty and loveliness of the earth.

'BB'

No fishing anthology would be complete without including Thoreau's account of fishing in Walden Pond. No other writer who has ever lived portrays the fishes' element more perfectly than Thoreau. There are many pearls within his masterpiece but the greatest of all is the chapter on Walden Pond. It is one of the chapters I read over and over again until I think I know it by heart. It has a rareness about it which cannot be diagnosed. Though Thoreau is describing an American lake, much of what he says holds good for many of our North country inland lochs.

Walden Pond

THE scenery of Walden is on a humble scale, and, though beautiful, does not approach to grandeur, nor can it much concern one who has not long frequented it or lived by its shore; yet this pond is so remarkable for its depth and purity as to merit a particular description. It is a clear and deep green well, half a mile long and a mile and three quarters in circumference, and contains about sixty-one and a half acres; a perennial spring in the midst of pine and oak woods, without any visible inlet or outlet, except by the clouds and evaporation. The surrounding hills rise abruptly from the water to the height of forty to eighty feet, though on the south-west and east they attain to about one hundred and one hundred and fifty feet respectively, within a quarter and a third of a mile. They are exclusively woodland. All our Concord waters have two colours at least, one when viewed at a distance, and another, more proper, close at hand. The first depends more on the light and follows the sky. In clear weather, in summer, they appear blue at a little distance, especially if agitated, and at a great distance all appear alike. In stormy weather they are sometimes a dark slate colour. The sea, however, is said to be blue one day and green another without any perceptible change in the atmosphere. I have seen our river, when the landscape being covered with snow, both water and ice were as green as grass. Some consider blue 'to be the colour of pure water, whether liquid or solid' but, looking directly down into our waters from a boat, they are seen to be of very different colours. Walden is blue at one time and green at another, even from the same point of view. Lying between the earth and the heavens, it partakes of the colour of both. Viewed from a hill-top it reflects the colour of the sky but near at hand it is of a yellowish tint, next the shore where you can see the sand, then a light green, which gradually deepens to a uniform dark green in the body of the pond. In some lights, even from a hill-top, it is a vivid green next the shore. Some have referred this to the reflection of the verdure; but it is equally green there against the railroad sandbank, and in the spring, before the leaves are expanded, and it may be simply the result of the prevailing blue mixed with the yellow of the sand. Such is the colour of its iris. This is that portion also, where in spring, the ice being warmed by the heat of the sun reflected from the bottom and also transmitted through the earth, melts first and forms a narrow canal about the still frozen middle. Like the rest of our waters, when much agitated, in clear weather, so that the surface of the waves may reflect the sky at the right angle, or because there is more light mixed with it, it appears at a little distance of a darker blue than the sky itself; and at such a time, being on its surface, and looking with divided vision, so as to see the reflection, I have discerned a matchless and indescribable light blue, such as watered or changeable silks and sword blades suggest, more cerulean than the sky itself, alternating with the original dark green on the opposite sides of the waves, which last appeared but muddy in comparison. It is a vitreous greenish blue, as I remember it, like those patches of winter sky seen through cloud vistas in the west before sundown.

Yet a single glass of its water held up to the light is as colourless as an equal quantity of air. It is well known that a large plate of glass will have a green tint, owing, as the makers say, to its 'body' but a small piece of the same will be colourless. How large a body of Walden water would be required to reflect a green tint I have never proved.

The water is so transparent that the bottom can easily be discerned at the depth of twenty-five and thirty feet. Paddling over it, you may see many feet beneath the surface, the schools of perch and shiners, perhaps only an inch long, yet the former easily distinguishable by their transverse bars and you think that they must be ascetic fish that find a subsistence there.

Once in the winter, many years ago, when I had been cutting holes through the ice in order to catch pickerel, as I stepped ashore I tossed my axe back on to the ice, but some evil genius had directed it, it slid four or five rods directly into one of the holes, where the water was twenty-five feet deep.

Out of curiosity I lay down on the ice and looked through the hole, until I saw the axe a little on one side, standing on its head, with its helve erect and gently swaying to and fro with the pulse of the pond, and there it might have stood erect and swaying till in the course of time the handle rotted off if I had not disturbed it. Making another hole directly over it with an ice chisel which I had, and cutting down the longest birch which I could find in the neighbourhood with my knife, I made a slip noose, which I attached to its end, and, letting it down carefully, passed it over the knob of the handle, and drew it by a line along the birch, and so pulled the axe out again.

The shore is composed of a belt of smooth rounded white stones like paving stones, excepting one or two short sand beaches, and is so steep that in many places a single leap will carry you into water over your head; and were it not for its remarkable transparency, that would be the last to be seen of its bottom till it rose on the opposite side. Some think it is bottomless. It is nowhere muddy, and a casual observer would say there were no weeds in it; and of noticeable plants, except in the little meadows recently overflowed, which do not properly belong to it, a closer scrutiny does not detect a flag or a bulrush, nor even a lily, yellow or white, but only a few small heart leaves and potamogetons, and perhaps a water target or two; all of which however a bather might not perceive, and these plants are clean and bright like the element they grow in.'

Thoreau goes on to describe the rise and fall of the pond and how these periodic fluctuations stunted the trees and bushes which fringe its shores.

By this fluctuation in the pond asserts its title to the shore, and thus the *shore* is *shorn*, and the trees cannot hold it by right of possession. These are the lips of the lake on which no beard grows. It licks its chaps from time to time. There have been caught in Walden, pickerel, one weighing 7lb. to saying of another which carried off a reel with great velocity, which the fisherman safely set down at 8lb., because he did not see him; perch and pouts, some of each weighing over 2lb., shiners, chivins or roach (*Leiciscus pulchellus*), a very few breams, and a couple of eels, one weighing 4lb. – I am thus particular because the weight of a fish is commonly its only title to fame, and these are the only eels I have heard of here – also I have a faint recollection of a little fish some 5 inches long with silvery sides and a greenish back, somewhat dacelike in character. Nevertheless, this pond is not very fertile in fish. Its pickerel, though not abundant, are its chief boast. I have seen at one time, lying on the ice, pickerel of at least three different kinds, a long shallow one, steel coloured, most like those caught in the river; a bright golden kind, with greenish reflections and remarkably deep, which is the most common here, and another golden-coloured and shaped like the last, but peppered on the sides with small dark brown and black spots, intermixed with a few faint blood red ones, very much like a trout . . . these are all very firm fish and weigh more than their size promises. The shiners, pouts, and perch also, and indeed all the fishes which inhabit this pond, are much cleaner, handsomer and firmer-fleshed, than those in the river and most other ponds, as the water is purer, and they can easily be distinguished from them.

A lake is the landscape's most beautiful and expressive feature. It is the earth's eye, looking into which the beholder measures the depth of his own nature . . . .

An old man who used to frequent the pond nearly sixty winters ago, when it was dark with surrounding forest tells me that in those days he sometimes saw it all alive with ducks and other waterfowl, and that there were many eagles about it. He came here a-fishing, and used an old log canoe which he found on the shore. It was made of two white pine logs dug out and pinned together, and was cut off square at the ends. It was very clumsy but lasted a good many years before it became waterlogged, and perhaps sank to the bottom. He did not know whose it was, it belonged to the pond.

THOREAU, *Walden*

The Trout's 'Window'

THE amount of the surface a trout can see is represented by a more or less circular patch over the head. The deeper the water in which the fish is lying the larger will be this circle and the less distinct (owing to the depth of water between) will anything on that surface appear. The closer to the surface it lies the smaller the area of surface it can see and the clearer its view of any object on that surface.

This circular patch of the surface is known as the 'trout's window,' since through it alone can the fish look upon the outside world. This is an important feature of the trout's underwater world for the angler to realise. As long as he keeps well back from the bank there is every chance of his being beyond the trout's window and consequently out of sight. If he approaches close to the bank he should keep low, drop on one knee, and cast if possible from that position, or take advantage of such cover as the bank affords. Since the outer world cannot well be very distinct to a fish, 'cover' may be taken to include background. An angler clad in sober garb will be much less visible to a fish through its window if he has bushes or a rise in the ground behind him than if he is standing against the skyline, and will also be less visible to a fish if the light is behind him (provided that his shadow does not fall on the water) than if it is in front; this is because the light, if in front of him, is reflected from his figure. It is particularly important if the sun is shining.

Invisibility is probably of more importance in fishing even than good casting.

But the 'trout's window' also explains the behaviour of our fish. Trout instinctively pick the position in the water which is best suited to their immediate purpose. The fish we have been watching poised itself some six or eight inches under the water. This gives it rather a restricted window but a clear view of anything which comes into it. The flies a few yards upstream which could be seen coming down by the angler were quite invisible to the trout until they were a couple of feet or so away; then, and then only, did they come over the trout's horizon, hence its animated movements to and fro as to cover a good breadth of the stream and its appearance of tense anticipation. At any moment a tasty morsel might come into its view and pass out again if not intercepted.

Had the fish been lower in the water, the flies would have come into its field of vision sooner, but it would have meant a greater effort to seize it.

9

Hence also its habit of moving from side to side like someone fielding a cricket ball. By allowing itself to be carried back a few inches by the current the fly remains longer in its visible area; there is more time to see if it looks edible and to take 'aim' before rising. Sometimes a trout will turn round and snap at a fly – a sort of last moment decision. In common with other anglers I have seen this happen when the whole movement of the fish could be seen, but as a rule, these late rises, I think, are due to a fish backing downstream while it takes a good look at the fly; a hint to the fisherman not to recover a fly too quickly. This is a lesson which cannot too soon be learnt by a fly fisher. I acquired it myself in a painful manner when I lifted a mayfly too soon from the Kennet and it was in consequence just missed by a fish whose roll over as it went down (for good) made the reeds on each blank sway in its wash.

The other noticeable feature about our trout's behaviour – its habit of getting in line with the fly before rising – is not easily explained. Trout's eyes are set on each side of their heads so that they are usually supposed to have no binocular vision – they see a fly with one eye or the other, not with both. Whether this is truly so, or whether there is a point just in the middle over the fish's snout, as it were, where both eyes can be directed on it is not yet definitely known. The general assumption seems to be that there is a 'blind spot' in this position. If this is so one must presume that the trout uses this blind spot as a sort of 'test position'; when the fly enters the blind spot the fish rises. That perhaps would explain why young fish in particular often seem to make bad shots at a fly, though the binocular vision theory would seem a more natural explanation of the trout's behaviour – anyhow, I have watched trout 'getting in line' with flies so often that I am convinced it is done on purpose, though exactly what that purpose is, apart from the suggestions above, I cannot determine.

If a trout can only see the surface, or at least anything *on* the surface, through this small area, what happens to all the rest of the surface of which it must obviously be able to see the underside? The late Col. E.W. Harding has done a great service to the sport in calling attention to this particular feature – the under surface acts as a mirror and reflects the weeds, banks, or bed of the river as the case may be; in fact, the trout's landscape when it is looking upwards is a mirror, more or less of a distorting mirror, according to whether the surface is calm or ruffled by wind or current, and in the middle of it is a circular window, with probably a rather dark and blurred edge, through which it can see outside the water.

H.D. TURING, Trout Fishing

One of the most delicious descriptions of *water* is to be found in *Earlham*, that classic book by Percy Lubbock. His graceful and distinguished style, akin to that of Charles Lamb, is in a class by itself. He is describing the Yare which flows past the park at Earlham in Norfolk.

The River at Earlham

BUT here meanwhile is the sphere of the water-world, with its strange and lovely treasures; trailing my hands in its delicious chill, I can soon be lost in the landscape of the river floor.

Shallow and pool, pool and shallow, the river coiled its way through the hollow land. Outside the boat-house the gravelly bottom was full in view, only blurred a little by the twist and swirl in the clear glass of water. Do you know that broad-leaved plant, bright green, translucent, that grows in thick drifts along the bed of the stream, never touching the surface? – and the fine feathery thing, a darker green, eternally pulled by the current, like a thicket through which a wind never ceases to blow? – and the stalks of the arrow head, that climb to the upper air and are shaken there by a constant little breeze, it would seem, which is not really a breeze but the same secret tug of the stream below? – and the perpetual flitting of tiny shadows over the gravel and sand, as the minnows dart from under our monstrous hull, the leviathan that pushes among their cressy islets?

The only sound in the quiet valley was the measured cluck of our clumsy rowlocks; the reedy pastures were deserted, there wasn't a house or a cottage in sight; the tawny cows stood stock still, solemnly eyeing us as we passed. And then, as we steered round a swinging bend of the river, the sunlit floor had disappeared and there was nothing but the blackness beneath us, thick darkness of water unbroken by reed or rush – a deep pool, and you could plunge the oar down and down, further and further into the bottomless mud; and the next moment, perhaps, the boat was almost scraping the clean gravel again, and the smooth bottle-green reed-stems stood out into the water away from the bank; and so the river went winding on its leisurely way, and after ever so long you still saw the boat-house within easy hail, just across the breadth of a single meadow.

PERCY LUBBOCK, *Earlham*

Floats

WHEN one is setting out to construct a philosophy of angling it would be proper, I think, to begin with the, float, the link which connects the contemplative man with the wonders of the deep. Everybody knows about floats; even the Philistine used them to support his inaccuracies touching the craft and the brethren.

A sound scholar, from whom I was privileged to receive the rudiments of humane letters, a man decidedly of opinion that fishing, for small boys, was an undesirable species of 'loafing,' used, I remember, to be particularly severe about the float; it was unfortunate, perhaps, that the word lent itself so kindly to alliteration, for your sound scholar dearly loves a phrase, and if he be a masterful man, is apt to make it not only define a situation but also determine a policy. Happily, there were more ways than one out of the school demesne, and the river bank offered several secluded nooks to which the eye of authority never penetrated. The float of those days was a fat, globular thing, gross in aspect, clumsy in movement, and although its painted cheeks were not unpleasing to the eye, so far as float can ever be legitimately condemned as a symbol of folly, it could. Even in that halcyon time, when fish were still unsuspicious, it needed at least a perch to pull its unwieldly form under, a roach no more than made it wobble. Had the sound scholar based his imputations on the ground of using, not a float, but such a float, I should not now be protesting.

For I readily admit that virtue lies almost wholly in using the right float. Shape is important, and so is colour, and it is pleasant at times to dally with material. I have heard many learned disputations on the respective merits of quills from different birds, one man favouring swan, another goose, a third peacock, and each maintaining his

12

opinion with epic accounts of past sport. But as a rule these disputants are a shade too practical; their floats are for use only, and they make no allowance for the element of beauty which should have its place in the consideration.

I used at one time to prodigiously admire a certain slender kind of float, fashioned cunningly out of twin sections of clear quill, amber varnished and silk lapped, and tipped at either end with a slim point of bone. I lavished a good shilling thereon (you can buy an admirable cork float for half that sum), partly out of respect for the ideal, partly from belief in the efficacy of the lovely object in pursuit of roaches. Certainly it rode the stream in dainty fashion, peeping slyly out like some modest naiad, and responding even to that bite, perceived by the men of Lea alone, when a fat old roach makes a round mouth at the bait and sucks it in, only that he may expel it the more emphatically, as a pea-shooter expels a pea. Out of the water, too, that float was a delight; it was pleasant merely to let it hang in the air and see the sunlight captured in its transparent body. Once we had a really great fishing together. It was a glorious August day, and the roach were on the feed in every hole of the backwater, which was a string of holes separated by short gravel shallows. With no more than a loose handful of ground bait scattered broadcast in each hole, and with a good, large, piece of white bread on the hook, we caught roach literally as fast as we could. The water was a clear brown, and it was most fascinating to see, down in the depths, the gleam of a broad side as the rod went up and the hook went home, and afterwards, to be able to follow every movement of the fighting fish. The man who has not yet played a good roach on gossamer tackle in eight or ten feet of clear water with the sun on it has a rare pleasure still to come. The roach that day were beauties, and of the twenty kept, three would have weighed two pounds apiece, had I trusted to instinct and not a spring balance which had neither heart nor soul, and was (I maintain it) rusty somewhere inside.

It was shortly after that day that the naiad float disappointed me by parting assunder at the junction of the two sections of quill, and leaving me floatless just when the fish were beginning to bite. The sections could be joined together again, but the float was never the same after. Sooner or later the water would leak in and the naiad ceased to be a float, becoming a thing of no classification – unless it belonged to the order of plummets. On the whole I prefer my plummets to be of lead, so I gave up the naiad float with a sigh of regret as a last tribute to its beauty. There remains, however, a certain habit of mind induced by it, and I still strive after floats which are good to look at both in line and colour. A slender body of cork can

13

be very gratifying. For colours give me scarlet above and green below, with a little knob of sealing-wax at the top of the quill. This last is for use as well as ornament. The uninitiated might suppose that nothing could be well more visible to the angler than the quill's natural white tip sticking out of the water, but what with the dazzle of sun and flicker of wavelets, it is often very hard to see, and it is surprising how the little red knob helps the eye. Also, with its aid, one can gauge a bite very, very nicely. Properly poised, there is half an inch above water and the half of this is white, the other half red. When the white has disappeared you have a noble bite as roach bites go, and you may strike at once. It is not often that the roach of these degenerate days takes one's float right down out of sight. For evening fishing, when the last faint light is on the water, a black-headed float is most visible.

At one time I used to fish occasionally through the dark hours, and I was mightily puzzled to find a float which I could see after dark. I tried adding a cone of white paper to the tip, and at first deluded myself with the idea that it was visible; but when, after intently watching it for a long time, I discovered that I was really gazing at nothing, I gave it up. The discovery was due to a horrid eel, which had taken my float off in a wholly opposite direction. Incidentally, that eel very nearly made me give up night fishing also. Let him who doubts, try to unhook an eel among thistles by the light of the stars and a wax match. Later in the same summer, however, I came upon an ancient bream-fisher at dusk, perched on a camp stool, and brooding over the quiet waters like some sad heron. Attached to the top of his float was a feather, blacker than the impending gloom, and therefore visible against the water-line longer than anything else.

A man of few words, that ancient. He may perhaps have been susceptible to the mysteries of night, the rustling and whispering of unseen creatures, the melancholy owls in the woods behind, the low murmur of the restless river, the reflected track of the stars growing ever fainter, as dawn approached, to the deathly chill of the darkest hour. But of these things he said nothing; his hope was a sackful of bream before sunrise.

I sometimes pick up out of a drawer a queer little black object with a fat white head which I am informed is a 'luminous' float, and so often as I do so I think of that old bream-fisher, sitting solitary through the nights, and wonder whether he ever met the river god face to face.

For my part I never could catch anything to speak of after dark, and the luminous float goes back into the drawer where it has lain all these years unused.

One old writer, by the way, two hundred years ago, commmended to his disciples the use of glow-worms imprisoned in a clear quill float, and is minute in his instructions as to getting the best light out of them! But I suspect him of depending on tradition rather than on experience. He is more practical when he comes to a floating reed:

'Note, if at any time the angler should be destitute of floats, when he comes to the waterside to angle, and there be 'ere a dry sound reed to be gotten, cut it close to the joints, leaving two joints in every float uncut, one at one end, and another at t'other, to keep out of the water; it will make a good float in time of need.'

Float caps are most pleasing when cut out of quill and stained a deep red, but most practical when cut from a length of fine black rubber tubing. A foot of this will last a season through.

You can also embellish your floats yourself if you please. A long swan quill can be given a coat of Lincoln green and a head of crimson with the aid of varnish stain or enamel, and it is then sufficiently attractive to be the companion of one's days. The true test of matrimony is said to be continued ability on the part of the persons involved to survey each other across the breakfast-table without weariness. If you consider that the angler has to watch his float motionless, 'a painted ship upon a painted ocean' for hours with no intrinsic interest beyond the float and the watching, you will perceive that a fair appearance has its value here also.

But, of course, one is best pleased with one's float when it vanishes from sight, so I will not seek to press the analogy too closely. Moreover, you can always change your float when you get tired of it, and try another with a new colour scheme. If luck counts for anything, it is sometimes worth doing.

But there is a thing about floats which I have noticed most sorrowfully and cannot explain. The one which looks nicest, and sits best in the water, and reveals most bites, always is to be found on the line of the other man. To comprehend this, one must, I fancy, plumb deeper depths than those of angling.

H. T. SHERINGHAM, *An Open Creel*

Food for Fishes

THERE is a huge agile worm, known to anglers as the lob worm, who takes his walks abroad only under the stars. Him you must pursue with guile and a bedroom candlestick to light your path. On a shining night, when the dew lies thick, you shall see him spread at ease inches long on the smooth lawn. He has both head and tail, and, while his head wanders abroad, for safety's sake he always keeps the tip of his tail in his hole, so that when he is alarmed he can retreat backward quicker than thought can fly.

It is your business to grasp him before he is frightened, and very sure and rapid you must be.

And you must know which end of him is head, so that you may grasp the other, or he will slip through your hand like an eel. Even when you have him firmly you will find his tail clings marvellously to the earth, and if you pull too hard he breaks in twain. But if you work him gently, as one works a loose nail out of wood, he will yield and gradually all his length is your own.

When you have him, you have an excellent bait to your angle-rod, but, as I have shown, in the catching he needs to be handled with as much love and tenderness as Master Walton's frog itself.

H.T. SHERINGHAM, An Angler's Hours

Worms

AND first for worms; of these there be very many sorts, some breed only in the earth, as the earth worm, others of or among plants, as the dug worm, and other breed either out of excrements, or in the bodies of living creatures, as in the horns of sheep and deer; or some of dead flesh, as the maggot, or gentle, and others.

Now these be most of them particularly good for particular fishes; but for the trout, the dew worm, which some call the lob worm, and the brandling, are the chief, and especially the first for a great trout, and the latter for a less. There be also lob worms called squirrel's tails, a worm that has a red head, a streak down his back, and a broad tail, which are noted the best, because they are the toughest and most lively, and live longest in the water; for you are to know that a dead worm is but dead bait, and like to catch nothing compared to a quick and lively quick-stirring worm; and for a brandling, he is usually found in an old dunghill, or some very rotten place near to it; but most usually in cow dung rather than horse dung, which is somewhat too dry and hot for that worm. But the best of them are to be found in the bark of the tanners, which they cast up in heaps after they have used it about their leather.

There are also divers other kind of worms, which for colour and shape, alter even as the ground out of which they are got; as the marsh worm, the tag tail, the flag worm, the dock worm, the oak worm, the gilt tail, the tawachel or lob worm, which, of all others, is the most excellent bait for salmon, and too many to name even as many sorts as some think there be of several shrubs or herbs, or of several kinds of birds of the air.

And now I shall show you how to bait your hook with a worm so as shall prevent you from much trouble, the loss of many a hook too, when you fish for a trout with a running line. . . .

Suppose it be a big lob worm, put your hook into him somewhere about the middle and out again a little below the middle; and having done so, draw your worm above the arming of the hook, but note that at the entering of your hook it must not be at the head-end of the worm, but at the tail-end of him, that the point of your hook may come out toward the head-end, and having drawn him above the arming of your hook, then put the point of your hook again into the very head of the worm, till it come near to the place where the point of the hook first came out; and then draw back that part of the worm that was above the shank or arming of your hook, and so fish with it.

And if you mean to fish with two worms, then put the second on before you turn back the hook's head of the first worm; you cannot use above two or three worms before you attain to what I direct you; and having attained it, you will find it very useful, and thank me for it, for you will run on the ground without tangling.

ISAAK WALTON, *Compleat Angler*

The Spent Gnat

BY now it was past six o'clock, and the spent fly began to come on the water. All over the surface mayflies were to be seen; they were in clouds in the air above, busy egg laying, now dipping down and just touching the top of the stream, then rising in the air and dipping again. They got thicker and thicker and so did bodies of dead mayfly floating down. If your eye followed an individual egg layer, you noticed, if you could pick her out from the swarms of her companions, that her trips through the air got shorter, and her visits to the water more frequent, and that, instead of just brushing the surface in order to lay her eggs, she began to sit for a second or so upon it until the time came when she could rise no more. Then, her work done, her store of six or seven thousand eggs safely laid, the future of her race assured, she settled on the surface and sailed down upright; but soon she would give a shiver, one of her wings would collapse on the water, until finally she died and fell flat, wings extended in the form of a cross.

Thicker and thicker grew the mass of fly over the water, more and more numerous those carried down by the current. At first those floating were present in all stages, sitting upright, or half collapsed, or dying or dead, but soon the dead predominated, until all that could be seen were their bodies, the dead fly, the spent gnat. These came down in ever-increasing quantities. In the backwaters and eddies they were packed nearly solid. In the main current, the quick swinging stream of the lower Test, they were separated only by inches. All the broad river was covered, and bore them seawards like a moving carrier. Now all these had escaped the attacks of trout and grayling, and swifts and swallows and martins and wagtails, and warblers and chaffinches and many other birds which prey on them, all of them had escaped, and had reproduced their species; when you looked at the countless thousands which floated down in the small time during which you saw only a small part of the river, you realised that the quantities of them which had survived were so vast that the assaults of all their enemies made no appreciable impression on their numbers.

J. W. HILLS, *A Summer on the Test*

The Mayflies' Hour

THEN we came out and lay among the meadow grass and watched the mayflies dancing. We were right down among the buttercups, the shiny yellow goblets were above us, and overhead floated the mayflies, *up*, with a flitting of gauze-like wings, *down*, with a parachute motion, their long thread-like tails turned upwards. A small heath butterfly appeared and chased one of them, the twain went dancing away over the flowers.

Then all at once the mayflies seemed tired of dancing, they all settled on the grass and looking up the course of the brook I saw that all the countless thousands had done the same, barely one insect was on the wing.

But after about five minutes the dance began again, as far as the eye could see, all up the course of the Folly. Some locked together in mid-air fell into the grass, others, whose brief life was over, winged back to the stream, closing their wings and falling on the surface of the pool. I watched one mayfly struggling, resting and struggling again, as it was borne slowly away by the current, sending minute rings outwards. A dim shape appeared beneath, there was a flash of silver, and a fat roach sucked it down. This happened to several other exhausted insects that drifted by.

What a lovely summer dream it is when the mayflies dance! For two years these fairy-like creatures have been living a worm-like grub existence in the sand and mud of the stream bed. Millions of other grubs must even now be below the water, waiting for just such another glorious summer day next year. Ice has roofed them in, covered with snow, the bitter winds of winter have blown across the dreary fields, long winter nights have given place to grey days. Two years for this, the mating dance in the June sunshine, this brief hour of glory!

'BB', *The Idle Countryman*

The Way of a Trout with a Nymph

THERE are two states in which the natural nymph is taken by the trout – first, in the active larval stage, and second (and to the angler far more important) in the practically inert stage, in which the mature nymph arriving at the surface to split its final nymphal envelope and to emerge as a subimago often reaches them.

The active nymphs may be routed out and pursued by the trout from their shelter in weeds or silt. This may be done in water so deep as to afford no clue or opportunity to the angler. In shallower water it is apt to produce the evidence of activity known as 'tailing,' giving the angler a fairly precise indication where he may cast to his fish, but the opportunities thus afforded are few and the angler is handicapped by the fact that the natural nymph which the trout are pursuing are in one or other of their active stages and cannot be accurately represented in action.

Where trout are 'bulging' in the correct sense of the word (i.e. rushing about over the weeds in comparatively shallow pursuing nymphs which emerge from their shelter in weeds and making a bulge in turning as each nymph is captured), the nymph may be more or less active or it may be almost inert. In his chapter on 'Nymphs and Bulgers' in *Fly Fishing: Some New Arts and Mysteries*, Dr. Mottram gives an interesting description of what he had observed on occasions when trout were bulging to nymphs. He writes:

'The nymph may be seen coming downstream, but often diverging to one side or the other, at the same time rising slowly to the surface, the motion is quite slow and even, not in the least fast or jerky, and a 'bulging' fish, although he is quiet in his motions, is obviously not chasing nymphs but moving now to this side, now to that, in order to meet the nymph coming down.'

He regards the nymph at this stage as swimming – and I think he is probably right, for I have often seen trout bulging furiously over weeds, as if the nymphs emerging from shelter were numerous, while the hatch of subimagines is scanty or almost non-existent; so that it seems that if there were occasions when the nymph emerged and if uncaptured by the trout, remained inactive enough to return to its fastnesses or to take refuge in others. Moreover, according to Dr. Mottram, the trout in these conditions is prone to take a dragging artificial nymph, a fact which rather suggests that he is in pursuit of nymphs of which some, at any rate, show a degree of activity.

There is another occasion on which the active nymphs may be taken, viz., after weed cutting, when the nymphs, feeling their weed homes cut away from their stalks, seek shelter in bays and eddies under the banks – and are there found by the trout. Often, too, when cut floating weeds are coming downstream, trout may be seen rising among them – undoubtedly taking the active nymph which are deserting or drifting out of the cut weeds.

The commonest occasion known in which the trout feeds on the nymph on its way to hatch is when he lies in position under a bank or run, poised to meet and accept without excitement or pursuit the mature nymphs brought to him helpless by the current. On such occasions it is often extremely difficult for the angler to detect whether the fish is taking nymphs or subimago, for there may be, and often is, a string of hatched duns coming over him on the same line of current as brings the nymphs. Yet quite frequently the fish will be found to be taking to the nymph to the exclusion of the winged duns, and that for hours at a time.

Dr. Mottram on his next page makes a distinction between the swimming nymph and the floating nymph which I call the inert nymph, and describes the way in which the fish takes the latter.

'The fish is taking just beneath the surface of the water nymphs which are floating down and about to burst their cases in order to change into duns.'

He calls the fish thus feeding on floating nymphs, a 'dimpling' fish in contradistinction from the 'bulger,' feeding on swimming nymphs. He adds a little later of the floating nymph: 'In this position they are motionless, with legs and tail extended in the position of rest.'

At times during a hatch of duns, trout, often large, may be seen questing about near the surface in mid-stream and taking the nymphs which are ascending from the river-bed as they find them generally breaking or 'humping' the surface when they effect a capture. And occasionally trout, when in the height of condition, may be observed hovering in the fastest part of the stream, not moving from one spot and intercepting just below the surface the nymphs on their way to hatch, and at times doing so without breaking the surface.

It will thus be seen that the occasions most favourable to the angler fishing to individual selected fish are those when he is taking the mature and, for the moment, practically inert nymph, on its way to hatch.

As a matter of fact, it does not seem to have been realised for many years after the advent of the dry fly, what a large proportion of the rising trout under banks, and indeed in the open (other than bulging) is to nymphs on their way to the surface to hatch, with the result that many a fish so rising has been vainly hammered by anglers with floating flies.

The due appreciation of *how* a trout is rising forms the very essence of fishing, whether it be with floating fly or artificial nymph – and it is often no easy matter. The late Colonel E. W. Harding in his invaluable volume, *The Flyfisher and the Trout's Point of View*, shows how the trout lying in wait with an upward gaze below a smooth surface is enabled to watch the reflection of the approaching nymph in the mirror made by the surface beyond the window through which he can see – and how, in order to keep the reflection in view of his upward gaze, he has to come to the surface to meet the actual nymph as it and its reflection come together there.

G. E. M. SKUES, *Nymph Fishing for Chalk Stream Trout*

Behaviour of Otters

IN June 1935, a water bailiff and an angler on the River Tavy in South Devon had an extremely interesting close-up view of an otter hunting in broad daylight, and one which showed in unmistakable fashion what was its favourite food. About 4 p.m. they were standing near the tail of a long pool just above an island which had been a regular holt for otters since time immemorial. Suddenly the keeper saw a wave going up the pool and whispered, 'Otter,' and they waited to see what would happen.

Presently a big otter poked his mask above water, and then, seeing and scenting no danger, began to quarter the water like a dog working cover for game. Although there were several salmon in the pool, it paid no attention to these. But four times in the next twenty minutes it landed on a flat rock within thirty yards of where the watchers stood, and each time proceeded to eat an eel, the crunching of the bones being plainly audible. Then it swam back downstream and doubtless went to sleep.

Such daylight hunting must be comparatively rare. Personally I have never seen an otter make a catch. But it is not by any means unknown for anglers fishing at dusk or after dark to see one come up holding a fish in its mouth. In one case a man actually had the herling he was playing seized by an otter, which went off with the prize too. This incident was reported in *The Field* several years ago.

The most usual time to see otters by day is when there is a sudden rise in the water. This, no doubt, has the effect of flooding them out of their holts, and they drop downstream, making for other hiding-places. Once in a spate I nearly foul-hooked one. The water started rising, bringing with it the usual flotsam of branches, bottles, and bits of weed and rubbish. I was reeling in my spinning bait when I felt something, which looked like a piece of half-submerged wood, touch the line, and then a flat head and two beady black eyes came out of the water on the other end of what I had taken for a log.

One of the prettiest sights I have ever seen was in 1927. Another angler and myself were sheltering from heavy thunder rain under an overhanging rock at the tail of a pool on the Tavy. Presently two smallish cubs of perhaps 7lb. apiece came up from below, hugging the shallow water at the edge, and passing within a few feet of where we were sitting.

They went into the pool above, and a few minutes later we saw a wave coming into the same pool from a leat which led out of the opposite bank, and then a big otter appeared. The three played about for some time, but presently the bitch must have winded us, for she gave a sharp whistle. Instantly they all dived and we saw the waves going back towards the leat.

MAJOR KENNETH DAWSON, *Modern Salmon and Sea Trout Fishing*

Food for Men

THE best eating of all coarse fish are gudgeon and perch. Mr. Marshall Hardy in his excellent little book, *Coarse Fish* (Herbert Jenkins), gives this recipe for gudgeon.

'First bring a pan of deep fat to the boil. Then take a wooden board and a sharp knife and decapitate each fish, open the stomach, and clean with the thumbs.

Now roll each fish in seasoned flour and cast each into the boiling fat for three minutes. Prepared in this way, eaten with a squeeze of lemon, and a sprinkling of red pepper and brown bread and butter, gudgeon will hold their own with the best of fish.'

Perch are firm-fleshed which has a slight bluish tint, and the bones are easily removed. From a pond or lake which has a clean bed they are of delicious flavour but this does not apply to perch caught in muddy ponds. Here is Doctor Starkie's recipe for cooking them and the same recipe might apply to roach and other coarse fish, with the exception of pike.

'Take a "hazel nut" of butter, melt in a frying-pan, put in two chopped onions and three chopped tomatoes, peppercorns and chillies, pepper and salt. Add three tablespoons of olive oil and bring to a nice brown colour over a slow fire.

'Wash the fish and clean them (but do not wash again when cleaned), flour each fish separately and put in pan with the mixture, add a tumbler of cider and fry gently over a slow fire with a cover over the pan.'

Fish cooked in this manner are delicious as the Editor knows from experience.

Pike vary in flavour and I have always found the young fish from two to four pounds are the nicest to eat.

There are many recipes for pike, pike stuffed with sage and onions are sometimes delicious but it is a fish which possesses many minute bones and these should be removed. My own personal taste is pike fish cakes. These are made in the same manner as any other fish cakes.

The fish is first boiled or steamed in the usual way and allowed to cool. To each half-pound allow a quarter of a pound of mashed potatoes, ½-oz. of fat, an egg, bread crumbs, milk, salt and pepper.

Heat the butter or fat in a saucepan, add the pike flesh coarsely flaked, potatoes, half the yolk of an egg, salt and pepper, and sufficient milk to make the mixture moist. Stir the ingredients over the fire for a few minutes then turn out on a plate. When cold, shape into round flat cakes and brush them over with egg, cover with bread crumbs and fry in hot fat. Time allowed – about one hour.

For baked pike take one small pike, 4 oz. of force-meat, one egg, brown bread crumbs, and good dripping for basting.

Wash clean and scale the fish and remove head, fins and gills. Fill the inside with force-meat, sew up opening, brush over with beaten egg, and cover with bread crumbs. Before putting the fish in the oven it should be well basted with hot fat. Baste frequently when cooking and keep covered with greased paper. Bake for fifty minutes and serve with sauce.

Trout may be cooked in the same way but I always consider that an unstuffed trout has a more natural flavour. Boiled trout are also delicious. For two medium-sized fish take a third of a pint of melted butter, one tablespoon of coarsely chopped gherkins, salt and pepper. Clean and wash the trout, barely cover them with hot water (not quite boiling) which should be salted. Simmer gently for ten minutes. Have the sauce ready, add the gherkins, season to taste, pour over fish, and serve.

'BB'

The Fisherman's Inn

THERE are many kinds of fishing inns, some are not 'inns' at all, but hotels, which serve six-course dinners every night and where the chambermaid, the waiter and the head waiter all expect a tip when you depart. These hotels are patronised by the wealthy fishermen, thickset, tweedy, red-faced men in knickerbockers and two-way hats. Their tackle is the best that money can buy, they consume great quantities of whisky, they are not concerned with what happens to their fish once their gillies have landed them.

These places are not true fishing inns. I knew a fishing inn in Bedfordshire which I call the Three Chubs. The first time I saw the place I realised that this was the real thing. I knew nothing about the fishing, which, after all, was the most important adjunct, but that was investigated later and found to be beyond my highest expectations.

It was a very small inn, the only one in the very small village. It lay back from the road with a small triangle of green grass before it on which stood the sign of the Three Chubs, three huge chubs standing on their tails. The sign was faded but attractive, those chub really *were* chub, they looked appetising too, which every good angler knows chub are not; it is the most bony, tasteless, freshwater fish that swims, whatever Isaak Walton has to say.

But there was something in that rude painting which warmed my heart, these were *big* fish, worthy of your skill, their fins faded red, their eyes still golden, their painted scales still suggesting a silver and green lustre.

Before inspecting the inn I leant over the three-arched bridge which was also very old. Under the arch nearest the bank the river ran shallow and quite swift, wagging cushions of poa grass. Three lusty chub, a trifle more modest of girth than those on the sign hard by, but nevertheless undoubted three-pounders, were lying, one behind the other, close to the waving tresses. Under the other two arches the river was dark and deep, and silver water beetles gyrated just in the back wash of the current as it crinkled against a stone buttress covered with bright green moss.

Up-river was a charming June evening glimpse of wet meadow and willows and hawking swallows, a frieze of ruminating red cattle by a pollarded tree and seven white ducks processing down-river towards a shallow ford. The place smelt of fish, big ones.

I turned and crossed the little green under the sign of the Three Chubs. The inn was thatched, coral-pink roses embowered the windows and bushed them in, they almost hid the top of the door so that it was like the entrance to a wren's nest. The windows were (of course) mullioned, and martins had their nests under the wide thatched eaves.

Over the door, almost invisible because of the roses, was a notice, lettered in old and graceful characters more suitable to a tombstone, 'Ernest Small, licensed to sell wines, spirits, and tobacco.'

On opening the door I found myself in a flagged passage of rose-red quarries. In front of me was a door labelled *BAR*, on the left another under a beam labelled, very grandly, *LOUNGE*, I opened this and went in. It was very different from other lounges I have known in other fishing inns.

Over the fireplace was a faded photograph in a very heavy wood frame. It depicted two gentlemen, holding rods, wearing straw hats and long, drooping moustaches. One was in his shirt sleeves. At their feet was a fishmonger's array of victims, some of them vast bream, larger, apparently, than the old-fashioned leather bellows. I thought this picture was very proper and right – now for the stuffed fish. Yes, there it was, sure enough, regarding me with affrighted stare from behind its curved glass front. A bream, a very large one, indeed I thought it was the largest I had ever seen, dead or alive. On the opposite wall, likewise regarding me with affrighted stare was a perch, a three-pounder, and one of his pectoral fins had dropped off and was lying on the silver sand under his belly.

At this juncture the door opened and the landlord stood before me. I recognised him as one of the straw-hatted gentlemen in the photograph, though the drooping moustache was missing and the years had given him more fat. And never in my life have I seen a man so like a chub! He had a round face, pink and rubicund, his eyes were slightly protruding, with a merry twinkle in them, but his mouth, which should have been thick-lipped and large to complete the simile, was like a cherub's. He had no teeth. I intimated that I had a thirst upon me and accordingly he led me down the passage to where three stone steps led into a cellar. There against a whitewashed wall was a cask and stooping down he turned a tap and there came to me the gratifying sound of beer trinkling into a pewter pot. And *what* beer it was to be sure! Ice-cold and full of nutty flavour, I have not tasted beer like it since.

I was hungry, so Mrs. Small ushered me into the parlour and bustled off to prepare the meal. Meanwhile mine host stood by the door and talked, he rolled his words as though they were bread pellets. Pike? Yes, there were very big pike. Chub? Ah, there was not better place for chub in the whole of the Ouse valley. Had he not caught one himself the day before, a fish of four pounds? 'Why, sir, the place smells of 'em.' I remembered the smell on the bridge and agreed.

Soon came Mrs. Small bearing a tray loaded with plates, a crusty cottage loaf, fresh lettuce plucked a minute ago from the garden, a dish of freshly caught gudgeon fried in bread crumbs and laced with watercress, and a flap of Small-cured ham on which was enthroned two 'half apricots' of fried eggs still sizzling! It was unbelievable!

Host and hostess then retired and I was left to discuss my supper. The mullioned window was wide open and the roses peeped in at me. It looked on to the garden and a small green lawn. Beyond was a low wall, a few apple trees and – the river. I glimpsed silvery willows and pallisades of sedge and there came to me the perfume of meadowsweet and river water. Somewhere a hidden weir was making a low murmur and patrolling martins and swallows kept up a continual twitter.

Beyond were water meadows and black poplars. You will always find black poplars in the haunts of big chub. My meal finished at last I strolled down the garden and leant my elbows on the low wall.

The June evening was softening, sedge warblers chattered and grated among the willows of a little island in mid-river, exactly opposite to me, and in the crinkling deeps beyond the sedge beds fish were rising after the dancing gnats.

It was all so perfect, all too good to be true, the whole scene – inn, landlord, supper, beer, river, and evening had something unreal about it, something not far removed from a fisherman's idea of paradise. Not far off were the remains of an old watermill and it was from there that the sound of rushing water came, a low, soothing murmur which later would lull me to sleep.

Here indeed could the weary man find peace and quietness, far from the turmoil of this troubled world.

'BB', *Fisherman's Folly*

A Corner of the Meadow

For ever, says the stream, must I
Along this sunny pebbled bed
Run light and swift and singing by?
Here, then, I'll change; a face of dread
I here assume, and past this oak
I slide in silence and I move
From shallow light like a grey smoke
To fill a deep and clayey groove,
And thence into a deeper pit
Where I will nourish a proud shoal
Of fishes that shall have the wit
To make the angler look a fool;
Not brainless, puny, darting things
But wise important water-kings
That have no time for hooks and lines.
Their progress on my twilight wave
Shall frighten solitary boys,
And in my patriarchal cave
I'll thunder terror, without noise.

The thing was done; the water-hole
Lies sullen under cliffs, and claws
Of trees bewitched; the bell shall toll
For those whom this Medusa draws;
And that far rose-reflection burns
On the dusk water far too red—
Our altered naiad ever learns
Some deadly trick, with eyes of lead.

EDMUND BLUNDEN

SALMON

King of Fresh Water Fish

THE records of great salmon are many and varied. It is actual stories of capturing record fish which are most likely to interest the reader. But a few may be picked out from history. Premier place is given to the Earl of Home's sixty-nine-and-three-quarter pounder, caught in the Tweed in 1730. But there is some doubt in some quarters whether this fish is authentic.

Next follows a sixty-four pounder from the Tay caught by Miss G. W. Ballantine, and which took nearly two hours to land, which is a notable performance considering the gigantic size of the fish. This was caught in October 1922. A salmon of sixty-seven pounds is supposed to be authentic. It was caught on the Nith in 1812 by a poacher and took ten hours to land. The 'Bishop Browne' story is recalled here, an account of which follows later. The Wye and the Tweed have yielded monsters in the sixty and fifty pounds category, all too numerous to mention.

The biggest salmon on record is one of 103lb., an incredible figure, which came from the Forth district (mouth of the Devon, in 1902). This was caught in the nets. And the heaviest salmon ever known in our rivers was the Wye monster, thought to weigh 80lb. when alive, a fish which measured no less than 59½ inches long by 33¼ inches. It had a minnow in its mouth. (May 1920.) This fantastic fish was not weighed when first found but nine days later *a portion of it* weighed 43lb.

No doubt it was a fish of such proportions which Bishop Browne played for so long and finally lost.

Much literature has been devoted to the great salmon mystery – i.e., whether or no they feed when in fresh water. There are conflicting opinions, and one of the greatest authorities on this subject of salmonology, Abel Chapman, writes at length on this deepest of nature's unsolved mysteries.

In his book *The Borders and Beyond*, there are several chapters which deal entirely with salmon and their habits. Chapman was able to study them at first hand on his own water at Houxty, and one always feels that what he says is the result of prolonged and observant study.

The whole subject of this species is so vast no attempt is made in this anthology to deal with every aspect of it. In some ways the fish is as mysterious as the eel. Abel Chapman seems to think with the vast majority that salmon do *not* feed in fresh water, the period of feeding and growing taking place at sea. Few people realise that these great fish, some weighing thirty pounds and more, penetrate in the spawning season up the smallest burns, where there is barely enough water to cover their backs. I have talked with a shepherd in Dumfriesshire who has seen them right up in the head waters of a tiny burn which I know well, and from which I have never caught any trout larger than a sprat. 'BB'

One very likely explanation of why no food has ever been found in the stomach of a salmon is advanced in the following extract, taken from the Badminton Library.

Salmon Feeding

It is commonly believed, because nothing has ever been found in the stomach of a salmon, that he does not feed. A friend of mine, who takes a great interest in the subject, told me that while fishing in Norway some years ago, he cut open every fish he caught (thirty in number) and did not find anything inside any of the salmon, but three of the grilse were gorged with insects, which he thought were daddy-longlegs.

This is the only instance I have every met with of food being found in the stomach of a salmon; it is, of course, an exception; but if evidence were wanting this of itself proves that salmon will feed, though how to account for the absence of food in their stomachs is a puzzle. I have often noticed, fishing with natural bait, when the salmon is landed the bait is torn from the hooks and sent up the line a foot or more. Does not this show that the salmon has marvellous powers of ejecting its food? Is it not probable that when he gets into trouble, either by being hooked or netted, he will disgorge the contents of his stomach? A trout that is full of food will, we all know, do so immediately after it is landed – and why not the salmon? My friend who told me that he found food inside the grilse also said that several Norwegian net fishermen informed him that after their nets were drawn in they generally found a number of half-digested fish amongst the salmon thus caught. He also said that he had heard the same story at Newcastle-upon-Tyne. If these fishermen spoke the truth it goes a long way in support of my theory.

The absence of food in a salmon has been accounted for in another way. A salmon may have such powers of digestion that whatever food he consumes disappears almost at once; but against this supposition there is the fact of what my friend found inside the grilse. As it is certain that grilse are only salmon in youth, this theory must fall to the ground, and I am inclined to think that the former explanation is the correct one.

BADMINTON LIBRARY

Here follows an account of spawning salmon from Abel Chapman's *Borders and Beyond*. It is included because it presents a very vivid and even awe-inspiring picture of these great fish in the throes of mating. No other writer has ever put into words such a thrilling description of one of the most dramatic happenings in nature. Scores of salmon fishers who have to travel far for their sport are, alas, entirely ignorant of what takes place during the close season.

Spawning Salmon

TYPICAL of hill-born streams in Northumbria, the Houxty burn springs from the wild moors of Cairnglassenhope, 1,023 feet above the sea – one of its parent hills bearing the curious name of The Naked Man – and runs a rugged course of seven or eight miles; the ascent of salmon therein, however, is limited to the three lowest miles, the 'linn' of Espmill being always insurmountable.

Though of no great depth, and barely averaging twenty feet in breadth (though it may reach twice that in flood) the Houxty burn in favouring seasons becomes a focal point and a rendezvous of love-lorn salmon; and surely it would be difficult to imagine a more striking biological spectacle than that of these huge fish – many running to twenty or twenty-five pounds, some beyond that – wallowing and weltering together within these narrow waters. In proportion, the sight of Greenland whales gambolling in the Thames at Richmond hardly seems extravagant comparison. The winter of 1916–17 afforded typical instances of these scenes, hence that season is here selected as an example.

Early in December the influx began, the first pair selecting a station at the Milestone Haugh, in a fairly strong stream easily commanded at close quarters. An hour or so later another pair appeared, splashing up the short rapid below. After a preliminary skirmish or two – never pressed home – both couples settled down about six yards apart and in some eighteen inches of water. The bed of the burn was composed of stones varying from the size of a hazel or a walnut up to that of a tennis ball, all fairly compacted amongst the gravel, movable by hand not without effort.

The hither bank being high and half hollowed, enabled me day by day to creep up unseen and take post – amidst impending icicles – almost in arm's length. These two couples I watched for the great part of two consecutive days. The two hen salmon, being dark in colour and harmonising on the moss-clad stones on which they lay, were none too easy to distinguish, even at so short a range. They lay constantly on their respective 'redds' in mid-stream – for long periods without visible movement. Then it became evident that one or the other was striving to rout out a stone with her snout, their tails at such times breaking the surface with their strenuous efforts. But at recurring intervals, say three to five minutes, each female would suddenly fling herself flat on her silvery broadside, usually athwart the stream, and thereupon followed a sort of convulsive spasm, her whole frame writhing as if in agony, while her tail, lashing out in vertical strokes, sent the water flying in spray.

This was the act of extruding ova, and after each such spasm her consort (who meanwhile had been lying inert a yard or two below) moved up alongside and gently pushed her sidelong off the 'redd' till, in the shallowing water beyond, she often lay half exposed, the pair nestling juxtaposed in tremulous emotion. At times, but not always, a sort of electric tremor visibly thrilled their whole frames especially that of the male, whose very fins quivered, and it was evident that the operation of fertilising the newly-shed ova was in progress. This situation might last for a half a minute. Then the cock fish slowly dropped back to his billet – beneath my toes. He was an eighteen-pounder, copper-red, and ornamented on the shoulder with three pale blotches – battle scars – and a huge white gib. This excrescence, projecting beyond the snout, prevented the mouth properly closing, thus producing a curious white line along the whole length of the jaw that was distinctly visible under water. His wife was twelve pounds.

This pair I named Jack and Jill. After watching these (and subsequently many other pairs) during several hours, it became obvious that no single trench was dug, as is often described and quite probably often may be made. The female, after each of these recurrent spasms, moved a yard or two upstream, and again set to work by shifting some of the larger stones to dig a slight hollow perhaps the size of one's open palms wherein she deposited a fresh batch of ova, the attendant male each time moving up to fulfil his functions. As the female worked, stage by stage, upstream, so automatically she filled the previous redd with gravel and sand. At first it seems doubtful if that result was intentional, or whether it followed as a merely accidental effect of further excavations above, till I noticed that on occasion a female, after filling a so completed redd, moved away without spawning to another spot.

It will be observed that it is the female *alone* that does all the work, her consort merely standing by to supply milt as required. As many as half a dozen separate nests might be completed by the female in a single day, the site of which was usually recognisable by the yellow upturned stones.

Now day by day, as their domestic operations approached completion, a stange familiarity ripened between these two contiguous couples. Twice during the forenoon the female of the upper pair dropped, tail first, down the short intervening rapid and joined her neighbours below in a sort of *menáge á trois*, the trio wallowing side by side in blissful amity. Presently the compliment was returned and there were variations too diverse in detail. Three days later the two old sultans had permanently fraternised, the pair lying side by side in deeper water, twenty yards below where their consorts still lingered.

The séance was over and its object achieved (at any rate this proved to be a semi-final scene, for heavy snowfalls, with severe frost followed and the burn was frozen half across so further observation was arrested).

15th December.

The intensity of the frost this mid-December morning has relaxed. The ice blocks, that last evening lay piled in glistening beauty, have been swept away, and the stream runs a good foot above yesterday's level. At once I observed that a big new run of salmon had arrived overnight. In one long rough pool – or rather a series of contiguous pools formed below a sharp elbow bend in the burn – quite a dozen big fish showed up in tumultuous evidence. Broad brown backs clove the torrent, each adorned with a dorsal fin as a gaff topsail, while the flukes of great shovel-like tails sheered to and fro athwart the current. All these I saw at a glance were new-run salmon, each spick and span fore and aft, and in conspicuous contrast with the scarred and battle-battered veterans that had already passed through the ordeal of love and war. The whole pool was a-wallow . . . was it polygamy or polyandry? or simply vulgar bigamy? A week's steady watching solved all problems. The bigger fish that lay in constant evidence on the farther shallow, varied from three, or four, to six in number, and these were all males. They lived in fraternal harmony only varied by an occasional half-hearted lunge as two rolled together side by side; even this I only saw thrice. But deep down in the dark torrent between us lay their six consorts, already engaged in the strenuous function of life. Motionless, and to all intents and purposes invisible, they lay, save that at periodic intervals each female underwent one of those convulsive spasms of violent energy which accompany the shedding of the ova, and during these moments a gleaming broadside revealed the appearance of each. At corresponding periods one or other of the awaiting males would quit his station on the shallow in order to effect the fertilisation of the ova. This it will be noticed is more or less identical with the operations already described at the Milestone Haugh, but with this difference. Day after day these six hen salmon kept persistently spawning on the identical spots, they never shifted their position upstream as did those others, indeed this small pool provided no space for move-ment, nor was there any visible indication of upturned stones. As I suspected at the time and subsequently verified by testing, the bed of the burn at this point is so strongly compacted that no power of a salmon's snout could shift them, neither was there any appreciable amount of small gravel or sand. The ova here, in short, was simply shed in the open current and were left to find for themselves such shelter and cover as they might chance upon. Here, no doubt, the rugged upstanding stones provided considerably more crevices than the smoother gravel at Milestone Haugh.

Still, it seemed a reckless procedure, but after all Nature has provided for such contingencies. For the fact has been established (by counting and weighing the spawn) that a female salmon will produce eight hundred eggs to each pound of her weight. Here, within a few yards were six females spawning. Assuming them to average ten pounds apiece, we would have near fifty thousand eggs laid in one tiny pool.

ABEL CHAPMAN, *Borders and Beyond*

Abel Chapman had, to my mind, an enviable life. He was able to travel widely to different parts of the world in quest of sport; to the tropics for big game (though I do not envy him his big game shooting), to Spain for the Great Bustard and wild-fowl, to Northern Europe for elk and deer, salmon and trout; all this apart from his sporting life in England.

With what relish he recounts his various adventures with rod and gun, how even the simplest delights of wildfowling appealed to him, and what use he made of his experiences with brush and pen! No better character could have been singled out for good fortune than this man, who has left behind him, after a long life, such a wealth of natural history writing and so many stirring tales of his adventures!

And here is an account of his battles with the giant salmon of Norway which cannot fail but to stir the blood of every true fisherman.

The Samkomme Pool

SAMKOMME Pool is formed by the junction of the Sur River with the main stream. It is easily commanded by wading the Sur; but when the latter is too deep and strong to wade, the pool presents some slight difficulty, owing to the opposite bank being inaccessible and the main current running at an angle of forty-five degrees towards the angler. Hence, in the temptation to cover the whole water, he is apt to lose control of his fly which then drifts drowned and helpless.

I had fished it down carefully with as long a line as I can manage, leaving untried the dangerous bit at the top, and proceeded to the pools below, while W. tried Samkomme again with a change of fly. He wisely reversed my attack and using a short line, almost at first case, a monster salmon lunged along the surface and seized the small Jock Scott in the strongest stream-head.

I had hardly commenced casting below ere a syren-signal startling the echoes, summoned me back to Samkomme.

This fish, while evidently convinced that safety lay in the strongest stream (whence he had first emerged) made continuous runs, short and sharp, down or across the pool, taking off twenty to thirty yards of line with a screech, but always returning to the heavier water close at hand. Again and again during these excursions he 'flowzed' or plunged along the surface, sending the water flying and exposing his formidable proportions – full four feet long by estimate – with massive shoulders and a depth which seemed disproportionate. But he never tried to leave the pool, which was about sixty yards in length. At the end of half an hour's fight, he hung more in the slack water, and once seemed disposed to go down the rapids below, the main stream of which ran far away under the opposite shore. But if ever that desperate attempt was in his mind, an equally desperate counter effort dissuaded him, and for twenty minutes longer the struggle continued without respite or breathing time, but within its original limits; yet after fifty minutes of this there were few, if any signs of submission – indeed it appeared an open question whether angler or quarry were in a more parlous state. Distress there certainly existed, and Erik now crept forward beneath the willows. Twice the gaff moved out in readiness, but the fish again sought the middle depths. Fifty-five minutes and he once more came sailing round the bushes – still on an even keel, and no inducement could bring him quite within reach. Then, without a moment's notice, the rod sprang upright, the line twirled backwards among wild cherry blossom, and the fish was gone – gone for ever!

The little Jock Scott hung unharmed on the gut; its hold firm as its puny size could grasp, had simply worn itself out, and the strong gristle and sinews of the big beast's mouth had given way under the strain and stress of the struggle, and of a three-pound pressure maintained continuously during an hour and five minutes. Those five minutes would probably have served to kill this grand fish, had only the hold held good.

ABEL CHAPMAN, *Wild Norway*

A Dee Memory

ON the Dee I was the guest of a boy whose father was tenant of a fine stretch. Early in the morning we were met at the riverside by a tall and shaggy gamekeeper; taciturn, business-like; not ill-natured to look at, but certainly not so cheerful as many a gillie is; resentful, I have no doubt, at having to attend on youngsters. When he saw my rod, that with which I had been successful on the Eden, his frown deepened into irritated contempt. I had come to think my rod, which was of greenheart and thirteen feet long, sufficient for all occasions. If I could manage a salmon in one part of the country, what had I to fear in any other? Thus, I had proudly reasoned, if at all, in setting out for Banchory. My satisfaction, it seemed, was foolish. Not speaking a word, the gamekeeper held out a hand for the rod, and, with a wave of the other, called my snubbed consideration to the grassy bank behind him. There lay two rods, salmon rods, with huge reels, lines run through the rings, and enormous flies ready to be used. I had never before fired a salmon fly in earnest; but with that majestic Highlandman looking on, still silent, and not complimentary in spirit, this was no time to seem confused or hesitant. Calmly, therefore, with aplomb, I stooped towards one of the rods. It was much less easy to lift than I could have supposed, but with an effort, while the gillie's back was turned towards me, soon I had it erect. Holding it against my right shoulder I stepped over the pebbles, steadily as I could to the water's edge. What was to be done next? The salmon were rising just in front of me. I saw them, I had never seen so many in one pool before, and I have never had such a spectacle since. They were not leaping. Merely they were constantly coming up, gently breaking the water with their heads, and in some cases, as they dropped, making swirls with their tails. They were exactly like gigantic trout feeding in a well-stocked pool. There was I standing gazing at them, inactive. That, however, was not for more than a minute. I knew that the discomforting visage of the Highlandman in the rear would be upon me and that it was not a white feather I held aloft. To work, then! Cautiously I let the long rod droop; unloosed the very large fly; with help from the torrent, let out a good many yards of line; and was prepared for action. I cast; it had been a sound intuition which made me hesitate. A salmon rod, even if it be an inheritance from times gone by, is not of insupportable weight; but if it be of the Shannon build, heavier in the middle than at the butt, it calls for a skill in balancing that is not yours by nature. Just as I saw the fly about to fall into the thick of the fish, about twenty yards out, I felt my bodily equilibrium being not less disturbed than the mental. The great rod, with the fat knob at the end wedged against the pit of my person was a lever. Headfirst, I followed it into the river. As the pebble bank was shelving, the water into which I went was not deep. I remember wishing that it were. Death by honourable drowning would be preferable to be beholding again the countenance of that Highlandman. His shaggy cheeks would now be relaxed in sarcasm. He helped me out and that by the ignominious heels. When I was once more upstanding 'You should go home,' he said, not ungently, his tenderness was cutting. Home indeed! Still, I could not well begin again just there. Yearning for solitude, to be unseen, I wandered off in the direction of Balmoral, leaving my host and the Gael to make the best they could of Banchory, I did not go far. Within a quarter of a mile I came upon a temptation. A ledge of scraggy rock stretched out into the river, from the point of this natural pier, I should be able, with ease, to cast upon an attractive patch of water. Thither I picked my way, and then let out the line. At the very first cast, delivered with desperate resolution, I found myself in trouble, which, though less unheroic, was more serious than that from which I had just emerged. In the black water, where the fly was stemming the strong current, I saw a heaving gleam from out the depths, and instinctively raised the rod. Lo! I had hooked a salmon. At first his behaviour was sedate, he ran across towards the other bank and slowly returned to his holt. Then, after a pause as if for reflection, he began a movement straight towards me. He came as it were foot by foot, deviating neither to the right nor to the left; I reeling up in strict accordance with his leisure; deliberately he came, until he was at my very toes, in the dark depths gurgling in the lee of the perilous jetty. There he rested; to keep in touch with him, I had to hold the rod straight up, sometime, as it moved slightly, or as I did, the taut line brushed my face. For many minutes the fish lay still, how long was this to go on? The query was not without dire suggestiveness. While the salmon sulked, I realised, I should, unless I took action, be imprisoned on the demn'd, damp, cold, uncomfortable Dee. There was no one looking, I would make a bolt for freedom. The ledge of rock was so narrow and so scraggy that I had had much difficulty in walking over it when comparatively unencumbered; but it was just possible that if I ran in bold long bounds fortune would favour my footsteps. Holding the rod so that the winch would be free to act, cautiously I wheeled right-about face, and made for the shore in haste. When I was half-way to safety the salmon turned tail and fled, and of course, my risky foothold failed. The fish was going downstream, and keeping well in towards our own side of the river, which, in water much deeper than myself could measure, helped me to keep afloat and gain a footing. There was now no lack of liveliness in the proceeding.

The line whizzed hither and thither through the broad flood; it was wagged in violent jerks from side to side; the salmon leapt again and again, and his splashings were heard above the breeze. Suddenly at a bend of the tree-fringed bank I came within sight of the Highlandman and my host. In the river and not well-groomed, I alone, it would appear, was for the moment visible. 'Tamnation! here he is again,' I heard the Highlandman exclaim. Instantly, however, seeing things truly, he changed his tune; 'Reel in, reel in!' he cried, 'or she'll be roond that rock and cut ye!' I saw the risk. Although manifestly affected by what had befallen, the salmon, head to the torrent, was moving steadily, sideways, towards the other bank, near which a jagged rock churned the water into foam. If he won his way beyond it on the upper side, and then dropped down, I should be undone. With all my might I checked him; rod, line, and cast stood the uncompromising strain; desisting, the salmon rolled over and over, as if in rage, lashing the water with his tail; and ere long, almost at the very spot where little more than an hour before he had landed the fisherman, the Highlandman gaffed the fish.

W. EARL HODGSON, *Salmon Fishing*

Salmon River

ONE May morning, before the sun had climbed high in the heavens, I went along the path that led beside the river, on my way to the pool most likely at that height of water to yield a fish. As I passed the backwater of an upper pool, I was tremendously excited at seeing a solid phalanx of salmon hovering beneath the unrippled sunlit surface. Four abreast they lay and three deep and there were yet more lying at a lower plane directly underneath them. I lay along the slanting bole of a tree overhanging the pool and watched them until the angle of light became unfavourable for observation. I saw one fish leave its fellows, swim easily up to the surface, gather a tremendous impetus and leap clear of the water. A moment later, it appeared from nowhere in particular and again took up its correct position in the phalanx. As the sun moved towards its zenith, the bodies of the salmon merged into the greyness of the depths, until only a number of slowly moving white mouths could be observed. I came down early the next morning but only to find the shoal had dispersed and salmon began to rise in the well-known places, where as yet that season none had been seen to show. The main spring run was very late that year.

If the river be running bank high, so that salmon have a clear road before them, the periodic rests every travelling fish must have are generally taken in a quiet lay-by, such as the inside of the curve of the river. Instead of contending with the racing torrent, they find a gently flowing stream, in which there is no need to look for a lodge.

Should spate follow spate and the river rise to an exceptional height the usual high-water resting-places will be swallowed up in

Salmon River

the general rush of water to the sea and salmon will lie in the most unlikely places.

When the fields bordering upon the river have been partly submerged, I have waded, where, even in high water, there is a low grassy bank, and, in wading in shallow water, have trodden upon a salmon, resting barely a yard from the river's edge. On another occasion, a salmon made a grab for a fly which I had allowed for a moment to hang in the water between me and the bank from which I had just waded. These two experiences have taught me not to risk treading on fish by wading in very high floods, but to fish from the bank and use only a short line.

The river has dwindled until there is hardly any current through the pools. Some of the rocks by which in good salmon-water, fish are almost certain to lie, stand lonely and desolate upon the river's edge – others rise up gauntly from the water and often their heads are crowned with grass and flowers, sprung from seeds that have been borne by the wind, or by the birds, and have chanced to fall into cracks filled with rich alluvial soil. The unwisdom of these flowers is no greater than the folly of the moorhen, which will often build a nest in the cleft of a mid-stream rock and back the continuance of the drought to the extent of her third brood of eggs. Wherever there is shelter, the Canada weed, pruned no longer by the flow of the water, spreads rapidly; and flannel weed clings to every stone, until the river bed is spread with a carpet of waving green. As the stream grows narrower salmon withdraw during the day into the recesses of the pools and show less often at those taking places where there is still depth of water. Yet they keep up their custom of jumping at the hour of dusk and frequently at midday as well, as though a signal were being acknowledged by all the salmon up and down the river. I have sat at the bend of a river and watched the fish in four distinct pools obeying for half an hour or so, at irregular intervals, this strange impulse. Mr. Menzies states he once noticed the same habit among fish cruising in the sea in Thurso Bay. The evening time of jumping in fresh water sometimes lasts until night has fallen, so that the splash of fish as they return to the water, comes with rather startling intensity to ears already straining to hear what the eyes can no longer see.

Outside these times, there is not very much leaping, until the fish grow really stale or 'potted.' During a late summer drought, a salmon, as though to get rid of fresh-water lice, or to ease the pressure of the growing spawn or, quite possibly, to obtain compensation for the lack of oxygen in the water, will be observed leaping almost vertically from the water, and returning on its side or on its back with a noisy smack. Or it will ricochet over the surface of the pool in several skips as a flat stone will do if it is thrown with a spinning motion and parallel to the water.

Shortly before the evening rising-time the fish become very restless and often swim at a great speed up to the neck of the pool. It is rather uncanny to see the V-shaped ripple, now straight, now wavering, of an invisible fish, or the following wave, reminding one of the curving water behind a fast launch.

At the head and at the tail of a pool, in the fast running stream, there is more oxygen contained in the water. A fish makes use of this fact when the river is low, by going up to the thin water and the stickles where the pools begin or by dropping down until its tail is hanging over the edge, so to speak, and within the rough water below the draw of the pool. Aeration in a river is all important; one of the deadly effects of pollution is the absorption of the oxygen contained in the water. Pollution is, therefore, less harmful to fast and well aerated rivers than to those which are sluggish; and more harmful to any stream when it is very low than when it is at its normal height. It should be remembered that the surface area of water, that is the surface of water coming in contact with the air, is the most important factor. Other things being equal, a river twenty feet across and six deep contains less oxygen than one thirty feet wide and four feet deep, although their volume is approximately the same. This is because the latter has a larger oxygen-collecting surface.

Late one afternoon the wind, which had been inconstant throughout the day, succeeded in gaining the west; the air grew warmer, almost to thunder point; the clouds for one moment lifted and the sun shone through. But the sheep upon the hillside lay low and the swifts flew across to the hedgerows. Then the clouds dropped and hung heavily upon the hill-tops; and the rain fell steadily in the gathering darkness. Or perhaps, as yet there has been no rain in the valley. A man from the hills has told us of it; we have seen it in the distance as a vast veil of greyness, hung in a moving heaven so that it sweeps gently over the screes, the bogs and the mountain plough-land, the grateful upturned face of the earth. All we know of it and much more is already old news to the salmon. As soon as rain is in the offing, the salmon in the pools become restless and often will not look at a fly. Conversely, this persistent refusal to rise is frequently taken as a sign of the coming of rain.

Then comes the spate. To a salmon this must seem like the opening of prison bars, as it sets forth on another stage of the journey to the spawning beds.

Whether the river rises slowly, or, adding two feet or more to its depth in the space of an hour, quickly becomes a raging torrent, the first signs of it are the tiny arms of water, stretching out between the boulders and around the grass hummocks to retake the lost territory. The river's edge advance haltingly, pile up until a sort of convex wall is formed and then reach forward, like drops of water upon a dry sloping surface, which hesitates and deepen at their lower edge, before they decide to run. This is a most useful sign of rising water that all fishermen should know. On every shingle beach the water, still clear, will soon cover a strip of stones, bleached by the sun; this also is a sign of a stream beginning to rise.

The flood grows and carries upon its bosom the vanguard of river flotsam; small logs of wood, bottles, cans, tins and other disfiguring garbage, thrown into the river when the bailiff's back has been turned, are also brought nearer to the sea. The water thickens and assumes a grey-yellow colour when the road-washings come into it – a turgid yellow or red (according to the soil) when banks crumble and are swept away; and a reddish-yellow when it is stained by mountain peat-water. Then the débris comes down from above; branches of trees and posts; arms of elms or ash and even the trees themselves. Sometimes dead pigs float down, legs uppermost; hens, more than usually foolish, and lambs or sheep, that have died high up in the mountains are lifted by the rising tide and carried away. All these and much besides go racing seawards.

The flood reaches its height, remains there for a short time and marks its highest level with a line of flotsam; small pieces of wood as thick as pencils, fir cones, chips of bark, corks, the refuse of domestic life and occasional slips of a fungus known as tree-sponge. The pressure of the water from above grows weaker, the river gradually subsides and, becoming less turbid, fines down to high clear water of a greyish colour, in which there is still much sand and sediment in suspension. Or, if the stream has been stained with black water from the peat hags, it turns to what is known in Ireland as porter; and foam sailing downstream gathers together to form large bergs in the backwaters. Later on, this water clears and turns to dark claret with a bluish tinge; and as the last of the foam is being drawn away by the current, the river runs a pale-brown sherry.

All that has gone before is but a poor attempt to paint in words the full wonder of a river in flood, when the pent-up water of the clouds has burst upon the uplands and races majestically onwards, divided by the arches of the bridge and yet united in its purpose. A spate is full of soft music, but its streams are dumb; it takes the weir in its stride and glides evenly over, down, down, down, always down to the sea, its mother.

ERIC TAVENER, *Salmon Fishing*

The Chef of Beauly Castle

THIS is the story of the Chef of Beauly Castle, a man who had greatness thrust upon him, who was singled out by the Goddess of Fortune for one of her richest jests.

The Chef knew right well how to cook a salmon but not how to catch one, nor yet how to throw a fly, and probably more for the chance of a little relaxation on the waters of the Beauly River he accompanied one, Frazer, a Pipe Major, in a boat. Now it is recorded that whilst Frazer was raising the anchor the Chef took up the rod unbidden, and rashly hurled the lure upon the bosom of the river.

And here the Goddess of Fortune laughed aloud and bade a mighty salmon to take hold of the lure. And forthwith it came to pass. There was a turmoil amidst the waters and the Chef found himself attached to the mightiest salmon ever caught on rod and line in those parts. The unhappy man knew not how to play a fish, Frazer could not lift the anchor. But somehow it was done, the anchor lifted by the Pipe Major, the boat was free, but the Chef and the salmon were, by the Goddess's command, still held fast, and connected one to the other.

At last the boat drifts against the bank and the battle wages fast and furious. All this autumn morning the fight goes on, three hours pass by until fish and Chef begin to weaken.

At last that monster salmon is at the bank-side and the Goddess laughed again and bade the rod to break. And it did so. But yet the fish was on. Now it came to pass that the net was put under the salmon and the Goddess laughed again and bade the net to break. And it was as She commanded. But yet the fish was on and the Chef could not get free of the fish.

At last the salmon was landed and the Chef obtained a big thick stick and carried the salmon to Beauly Castle.

And thereafter it is on record that he ran about the castle like one demented saying 'I am the champion fisher of the Beauly. I can catch a salmon as well as cook one,' and what he said was true.

That salmon weighed fifty pounds. So does the Goddess make sport of us poor mortals. This is a true story told by one, MacKintosh, who was there, and sent by him to Mrs. Cameron of Clunes, who kindly passed it on to me, on the twenty-second of February, in the Year of Our Lord, MCMXLIV.

MRS. MURIEL CAMERON

A Salmon from Loch Awe

IN May 1935, my wife and I were on our honeymoon. We had been married at the end of April and after a week or so in Devon, where my wife duly killed her first – and following on that several other – salmon, we progressed by easy stages up the west coast in Scotland and put up at the Loch Awe Hotel.

It had not been my intention to do any more fishing, but rather to devote ourselves to motoring about, picnicking and so forth, and generally to relax after the excitement of the wedding.

On the morning following our arrival, however, the sight from the hotel windows of various boats trolling steadily round the loch and more, the sight of several fish jumping, proved too much to be borne. A boat was soon forthcoming, together with gillie, by name Peter, and by nature 'verra dour.' However, as events were to prove, he was a man of great resource and on better acquaintance a most delightful companion. On that first morning luck was with us as before lunch I had hooked and killed a nice fish of 11lb., trolling a 2¼-in. blue and silver minnow.

The next day was one which will be remembered in that part of Scotland for the very severe snowstorm which did untold damage to the nesting grouse. The cold was intense for the time of year and not a boat appeared on the loch.

It had, however, always been my experience (and was a fact always maintained by my father and his friends) that salmon will take in a snowstorm almost more readily than at any other time. Accordingly, I somewhat diffidently, suggested to my wife that we ought to give it a try. She, to her lasting honour, replied that she was quite game and so we set off – dour looks on the face of Peter and also on those of the others in the hotel which told me quite plainly their opinion of me as a bridegroom if I was prepared to take my bride out fishing on a day like that!

The eastern end of Loch Awe below the hotel shallows gradually to the mouth of the Orchy and there is then a short stretch of the river itself – about three hundred yards – before one comes to a big still pool below the railway viaduct carrying the line to Oban. Here a great number of the Orchy fish congregate, and Peter assured us that it was well worth a trial despite the fact that it is choked with snags of every description brought down by the river. In addition the soft bank on the pool's south side was crumbling away and allowing a number of dwarf oaks which grew there to fall into the water as well, thereby adding a hundredfold to the hazards should one by any chance get into a fish there.

Conditions on the open loch were pretty bad, with quite a considerable sea running – not to mention the wind and the snow. We turned gratefully, therefore, for the shelter of the river mouth and pulled up towards the pool, Peter and myself at the oars as it had been quite impossible for one man alone to compete against the wind and sea on the open loch. My wife sat on the stern thwart, wrapped in many coats, and with a rod out on each side of her, armed respectively with a 2¼-in. blue and silver and a 2¾-in. brown and gold minnow.

At this stage I should add that the rods which we were using were not in the least suitable for the job in hand. Not having intended to fish much in Scotland on this trip, we had sent off most of the rods back to my father in the rod-box when we had left Devonshire, only taking with us those which were most easily taken in the car and consisting of a light twelve-foot greenheart grilse rod and a very short split-cane spinning rod, really designed for pike fishing from a boat.

Peter and I rowed steadily up the river and along the south side of the pool just clear of the sunken trees. Suddenly, bang! – the grilse rod top went down with a terrific jerk. Both Peter and I thought that it was undoubtedly one of the sunken trees, but the next instant there was no doubt what it was as the line was making tracks for the centre of the pool at high speed despite all my wife's efforts to hang on to her fish.

For a time the fish did little except cruise about at a good pace all round the pool but did not, for some odd reason, attempt to entangle us in the trees. After some considerable time my wife had lost all feeling in both hands in the intense cold and turned the rod over to me for a spell. Knowing that I could rely on the line and also that the 'Killin' wire trace was new and unkinked, I pulled at that fish for all I was worth in an effort to make it display some greater measure of activity and thus give us some hope that we might sometime tire it. It was however, a thin hope as we continued to go steadily round and round the pool despite constant shiftings of the boat in order to alter the angle of strain.

Eventually, after about forty minutes of the game of 'pull devil, pull baker,' with never a sight of our adversary, he made a sudden rather faster run across the pool and rolled over on the surface at a distance of about fifty yards from the boat. The view was only momentary but the impression gained was of a nice fish, quite clean, of about twenty-five pounds. Then down again into the deep water as before and despite anything I could do to the contrary the slow procession began again. It was by now quite evident that the little grilse rod just had not got the power to lift the fish in that stagnant water and we were all beginning to get a little desperate with the cold and generally awful conditions. My left hand, on which most of the strain had fallen, of course, had long ago gone quite numb and I was wondering vaguely to myself how long it would be before it became frost-bitten, when I was aware that the pull on the fish had changed and had now become quite 'dead.' We were, at this time towards the southern side of the pool and rowed slowly towards the place where it was by now abundantly obvious that we were snagged!

This fish had now been on for about an hour and twenty minutes and our feelings in the boat can be imagined as it dawned on us that we were almost certainly going to lose it after all! Slowly we approached the spot where the line was immovable, and presently it lead straight up and down. Peter leaned out far over the water while my wife hung grimly on to his legs. Cupping his head in his hands he put his face right down to the surface of the water and peered down. For a long time – silence – then: 'Man, I can see the fish line!' He scrambled up then and told us that the line appeared to be fast round an old piece of pipe or something of the sort, and that the fish he could just make out lying belly up on the bottom alongside it. Anxiously I asked him how far down he thought it was, but he seemed uncertain, and so I hurriedly leaned over and peered down for myself. For a moment I could see nothing in the dark amber-coloured water, but shortly could just make out something vague and white at what seemed to be a great distance.

Sitting up again I held a hurried council of war and we decided that our one and only hope was to try and gaff the fish where it lay. My gaff was one of Hardy's longest size telescopic which, I believe, measure fifty inches fully extended. There did not appear to be any suitable material for binding readily to hand in the boat, but by good fortune I had on a pair of shooting boots with almost new leather laces! It was the work of a moment to whip them out and with their aid the gaff was securely lashed to the loom of an oar. Then commenced the great attempt. Cautiously Peter lowered his unwieldy weapon overside while we waited – as still as mice and with our hearts in our mouths. Down and down went the oar till there were only about eighteen inches left above water.

Then, for what seemed an age Peter remained absolutely still until, with a jerk he struck, and began to wriggle violently, trying to work himself back into the boat. My wife seized him while I endeavoured to trim the boat what time the oar rose rapidly into the air. A moment later an enormous tail broke the surface beside the boat and in the same second the whole fish. Never shall I forget what a great brute it looked in that first instant, but what was more important was that it was apparent tha the gaff was no more than just 'in and out' close to its ventral fin, and that any attempt to heave it into the boat would undoubtedly break the hold out. In addition, the trace had broken and so the fish was to all intents and purposes, free. Yelling to my wife to get to the other side of the boat and trim it, I leapt wildly across to Peter and managed, by great good fortune, to get my hand into the fish's left-hand gill at the first attempt. Peter at the same moment seized the tail and with one heave we had it in the bottom of the boat.

It really seemed then as if the fish woke up for the first time and realised that something was amiss! It jumped and kicked and flapped and heaved and Peter and I got in each other's way and cast wildly round for a stretcher or something to kill it with. Eventually it was given the 'quietus' and we sat back and looked at it and at each other. Then we got out a flask and finished it and, when we had straightened out ourselves, the boat, and our gear, pulled slowly back towards the hotel.

That is really the end of the story except for one or two details as regards the fish itself. The weight was 36lb. and it was, as far as I could gather from local sources, the second largest fish which has been killed in the loch – at any rate of recent years – a 39-pounder having been taken some years earlier.

The most interesting thing, however, was that it was a heavy hen fish, and an unusually large one, and was very heavily spotted indeed around the gill covers. I took some scales, and with the aid of a rather indifferent magnifying glass thought I could clearly make out three distinct spawning marks. This seemed to me so unusual that, having despatched the fish to my father in London by the night train, I asked him on the telephone to arrange for some further scales to be sent to the *Fishing Gazette* for expert opinion. In due course the answer came back that we were quite correct in our guess and that the fish was certainly returning to spawn for the fourth time.

The fish was hooked at a few minutes past eleven and was landed, or rather boated, at a quarter to one. The depth of water at the place where it was gaffed was eleven feet three inches.

LT.-COMMANDR. H. C. NORTON. R.N.V.R.

A Lucky Day

THIS is the story of my first fresh-run salmon, a giant only because of the light tackle in use.

It was the first day of a week's welcome break in the early part of May 1940, and the River Usk at Abergavenny was still fishable although fining down somewhat. The weather was perfect, being fairly mild with some sun and light cloud. There was a light westerly intermittent breeze and a delightful freshness in the air that invigorated and made one eager to commence.

The previous winter I had partly bought and partly made salmon spinning and fly outfits and had so far obtained nothing but kelts. This was not discouraging as no fresh-run fish had been taken on this stretch, the Town Water, which was excellent for trout but lacked a good pool. In fact the only chance of a fish was in three 'lies' that yielded an average total of six fish per year.

At about 10.30 a.m. on the day in question it was decided to fish down-wet for trout, and, fixing up a 10 ft. Walker, a No. 2 Kingfisher and Hardy Houghton cast tapering to 3X, a Greenwell was tied as a dropper. In May, Usk trout do not always rise well, the chief attractions being apparently the larvae of the stone fly, which hatches in considerable numbers, and elvers which run in April and May. In an endeavour to meet these contingencies, without sight or photograph and only the male and female fly as a guide, I tied a truly weird mass of silk with colours varying from dirty yellow to dirty green, and with two turns only of a small red hackle a third of the length from the head. The whole almost covered the shank of a long mayfly hook and this was tied to the point, and be it said, confidently fished without result down the first stream, just below Llanfoist bridge.

A few hundred yards below, after passing some rapids, the bathing stretch is reached. This is really good trout water and occasionally a salmon rests here on its journey upstream. Wading out at the head of the stream, every yard was carefully searched across and down. Soon the line was sinking well and hope rose as it was evident that the best chance of a fish was near the bottom. About half-way down and just above the bathing house *it happened*. The line stopped and a wristy action followed. At first there was no movement, just a tight line into something heavy. Then a slow, very slow, move against the current. A whacking trout this, I thought. Putting on all the strain I dared, I could make no impression – just the slow, steady movement upstream. I thrilled! Was it a 'daddy,' an eel or simply a bunch of weed? Was I fancying the movement? No! definitely it was a yard or two higher now than when hooked. Could it be – was it – a salmon? In any case, what chance of a kill was there? If only I had put up a reservoir cast to 2X! The gut would soon wear in the jaw – it *is* a salmon! With a rush it went almost to the head of the stream. With butt well up and light pressure on the reel, the fish was 'tops.' Whatever it said – went. There was only forty yards of backing, making seventy in all and immediately below was a row of trees with deep water and high banks. I had to keep in the water and then had only twenty yards in which to manoeuvre. The fish turned and tore madly downstream – on – on – on – the test was surely coming very quickly now – wait! It has stopped – near the far bank about thirty yards below – phew! would my heart never stop pounding? What to do now except to keep up as much strain as 3X would allow? I wondered if the fish was feeling it.

Fortunately I had caught several large reservoir trout in the 4lb. region, and was not entirely new to a fish that really took charge – but this was different. Voices broke in from behind. Two anglers whom I had passed earlier offered to go back to the car for a gaff, but then I thought it a waste of time. After about twenty or thirty minutes I began to hope. The fish must be lipped only and the jaws in that case would be bearing on the long shank. My heart leapt. There were quite a few spectators on the opposite bank and one offered to send his boy for Charlie (Mr. Charles Morgan, mine host of the Bridge Hotel at the top of the water and a good river man.) It was a good three-quarters of a mile away and the boy would not be back for at least forty minutes. I accepted and he trotted away. By now my arm was aching and the fish had left the far bank and was boring easily just below and about ten yards out. Things were not entirely hopeless. Could I recover some line? Was it tiring?

I went to the bottom of my twenty yards beat, hoping to get the fish above when it decided to take charge again. Down the river it rushed and why it stopped when only a few turns remained on the reel is just 'one of those things.' I could see the reel drum plainly. It just had to be. Stop it did, however, and back it came at almost the same speed. I backed and recovered frantically and luckily was able to maintain contact. How my left arm ached! It had been locked at the elbow for nearly an hour. The fish started to bore almost opposite again. I took a welcome rest, just keeping contact with the butt still perpendicular.

'Here comes Charlie,' I heard someone say. I looked round. Yes, it was he, hurrying with a long gaff. I had an attack of nerves. Would I really be lucky enough? I started day-dreaming. I visualised walking into my friend's engineering shop and placing the salmon and cast – I woke up. The fish was off again – up and towards my side and Charlie was entering the water. I trembled. Charlie was asking questions. What fly? Where? I answered in monosyllables. The fish was now well upstream and on the other side of the stream. Charlie was issuing orders. 'As soon as you can, bring it near and I will take a chance.' It came over under the relentless if comparatively slight pressure I was able to bring to bear, and was now near my bank only twenty yards up.

I tried hard to bring it towards me and sure enough it was coming down and out. 'Get out farther, Charlie – and don't miss.' He 'got out' and when, with only a few yards off the reel and within six feet of the gaff, the salmon saw him. There was a step forward, a lunge – and up and sideways shot the fish for quite two or three yards. It was the first time it had broken water. Experience only saved a break. I had dropped the point and thus eased the pressure. I tightened. With relief I found it was still there and taking line fast. Out and down-stream again – it could have gone three hundred yards without hindrance – and then it turned towards a collection of brushwood under the roots of trees immediately below me. If it gets there its *finis*. 'Pull him back,' shouts Charlie, forgetting. I held on and watched. It approached the brushwood, turned inches from it and came towards me. The agony in my arm had been temporarily forgotten in the anxiety of the moment, but now forced attention to the need for getting the fish in quickly. I could stand little more. The fish was tiring; there was no doubt about it. Surfacing in deep water out and below, it showed its side for an instant or two before again slowly moving upstream.

'You've got him,' says Charlie. Again that thrill despite my left arm. I got out of the water. The fish was up and out. 'It's now or never,' I said and tried light pumping operations.

The fish gave and gave ever so slowly and then it temporarily stopped struggling and drifted down with the current. A quick upward movement and Charlie had the fish in the air and on the bank in a jiff. He dropped the gaff and picked up the fly from the grass. It had not pierced the skin apparently and simply dropped out when the tension was released. What luck – and what a sight! I dropped the rod and could not straighten my arms for hours afterwards. Spectators agreed at a ninety-minute fight, but to me it seemed ages. The sight of the fish and the unstinted praise of the anglers present was ample compensation however, and it was a very happy being that was dragged back to the hotel to celebrate.

The weight was only 10¼lb., but to those who have not experienced the joys and the agonies of such a fight, I say they have missed something. Exactly a week afterwards I got another in the same spot on salmon tackle. It was killed in under twenty minutes, fought well but is now almost forgotten.

The trout cast with the original flies attached is a possession I shall cherish always.

W. E. B. SMITH

The Monster of the Stein Pool

IT was a Sunday evening. As the end of the week drew near we had been anxious as to local customs with regard to Sunday fishing – these varying in different parts of Norway. Erik had told us we might fish after dinner; and Gjertrud, our laughter-loving handmaiden who happily seemed to find something comical in almost everything we said and did, propounded the brilliant idea. 'Yes, but you can dine at ten and begin fishing at eleven o'clock.' There was subtlety about this capable of infinite development, but it struck us as too refined, so we delayed starting until four in the afternoon; the greater population of the village, we observed, accompanying our stolkjaer or making short cuts through the woods. When I commenced to cast Stein Pool from the platform, there was an audience of thirty-four folks, lads and lassies, old men and maidens, assembled on the bank behind.

Stein Pool is dead and deep , with a moderate stream running in beyond mid-river, and the fish lying well in towards the opposite bank, which was heavily wooded down to the brink. The nearer half of the river is (in fine water) a deep black set where the line, if allowed to enter, is instantly drowned. This combination necessitates not only long casting, but rapid long throws and quick returns, which means hard work, especially as a high bank, twenty yards behind, involved lifting the line well up in the air.

The swish of the line in the faces of the spectators soon cleared them off to safer distances, and about half-way down the pool there came that tug – no, it is not a tug, but a sudden inflexible resistance as of a tree trunk or solid rock. But I knew that a big fish had annexed the fly, deep under and without showing, and delayed not to drive the small double hook well home into his jaws.

Five minutes later, after a prolonged period of bottom fighting, jagging and sulking, alternated with sub-aquatic gymnastics and contortions that kept me trembling for my tackle the captive came up with a sudden rush to the surface, ploughing alone flat on his bent broadside for twenty yards. Then we saw that this fish was even bigger than the lost monster of Samkomme. Was it possible to subdue such a salmon on that paltry hook? True, it was double, that reflection seemed inspiring. But then the hooks were smaller than that which had already failed, being actually the smallest (No. 5) in all my collection and therefore specially selected for fine water in a streamless pool.

I determined rightly or wrongly to play for safety, to act solely on the defensive, and to leave the fish to kill himself, even though it involved my spending the night with him in the process.

I pass over details which would involve repetition. Suffice it that the fish, persistently dropping downstream obliged me to follow. This for some distance was easy enough, but lower down trees grew to the water's edge. Still it was necessary to follow, having some fifty yards of line out. The fish was now in the shallows, rolling heavily at intervals with short sullen rushes, during one of which I felt a slight 'draw' – perhaps the hold of one hook had failed. W. going down through the trees to reconnoitre reported the fish *'meget tret'* – tired. For almost minutes at a time he lay inert in midstream, suffering himself to be towed ahead in the slack pool tail without resistance. Had it now been possible to incline the rod inland an opportunity to gaff might, it seemed probable, be secured. But the thickset branches projecting far across the stream forbade this and two alternatives remained. One was to drop still lower downstream trusting to find shallows and get in the cleek at the foot of the pool. This, however, I rejected, first, because the fish was yet in no sense under control and the danger in the stronger stream obvious, nor was there any reasonable certainty of gaffing there. Secondly, because I knew nothing of the depth or nature of the water below, beyond seeing that there was a strong rapid at least two hundred yards long, with an island in midstream and thick wood on either bank. Hence I elected the other course, and endeavoured slowly to tow the half-beaten fish upstream and thus clear the trees. A stone thrown in below the fish's tail at this point might have served the purpose, but we did not think of it at the time.

While thus engaged, though exerting no special pressure – indeed, humouring the captive in all his little runs and lunges – the rod flew up and the fly came home unharmed. The fight was over and the fish the victor.

A few days after in the Stein Pool, I hooked a third monster. I felt him come, struck at the right moment, yet in rather less than a minute, for some reason unexplained, the hook came away. During his short captivity he had made one long surface run thus showing us his size.

The conclusions we came to were these. That these very heavy fish given the best of holds on single gut may take an hour to kill and possibly more, and that during so prolonged a pressure the hold of a small hook (in fine water no other is of any use) must almost necessarily wear itself out.

I give for what it may be worth, the quality and rank of the two above-named fish, these points being set down by estimate by the local experts.

1. The Samkomme fish, forty pounds, fresh from sea the night before.

2. The Stein Pool fish, a larger salmon, probably from forty-five to fifty, but of some fourteen days sojourn in the river.

These estimates I take to be fairly near the mark. After handling heavy fish one comes to know the strength and style of the twenty-pounder and of fish ranging between that and thirty pounds.

There are old hands among anglers who never fail to lose a fish. They may smile at this record of disaster, pointing out things done that should have been avoided or neglected that should have been tried. Well, to criticise is easy; so, too, is it to haul out heavy but ill-conditioned autumn fish from the depths of some sluggish hole. But with fresh-run springers in Scandinavian streams the case is different and the difficulty greater and more varied.

ABEL CHAPMAN, *Wild Norway*

The 'Bishop Browne' Story

IN that part of the Tay where the Earn flows in to join the larger stream and where the real estuary begins – three-quarters of a mile long at high tide, no salmon or sea trout had, until 1867, been taken by means of rod and line. After various experiments the late Bishop G. F. Browne, Bishop of Stepney, discovered that salmon could be taken with a blue or brown phantom minnow, and in the early morning of the last day but one of the rod season of 1868, a small expedition set forth from the mouth of the Earn, in a boat, with a personnel of three rods and a dour Scots boatman.

High tide that morning was at 10 a.m. and at 11.30 a.m. operations commenced. At 12.30 p.m. the middle rod was seen to drag and two seconds later the line went out at a speed that threatened to dispose of the rod and its owner. It is incidentally noted at the time that the middle rod was the weakest and that the line consisted of two trout lines spliced together to form a length of a hundred and twenty yards.

The fish decides to pull the boat all over the middle channel of the Tay before making at full speed for the mouth of the Earn, vigorously pursued by the boat. At the end of an hour and a half the fish decides to leave the Earn and makes for the north bank of the Tay, but on getting into the shallow water decides on a violent race to the southward, and at the first pause for breath the party finds itself among the shipping of Newburgh.

The fight goes on but at 3.30 p.m. there seems to be a definite weakening on the part of the fish. But alas for false hopes, the tide turns, a new surge of life begins and back we go to the westward with the tide, at a merry pace, and the party begins to think of food.

A cold rain begins to fall in the late afternoon and after four hours of gruelling fight all over the estuary the fish is seen. He leaps two feet out of the water, a monster, 'as big as a well-grown boy.' But the constant friction of the wet line on the rings has worn the threads and a strand breaks with a snap, leaving only twenty yards of whole line to defeat the biggest salmon ever seen.

Night falls and it is now 6.30. A strong salmon line has been spliced on to the trout line after frantic efforts and the party prepares for an all-night sitting. Various attempts are made to land 'a non-combatant' who has had enough, to go in search of food, but it is not until two hours later that our friends are fortified with whisky and scones, after prodigious manoeurvring with the victualling boat. At nine o'clock the rain begins to feel colder. There is a wild feeling of temptation in the air, and wild throughts of gaffs and lanterns on the water, are abroad.

However, by ten o'clock we still find them faithful, and we are now back in home waters, with still no sign of yielding on the part of either side. The fish still appears to have his strength and his opponents are now stoically committed to an indefinite life on the waters of the Tay.

At ten-thirty the line falls slack, the fish has come under the boat again. There is a frantic clicking of the reel, and the line comes in and in . . . . Alas for our gallant friends and our British Sporting Records, the tail-hook has broken.

A year later in 1869, near Newburgh where the Tay flows into the sea, a gigantic salmon of seventy-four pounds was taken in the nets, and in his mouth was the scar of a tail-hook.

DEREK BARBER

Salmon

THERE are stories of monsters that inhabit the deep holes in the Blackwater, Co. Cork.

About twelve years ago a man of the name of Maurice Hallahan, was trailing a bait out of a boat at a place called Hallahan's Rock, between Clondulane Weir and Fermoy, where the depth of the hole is supposed to be at least forty feet. He hooked a big fish, and having no one to help him put down the oars and held on to the rod, the fish dragging boat and man after him down as far as Ballydoroon stream, up again past the rock as far as Mount Rivers, and back again to the Rock, where, after sulking for hours, he took up the Funcheon River hard by, when, getting into shallow water, Hallahan put the gaff into him, but the fish was so heavy he could not get him into the boat, and was obliged to let go. The fish in his struggles broke the line and made a bolt down the Funcheon again to Hallahan's Rock and was seen no more that year. The year after a gallant Major, quartered at Fermoy, was fishing the same hole and hooked a fish which was gaffed after a long play – Hallahan's gaff still in him and enough wattling growing upon it to make a basket to carry him home!

The weight of the fish was never ascertained, and it is justly supposed it never will be.

BADMINTON LIBRARY

The Char

THE char is of the blood royal, is of the *salmonidae*, and he comes from very long ago. He is Arctic in origin, and his colours – his pinks, his greens, his vermilions – have been borrowed from the Northern Lights. And he came – how did he come into dark tarns and

Highland deer forests and the deep places of the bonny land of lakes?

It is said that he came with the push of the icepacks, with the glacier waters of the Age of Ice. And that when the pale blue glacial rivers, in the terrible days of the ice-melt, could run no further, some of their waters remained to mingle, here and again, with lakes, tarns, and lochans, in the deep beds that their mother Ice made for them in her final harbour. And therein stayed the char, men say, and there he stays still.

And did ever he come to those cold surfaces to feed on flying-ants and straddle bugs (only he rarely does) he might have seen the great survivors of the Pleistocene come down to drink. The giant fallow, perhaps, walking like an oak tree in his antlers; the cave bear shuffling and mountainous; the sabre-tooth tigress and her two savage golden-coated cubs; the mammoths, grotesque and solemn, who knows what awful else?

But the great brutes went, while the little char stayed and stays still. Listen then.

It was after the Ice Age, but before that of the motor-car. It was July, and it was 6 a.m. when the waking sun walks on all his tiptoes like a golden crab, that two little boys, a bundle of fishing-rods and easel legs, and an elder person with a paint box, packed into a wagonette to drive twenty miles, up from the laigh, into the very shadows of Lochnagar, all to catch little trout, or impressions, in the fastnesses of a deer forest. An adventure indeed.

And the loch, that is in the heart of the forest, is like a black opal to see as it lies, walled and encompassed by cliff and precipice, and flawed by a mystery of little winds and by the blue reflections of heaven. And, when its ramparts of naked rock have done with it and their climb, they cause the summer sky that roofs it to appear from the boat to be more purple than pansies. And it is no fable that has been told concerning the creels of little trout that may be caught here, of the pictures that water-colours may paint.

The loch is nearly a mile long and about a quarter broad but it looks no bigger than a dish, because the hills are so high. And wherever you look, its surface is ringed with rising trout. Their average is a bare quarter of a pound if I remember aright, I, who (it seems more remote than any ice age) was once a little boy, and one of the two anglers. But those small mountain trout fight like tiger-cats, and take by twos, sometimes threes, at a time.

The head stalker himself (for the sake of Auld lang syne and of the elder person, who will bide ashore and be painting) rows the boat. He is old, or he seems to be so to the anglers, but he is the fine man to see, eagle beaked, and splendidly bearded. . . . The boat drifts on. 'Is it deep here, Chisholm? Are there big fish here, Chisholm?' inquire the two anglers, suddenly and as one. Says Chisholm, 'I mind that his lordship was fishing himself at night and a fish took him . . .'

'Ooooh, what sort of a fish was it that broke him, Chisholm?'

'God kens, sir, a muckle fish – a fairack maybe!' The boat drifts on. The rise, for the moment is done. Then, suddenly, I am playing another, but? But? The quarter-pounder that comes fighting to the net is scarlet and green and orange – oh surely here is such a capture as never man made before! And yet, 'It's jut a bit char,' says Chisholm dispassionately. 'There's ay an odd yin in her.'

There is a pannikin, a bailer, in the boat and, moved by some precocious sense of beauty, the angler scoops the same full of the cold, deep, water, enlarges the char in it alive, and desires that the boat may be rowed to the beach that the elder person may at once wonder and mark.

And wonder and mark he does, telling the while of the loveliness and antiquity of chars.

And, 'What are you going to do with it?' he asks. An awkward question that. 'Oh, I dunno; kill it, I suppose.'

'Nonsense,' says the elder person, 'why, you've made a pet of it now, one simply *doesn't* kill pets – far better put the poor little chap back into the loch again.'

So, a trifle, perhaps, in the devotional spirit of David the King when he 'coupit' the water of the well of Bethlehem, outboard the bailer is inverted, and, with a kick of colour, the char is gone.

PATRICK CHALMERS, *The Angler's England*

The Salmon Poachers

ONE lovely spring day I set out on a week-end cycling trip. I had lately become the proud possessor of a new Raleigh bicycle and this was my first long run. I passed along the south side of the Pentlands and noticed that far to my left the Moorfoot hills were showing a faint powdering of snow which made me wonder what the road would be like farther on. Soon I was at Broughton and there had the choice of going down to Peebles, or the harder way via the Devil's Beef Tub. I decided on the latter and was soon at the little village of Tweedsmuir. Turning left at that place I headed for the heart of the hills, beside Talla Reservoir and up the terrific gradient beside Talla Linn.

I was very weary and looked about for a place to camp. To the lone wanderer this choosing of a suitable pitch is always difficult, but after searching about for some little time I settled down for the night beside a snow patch. I got out my frying-pan, lit a fire, and grilled myself some bacon. The meal finished and the pan stowed away, I drew my cape about me to serve as a blanket and burrowing into a deep bed of heather I made myself as snug as possible. About me were the great hills, infinitely ancient, already growing dim in the gathering shadows of coming night. Close by was the river, the voice of its tumbling eddies seemed to intensify my sense of loneliness. But after a little while a dipper came and, perching on a stone mid-stream, sang its evening song, which I could clearly hear above the murmur of the waters. Soon, however, it whirred away, the sense of loneliness returned and, a little later, I fell asleep.

I slept soundly enough and was wakened soon after dawn by the croaking of a pair of ravens who, no doubt, imagined they had spied a corpse lying there among the heather.

Breakfast over and the gear stowed neatly I was soon on my way once more, heading down the long valley beside the stony Megget water and so up the side of beautiful St. Mary's Loch. Near Mount Benger I saw a large flock of golden plover feeding in a field, quite the largest flock I have ever seen. The sward was dotted with the innumerable greeny-gold dumpy birds which tone so cunningly with the tints of the sward. I pushed on and was soon coasting down the long miles of the 'Paddy's Slacks' into Innerleithen. Evening found me in a little haven among some fir trees, on Tweedside above Peebles, and here I made a few casts with a fly. Soon three trout were captured and were speedily in the frying-pan. I built a wind-break to keep off the chill night breeze which was blowing across the river and, supper over, watched the glowing embers of my fire turn from brilliant yellow to orange, and finally to pink. I thought of Robert Louis Stevenson's camping place among the pines and the immortal words he wrote. I must have dropped asleep, for the next thing I knew was the sudden whirring sound of wings and a guttural quacking as a pair of mallards rose from the river hard by. I am a hunter by instinct and I knew something had disturbed the birds. Wide awake now I was up on my feet in an instant. Something made me step aside behind the rough trunk of a pine tree. Three dim figures were coming up my side of the stream.

I immediately thought of the fire which still showed a few winking embers, and of my cycle which was lying on a small open space near by, but the men came on, passed below me, and disappeared round the corner of the fir wood in which I was encamped. They were still in my close proximity, for very soon I heard the unmistakable sound of someone climbing a tree. Peering out I made out the form of a man at the top of a pine close beside the river, from which vantage point he began to direct operations. I heard him call out, not very loud: 'Here he is, doon here!' His two companions then appeared, one carrying a short rod in his hands. The latter, following the instructions of his mate up in the tree, began to cast over the deep pool immediately below.

'You're too far doon mon, about eight feet, he lies jist ayont that ledge!' Again the weighted hooks swung out. There was a sudden snatch and a great gleaming fish broke surface, plunged twice, and vanished, accompanied by the muffled oaths from the poacher in the tree.

The men again disappeared round the corner of the wood, evidently following the fish, and they must have hooked the same salmon (or another) for there came subdued shouts of 'Hold him, mon! no sae sudden! let him gang a bit,' and soon, round the bend of the stream, I saw the mad rush of a frightened salmon and the whip of the line like a lash on the surface of the water. The fish leapt clear and was off once more. The men searched up and down the pool for some time like hunting otters. But the look-out in the tree, who had not left his post all this time, again spied the quarry back again in the pool below, and this time, with a well-thrown line, it was securely hooked. A terrific fight began, the great salmon leaping, splashing, sulking, and boring, the poachers cursing and stumbling, until at last, men and fish vanished from sight behind the angle of the bank. All this time I had been standing quite still behind my tree trunk, though at times the two poachers must have been within twenty yards of me.

By the sounds around the corner I judged the battle had been won, for the man in the tree came scrambling down and joined his companions.

I heard a voice say: 'Aye, he's a guid yin – the biggest I've had yet, thirrty pounds if he's an ounce!'

After unhooking their prize they stowed it away under the bracken, no doubt planning to return later after raiding the river farther down. Had any of them turned about they must have seen me standing behind my tree, but they did not do so.

When all was quiet – save for the melancholy hooting of an owl in the dark firs over the river – I stole down to the scene of the fight, and, parting the bracken, beheld lying there the dim monstrous shape of the silver salmon. The poachers were right in their estimation of his weight, he was every ounce of thirty pounds.

I must confess I thought how nice a middle cut would be for breakfast, and moreover my night's sleep had been disturbed. And then I thought also what a difficult position I should be in if the bailiff happened to pounce upon me. And so I left it for the poachers to retrieve.

But I had witnessed a scene which would have delighted St. John or Scrope, and for me it had truly been an unforgettable and adventurous experience.

ALEXANDER BARCLAY

William Scrope wrote only two books, *Art of Deer Stalking* and *Days and Nights of Salmon Fishing*, from which work the following extract is taken.

Scrope, like Abel Chapman and Millais, was one of the fortunates. He had ample means and leisure and because he had no need to write for a livelihood, what he has to say is always readable, it never becomes 'hack work,' nor has it the heavy and verbose style of many of the Victorian writers. Born in 1772, he inherited the estate of Castle Coombe in Wiltshire. His interests were divided between literature, field sports, painting and travel. He was a friend of Sir Walter Scott, who incidentally had a high opinion of his artistic efforts declaring him 'one of the best amateur painters of his acquaintance.'

Things have greatly changed on Tweedside since Scrope's days but, as Sir Herbert Maxwell says in his introduction to Edward Arnold's 1898 Edition of *Days and Nights of Salmon Fishing*: 'Still, season after season the great fish rest in the Willowbush, Craigover, the Webbs, the Bloody Breeks, the darksome Holy Well, and the roaring Gateheugh, and resting, show the same caprice in refusing, the same incaution in seizing, the angler's lures.' Those words were written in 1898, and no doubt, they still hold good.

Scrope is here describing 'burning the water,' the finest account of salmon poaching I have yet come across.

Burning the Water

THE boat in general use for burning at night is larger than the rod-fishing boats, as more room and steadiness is required. In the centre of it, close to the side of which the 'leisterers' strike the fish, is a pole fixed vertically with a frame on top of it formed of ribs to contain combustibles.

Three men were sufficient to man the boat; one at the head,

another at the stern, as boatman and leisterers, and the third at the centre to kill the fish and trim the fire. But it will contain more men if necessary.

The remainder of the day having been spent in making arrangements, and the proper hour now being come, Harry Otter and Charlie Purdie went out from the pavilion to meet the party, who were to assemble at eight o'clock about a mile and a half up the river. The night was most favourable, it being utterly dark, and not a sough of air stirring. With caution and difficulty they felt their way step by step at the rocky base of the Scaur, where it dips into the river, till they descried the boat which was to take them across it at the Brig-end Pool. The clanking of the chains as it was loosened and flung on the planks sounded harshly in the silence of night; the oars dipped duly, and they were soon on the opposite side of the river, by which means they cut off a great sweep of the haugh, 'a huge half-moon, a monstrous cantle out,' and proceeded in a more direct line to their mark. They went on in darkness through the chilly dews, now and then stumbling into patches of furze which were scattered over the haugh; soon they begin to hear the rushing of the waters through the gorge of Carrywheel; now it breaks full and loud upon the ear, for they are arrived at the base of the wooden brae that overhangs the cast.

Two groups of men, but dimly seen, here await their arrival; one consisting of spectators lying on the ground with their plaids thrown athwart their bodies, and the other of the heroes who were to figure in the grand operation, these latter were sitting on the boats, and on the masses of rock beside them at the water edge.

All being now ready, a light was struck; and the spark being applied to rags steeped in pitch, and to fragments of tar barrels, they blazed up at once amidst the gloom, like the sudden flash from the crater of a volcano. The ruddy light glared on the rough features and dark dresses of the leisterers in cutting flames directly met by black shadows – an effect which those will best understand who in the Eternal City have seen the statues in the Vatican by torchlight. Extending itself, it reddened the shelving rocks above, and glanced upon the blasted arms of trees, slowly perishing in their struggle for existence amongst the stony crevices; it glowed upon the hanging wood, on fir, birch, broom, and bracken, half-veiled, or half-revealed, as they were more or less prominent. The form of things remote from the concentrated light was dark and dubious; even the trees on the summit of the brae sank into obscurity.

The principals now sprang into the boats. Harry Otter stood at the head, and Charlie Purdie at the stern. These men regulated the course of the craft with their leisterers; the auxiliaries were stationed between them, and the light was in the centre by the boat side. The logs, steeped as they were in pitch, crackled and burned fiercely, sending up a column of black smoke. As the rude forms of the men rose up in their dark attire, wielding their long leisters, with the streaks of light that glared partially upon them, and surrounded as they were by the shades of night, you might almost have fancied yourself in the realms below, with Pluto and his grim associates, embarked on a Stygian lake.

But as the sports began and as the Scotch accent prevailed, the illusion passed away, for no poet that I am aware of has made the swarthy and mysterious personages express themselves in the language of Tweedside; nor could one fancy salmon in the Styx, though they might well disport in the streams of the happy fields beyond.

'Now, my lads,' says the master, 'take your places. Tom, you stand next to me. Sandy, go on the other side of Tom, and do you, Jamie, keep in the middle, and take tent to cap the boats well over the rapids. Rob, do you and Tom Purdie keep good lights and fell the fish. Hallo, Tom, you have smuggled a leister into the boat for your own use!'

'Aye, aye, that have I, joust for mine ain deversion, ye ken.'

'Well, well, you may just keep it, for you are a stout chiel, and it would be hard work to get it from you, besides, no one can use it more dexterously than yourself. Now then, we will push the boat up the cheek of the stream till we come to the head of it. That will do. Now shoot her across the gorge, and down she goes merrily, broadside foremost according to rule. Cap, Charlie, cap, man. We are drifting down like mad; keep back your end of the boat.'

'Awheel, awheel, she gangs cannily noo, look, uncle, a muckle fish before ye or ever ye kent, the maister's leister gaed through him, and played all dife. That side, that side, Jamie – he's rinnin up to get past. Od ye have him and I hae anither, and anither. Keep a gude light, Tom. Now let us take up the boat to the head of the stream, or ever we look the stanes, for there war a muckle fush gaed by that nane o ye gomrells ever saw. There, we are nigh enough now haud your hand, and let her faw doon again; hey, but I see him the noo afore me – ou, what an awful beast!'

So saying, Charlie drove his leister furiously at him, but whether one of the prongs struck against the edge of the rock above him, which prevented its descent to the bottom or whatever other cause, the stroke was unsuccessful, and as he lifted the barren weapon out of the water, there arose a merry shout and guffaw from the spectators on the shore.

'Cap, cap,' cried Charlie, 'now haud yer hand, gie me up the boat – od, but I'll hae him yet, he's gane amangst thae hiding stanes.'

So saying, Charlie brought the head of the boat to the stream, pushed her higher up, and pulled her ashore; he then landed, and seizing a brand out of the fire, put it into Jamieson's hand, who preceded his eager steps like a male Thais, or one of the Eumenides in pantaloons. He now stood upon a rock which hung over the river, and from that eminence, and with the assistance of the firebrand examined the bottom of it very carefully. His body was bent over the water, and his ready leister held almost vertically as the light glared on his face you might see the keen glistening eye. In an instant he raised up his leister, and down he sprang from the rock right into the river, and with wild bound nailed the salmon to the channel. There was a struggle with his arms for a few seconds; he then passed his hands down the pole of the weapon a little way, brought himself vertically over the fish, and lifted him aloft, cheered by shouts from his friends on the shore.

Two or three more fish were taken amongst the stones at the tail of the cast, and the sport in the Carrywheel now being ended the fish were stowed in the hold of the boat, the crew jumped ashore, and a right hearty appeal was made to the whisky bottle.

It was first tendered to the veteran Tom Purdie, to whom it was always observed to have natural gravitation, but to the astonishment of all, he barely put his lips to the quaigh, and passed it to his nephew.

'Why, uncle mon, what the deil's come owre ye? I niver kent ye refuse a drappie afore, no, not sin I war a callant, I canna thole to see ye gang that gait.'

'Why, I'll tell ye what it is, Charlie. I got a repreef from Sir Walter for being fou the ither nicht.'

'Eh, uncle, how was that?'

'Why' said Sir Walter, 'Tom,' says he, 'I sent for ye on Monday, and ye were not at hame at aight o'clock I doubt ye were fou Tom.' 'I'll joust tell ye the hale truth' says I, 'I gaed roond by the men at wark at Rymers Glen, and cam in by Tarfield, then I went to Darnick, and had a glass wi Sandy Trummel at Susy, and I war joust coming awa when Rob steppit in, and cried for half a mutchkin. I wasna for takking mair, but the glasses were filled, and I did not like to be bat wi them, so I tuk mine.' 'And is that all ye had, Tom?' said Sir Walter. 'Aye, indeed it was,' said I, 'but Heaven have a care o' me, I never was the war of it till I was ganging up by Jemmy Mercer's by Coats Green and when I cam up by Kerr side I wanted to see Maister Laidlaw, but I thocht I dirstna gang in and how I got hame I dinna ken for I niver minded it nae mair, but our wife in a terrible bad key the morning, because I was sair wanted last nicht.'

'"Well," said the maister, "you mun never do the like again, Tom." We then ganged to the woods, and thinned the trees and I laboured with the axe at thae Sir Walter marked.

'"No, Tom," says he, "you will go hame with me, for you have been working very hard, and a glass of whisky will do you good"; and he cawwed to Nicholson to bring Tom a glass o' Glenlivet. I tuk it doon, and mon, if yed found it – it beat a' the whisky I ever tasted in my life. "Well, Tom," says Sir Walter, "how do you feel after it? Do ye think another glass will do ye ony harm?" I said naethin, but I thocht I would like anither, and Nicholson poured out ain, and I tuk it. Then the maister said: "Tom, do ye feel any the war for it?" "Na, na," said I, "but it's terrible powerful and three times as strang as ony whusky I ever drank in my life." "Then, Tom," says Sir Walter, "never tell me that three glasses o' Susy's whusky will fill ye fou, when ye have drank twa o' mine, which you say is three times as strong, an' you feel a' the better for it."

'Hey, mon, I was niver so ta'en by the face in a' my life! I didna ken where to luk. The deil faw me if ever he cotcht me so again!'

Tom Purdie's forbearance, however, was not of an enduring quality; his eyes glistened as he followed the course of the bottle; three times was his arm extended to make a grab at it, and thrice did he draw it back with modest confusion. At length when all were served he could hold out no longer, but elongating his dexter, he laid fast hold of the bottle, and filling the quaigh to the brim, 'Here goes,' said he, 'to the lousy stranger,' After he had drunk, and mended his draught, he kept the bottle in his own custody with a pretty smart allowance in it, in character for residuary legatee. I had an account, however, to settle with him; for being the only stranger in the company, I fancied his toast meant a reflection on my cleanliness. What did he mean by the dirty and degrading epithet? This I demanded, advancing with a war-like countenance and leister at rest; and had not Tom been in a very benign humour this book might never have been inflicted on the public, for the man was well armed and resolute, and might have leistered me according to his art. But putting on his sweetest smile, he assured me that by the 'lousy stranger' he meant a newly run fish with the tide lice on it, 'which' said he 'as far the best ye ken.' This I well knew, though the application did not occur to me at the moment. And here, by the way, I beg to observe that you may know the best clean fish by their having tide lice on them.

After describing some riotous behaviour that went on in the boat, probably caused by too liberal attention to the whisky bottle, the fishing is continued.

'Come, come, lads,' says the master, 'hold your clish-ma-clavers, for we are just going into Brig-end Pool; so keep back the boat as well as you can, or we shall go fiery fast over the stream.'

As the boat neared the pool, the men shouted: 'Auld Michael! Auld Michael! the charm for auld Michael Scott; trim the boat, and take care the muckle wizard doesna loup intill her.'

'Od lads!' cries Tom Purdie, 'pit yer best fut foremost; they are lying afore us like sacks, and will be as thick as you can dab them up. Mind the licht, Sandy, and take care that kipper doesna wallop out of the boat. See what a muckle fush Charlie has got!'

In fact the men were making great slaughter, and when we had gone over the pool two or three times, had half-filled the boat with spoil, so as they found they were well laden, they called to Rob Colyard to come forward with his cart to take them home.

'Shove the boat to the shore; Colyard come forrard wi' the cart; that'll do, mon, aw honds to wark; count the fush as ye put them in, Charlie, how mony hae ye counted?'

'There jest be a hunder and twa, great and sma' – whitling, bull trout, sammots, and a' thegither!'

Here the whisky bottle was again passed round with the not surprising result that later the boat turned over on a sunken rock and fish and 'leisterers' were thrown into the water which, fortunately, was not deep. After hunting an otter this riotous poaching affray came to an end. Scrope concluded his account as follows:

'We now marched home with out spoil triumphant – Sandy in front, with a blazing beacon over his shoulder to light our steps, as has been practised from time immemorial; the others with the fish and leisters. One of the spectators began a *concordia discors* with his bagpipes, but bade us adieu at Melrose Bridge and the dulcet sounds died away among the pine woods and furze brakes of the Elidon Hills.'

WILLIAM SCROPE, *Days and Nights of Salmon Fishing*

A 50-lb. Salmon

I RETURNED from a business trip to New Zealand in the spring of 1927. While there I had seized the opportunity of trying out Mr. A. H. E. Wood's greased line method for rainbow in the Tongariro River.

It was quite new out there, and I had one particularly good day which caused quite a stir in the local press. I had the opportunity of picking up what little I know of this method straight from the horse's mouth at Cairnton.

In August 1927, I went to the Eira River in Norway – a river famous for big fish. On my first day, feeling rather tired after a long journey by boat and car, I decided not to overdo things and so took out a 14-ft. Grant Vibration Rod instead of the heavy 16-ft. rod which is normally used on a big river like the Eira.

My line still had a lot of grease on it as I had last used it for greased line fishing on the Dee.

I was fishing a pool about eighteen to twenty feet deep, and using a 2/0 Tilbouries Fly. Why I put this fly on I can't imagine, but it was given me by a friend who used to fish the Tilbouries beat on the Dee – hence its name. The line would not sink and in my ignorance I thought that in this deep water (clear though the water was) no fish would see the fly, so I was poking my rod tip under the water and watching the line gradually go under the surface, when a thing like a submarine appeared on the top. First a head, then a back fin, and finally a tail, and it seemed ages before everything disappeared and I raised my rod and drew the hook home.

I, of course, knew that I was into a salmon far larger than I had ever dreamed of. However, the fish was a gentleman and never sulked, but on the other hand never did anything spectacular, and I landed him in twenty-seven minutes.

I had never seen a fish approaching this size before, but began to realise the possibilities when the gillie, who could not speak English, refused to carry it the two miles home and sent his pony and trap for it later on. It turned the scales at just over 50lb.

I sent a letter and some scales to Mr. J. A. Hutton, who reported that it was a male fish, fifty-two inches long, twenty-seven inches in girth, two years river life and four years feeding in the sea; had not spawned before as is usual with these big fish.

I wonder if anyone else has been lucky enough to catch such a large fish on the fly with a greased line?

NEVILLE BOSTOCK

TROUT

The Muckle Troot o' the Dulnain

It was the 27th of July, I was a guest for a few days at Dulnain Bridge, near Grantown-on-Spey, which nestles among the hills and pine woods on the Seafield estate, within easy access of the rivers Spey and Dulnain.

It had rained incessantly for at least three days and the rivers were in fine condition. The morning had already accounted for one small salmon and several fair-sized sea trout from the pool at the junction of the Spey and the Dulnain, and the breeze was still from the south-east.

Returning home at lunch-time, a letter greeted me from an angling authority on the outskirts of London, who on former occasions had stayed at Dulnain Bridge. This letter strongly urged me to fish a stretch of the Dulnain known as 'The Sandies' below the estate of Clury. The river Dulnain rises in the Monadhliath Hills in Badenoch and falls into the Spey near Dulnain Bridge. The Dulnain is roughly thirty miles long and is famed for its size of trout. Fishing is free near Dulnain Bridge. Salmon are frequently caught at the end of September and October. Among the best flies are the Blue and Silver, Peter Ross, Thunder and Lightning, and the Black Doctor.

The afternoon was bright and sunny, while little clouds lined the skyline. With rod in hand I sallied forth after tea accompanied by a friend, who was also staying at Dulnain Bridge, determined to try our luck at the place indicated.

As we approached the river we saw the water was in prime condition, just having fallen sufficiently to assume a delightful port-wine colour. It wimpled over its sandy bed as the early evening rays of the summer sun, which was sinking in the direction of the Monadhliath Mountains, penetrated the inky water.

We had scarcely reached the stream when, at the head of the pool, at a point where the river takes a right-angle bend in a southerly direction, we were astonished to see a large fish show itself for an instant, doing a kind of porpoise roll on the surface of the water about mid-stream. The fish was evidently on the feed, so there was no time to lose. Producing at random an ordinary Loch Leven cast from my pocket, I fixed it to my line and quietly plodded my way through wet sand, sinking knee-deep in places towards the spot where I fancied the fish to be. As I was in the act of stalking him he rose again a few yards from where I stood, with a mighty splash, filling me with breathless excitement.

The wind was in my favour, and with a steady aim my line landed lightly on the surface of the water about four feet above him. I let it sink a little, and in the twinkling of an eye I felt him take me under water. I struck hard, and my rod bent almost double, while the reel screamed out as the fish made a wild rush for the opposite bank, where I could feel him sawing, but I kept a steady strain on the line.

Suddenly downstream he charged, running out a considerable length of line; then back again upstream at lightning speed; then over the other side, and latterly changing his direction he came straight for the place where I stood, almost striking my legs. Finally he showed himself by leaping right out of the water in a frantic effort to escape by falling on the line. He was a much heavier fish than I anticipated and up to all the tricks, churning up the water and lashing out with his tail at the fragile casting line, which threatened to give at any moment under the strain. For minutes which seemed hours I played the fish carefully, until at length my friend came running to my rescue with the landing net. We had, alas, forgotten the gaff in the hurry, and a glance at the fish as it struggled in the water, and another at the net was sufficient to show how useless the net would really be for landing a fish of such proportions.

To my horror, before I had time to utter a word of command, my friend made a blind dive at the fish with the landing net and missed. Away went the fish again in mad confusion, but with some little difficulty I got him alongside again, and once more, despite my protests, my companion in distress made a further lunge at the fish, this time getting its head into the net, and lifted him about two feet into the air with the latter half of his body flopping over the brim of the net, when, with a splash, he tumbled into the stream again and made off into the deeps.

Once more I played the fish in towards the spot where my friend stood. This time my friend got him tail first into the net, and with a gigantic effort attempted to scoop him up the sandy bank, but again he wriggled out into the water at my feet. To my distress and horror my line went slack and I suddenly realized the hook had come out of the mouth of the fish. There was no time for thinking. I flung myself on the water on top of the fish and as if by a superhuman effort I shot both hands underneath him and flung him up the sandy bank to my friend who administered the *coup de grâce*, while I scrambled as best I could to terra firma.

Without waiting to fish longer we packed up, and after a brisk walk reached Dulnain post office, where, by the courtesty of the postmaster, we examined and weighed the fish. He was a beautiful brown trout of four and three-quarter pounds, over twenty-five inches in length and slightly under half that in girth – the record trout for the season for the Dulnain.

R. MACDONALD ROBERTSON, *In Scotland with a Fishing Rod*

Tussle with a Salmo-ferox

We were sitting, lazily chatting and striving to combat the delightful lassitude induced by hard exercise on a stormy loch, followed by the luxury of a change to the skin, a hearty dinner and a crackling log fire. It was mid-September, and the equinoctial gales appeared to have set in permanently, accompanied by lashing rain, which was causing the loch to rise rapidly. To us was announced Nichol Macintyre, our boatman, who for more than forty years had materially assisted in thinning the piscine inhabitants of Loch Awe, and who could never be induced to lay down his oars until all hope of 'adding a fin to the gentleman's creel' had vanished. We were in the dining-room of Auchnacarron Lodge, on the north shore of Loch Awe, when Macintyre, our boatman, entered. He suggested that we should next day try the river; we must start about eight o'clock, as we had seven miles to pull, and, if the gale held from the west, it would take all we knew to pull the three miles to the Pass.

Next morning I was awakened by a shower of gravel. Tumbling into my clothes, I hurried downstairs, and put up a substantial lunch, while breakfast was being prepared. By eight o'clock we were ready to start.

Wet work it was getting an offing, but when once clear of the shore, we had the wind dead aft, and a clear run of four miles before us. I sent Nichol forward to trim the boat, and then, with the sheet in one hand, and an extemporised tiller in the other, our little craft, with the aid of a tiny lugsail, performed the run in half an hour. Having reached the entrance to the Pass of Brander, we crept up the weather shore with a minnow on my salmon rod and an ordinary loch trout cast and flies on my trouting rod. On reaching the last sheltered point I took in my minnow, but allowed the flies to remain out with a very short line. We then settled down to a hard pull.

When we had gone about another mile and had reached the part of the pass where the shale comes sheer down to the edge of the loch – I believe the locality is pronounced Schloch'n ewer – a heavy squall was causing us to lose way and my flies must have sunk six or eight feet, when whir-r-r-r went my reel; the water parted close to the boat, and a great thick rosy-brown fellow leapt three or four feet into the air. I had just time to lower the point of my rod, ease the line, and so frustrate the obvious attempt on the part of the fish to break my fine trout cast by a slap of his great tail. Nichol had gained possession of my oar by this time, and was straining every sinew to hold the boat. Which way would he go? Thank goodness he was off downwind. Had he gone the other way Nichol could not have followed him; a few seconds' run would have exhausted my short line, and the first salmo-ferox that I had hooked in my life would at this moment have probably been enjoying life in the deep, dusky recesses of the weird and rocky pass, instead of undergoing a course of mummification in the garret of a taxidermist.

On we went, our friend steering an almost straight course for half or three quarters of a mile, which gave me ample time to recall the words in the *Sportsman's Guide* relative to ferox-fishing on Loch Awe. I had then only about one fourth of the requisite length of line on my reel, small flies, and correspondingly fine gut. I thanked my stars it was a fine-drawn four-yard cast, which had been specially made for me a fortnight before, and the soundness of which I had carefully tested. If I was severely handicapped in many points, I had at least the advantage of the services of one of the most experienced boatmen the countryside could produce. It was quite a treat to observe the dexterous manner in which he followed and seemed to anticipate, the movements of our spotted antagonist.

On went the fish with never a check, utterly ignoring the two or three pounds of pressure I steadily maintained, the bit fairly between his teeth. Soon I found myself trying experiments based on the assumption that our spotted hero had stubbornly made up his mind to prevent me from having my way even in the smallest detail of the fight; hence, when we began to swerve slightly out of his straight course, I turned the point of my rod to that side, as if to assist him, when he would immediately change his mind and go the other way. Can I have been mistaken in this? I think not, for we enacted the same game over and over again, until apparently our friend found the occupation of towing pall upon him, and he straightway sounded and sulked.

Nichol held the boat while I 'pumped' as strongly as I dared, but without result. My antagonist lay sullen and motionless, in the highest of dudgeons. After trying every means of civil persuasion in vain, and after expending every epithet in the vocabulary, both sacred and profane, and fairly driven to desperation, I ultimately decided to bombard the perverse brute with stones until I should succeed in dislodging him.

As we had been skirting the shore all the way, I told Nichol to edge the boat against the precipitous shore, only some five yards distant, where, without landing, we were able to gather a few large stones; then, pulling out again to windward of old brownie, we fired one missile after another. At the fourth discharge, his scaly majesty made a slight movement, then rushed forth like a boy discharged from school, and nearly emptied my reel before Nichol could get into his wake; and, if we might judge from the pace, he had fairly gained his second wind. This time he made for the opposite shore obliquely down-wind, but just before reaching it, made up his mind to return, and back we had to go.

All this time I had been sitting huddled up in the bottom of the boat, so as not to make pulling harder than necessary by exposing my surface to the wind. Now for the first time, I took a hurried glance to see how Nichol was standing the strain, and when I saw his exhausted but game-to-the-last look, I longed to give him a dram from my flask, though this was impossible under existing circumstances. Nichol seemed to read my thoughts, for he exclaimed: 'Dinnna tak' your eyes off him. I'm doing fine!'

The mad rushes now ceased, and our good boat was steaming at half speed, with an occasional slow down. As if to favour us, the wind lulled somewhat, and we could follow, when it was necessary, upwind. It must have been at the end of three-quarters of an hour that I first brought the quarry to the surface, where he came grudgingly, tugging and straining intermittently; but sight of us seemed to give him new life, which it took some ten minutes to exhaust. During a quiet interval, I said: 'Get the gaff handy, Nichol.' No answer.

'Nichol, have you got the gaff?'

Then he replied: 'No, sir, we've left both gaff and net. I took everything out of the boat last night when I hauled her up out of reach of the waves, and must have forgotten to put them back. I remembered it all the moment you hooked him, but I darn't tell you for fear it would upset you and spoil your hand, whereas if he broke away without your knowing the gaff was left behind I wouldn't have felt so bad.'

I supposed I must have ejaculated something, for Nichol said: 'Yes, sir, that's just how I felt, but I gave it up, as I couldn't find words to do the subject justice.'

'What shall we do?' I asked.

'When he's not able to sit upright, we'll slip ashore, sir.'

By this time the hardy warrior's strength was almost spent and as he came again to the surface, lying on his side, the keen pleasure of seeing him almost ours was momentarily marred by observing him once more open his mouth and gasp heavily before he once more gave a sweep of his powerful tail and dived nearly to the bottom.

'Poor beggar, he's hard up. I almost thought I heard him sob that time he opened his mouth,' remarked Nichol, who, by this time, was edging the boat towards the shore. The fish, having again surfaced was following quietly, lying on his side. Our difficulties were not yet ended, for the shale on the steep hillside afforded very insecure footing. I managed, however, to scramble up a few feet, and, reclining with my feet well buried among the loose stones, I began to wind up slowly.

'He'll come now, sir,' said Nichol, as he lay crouched at the water's edge. In he came, inch by inch, till he touched the stones.

Contact with them, however, seemed to infuse new life into him, and I could not check his efforts, feeble as they were, though I put on all the pressure I dared. It looked like having to make a hasty run for the boat – no, he was turning; the strain that he scoffed half an hour ago was too much for him now.

Lying on his handsome broad side, he allowed me to tow him gently towards Nichol who lay motionless. Almost before the stones were reached Nichol's right hand was buried under the great spotted gills, and the possessor of them was high and dry, struggling under

Nichol's prostrate form. Neither would the latter move until I had put down my rod and passed a string though the still gasping gills.

'Don't take the fly out, sir,' said Nichol. 'Cut the gut and leave it in his mouth when you get him stuffed.'

Still embracing the fish, I followed holding the string, we scrambled back to the boat and laid out the trophy tenderly.

'Well, I've never seen a trout in grander condition, or finer marked,' said Nichol, as I poured him out a good stiff dram. This felicitous and gratifying remark might have added a 'finger' to the depth of the dram, but I entirely acquit Nichol of any ulterior motive in this respect.

'What is he – fifteen pounds?' I asked.

'More than that, sir. He's as near twenty as fifteen,' was the reply.

When the fish was cosily wrapped away in Nichol's oilskin in the prow of the boat, we rowed on to the river and landed at the little red shelter where luncheon was quickly disposed of and work recommenced, but neither minnow nor fly elicited any response, and at 5 p.m. we made for home.

Great were the rejoicings that night at Carron Lodge, and many a toast drunk. Nichol, getting the scales, said: 'You hold him up, sir, your arms are stronger than mine. Now, towards the right. Fifteen and a half pounds! But I had thought he was more, and so he was when he first left the water. I'll pack him early to-morrow morning, and send him off from the Taychreggan Hotel by the boat to the stuffers for you, sir.'

When the pipes were finished and glasses emptied, candles were called for and I, for one, slept none the worse for my eighty minutes' exciting tussle. When shall I have such another I wonder?

This specimen was carefully stuffed and is preserved in a glass case at North Berwick, the identical fly with which it was caught being still deeply embedded in its jaw.

R. MACDONALD ROBERTSON, *In Scotland with a Fishing Road*

After reading Mr. Macdonald Robertson's thrilling account of capturing a salmo-ferox from Loch Awe, let us read what Charles St. John has to say about these highland lochs and the huge trout they contain.

Though netting the lochs cannot be regarded as 'sporting,' and it is to be hoped that such practices are no longer employed, save to exterminate the pike, his picture of a loch in Inverness is a very haunting one and especially I like his description of the wild Gaelic songs coming across the quiet waters as the fishermen rowed their boat under the pine-clad cliffs. Where this particular loch is I do not know but suspect it to be the loch which lies to the west of Dava, in Inverness.

With reference to fishing for the great lake trout it is interesting to note that these very big fish only appear to feed in the late evening and at night. I do not know whether it would be worth trolling for salmo-ferox on moonlight nights. I should imagine that Loch Awe and Loch Ness might yield some very big fish if this experiment was carried out. I have not yet met anyone who has tried it.

Highland Lochs

In the quiet summer evenings it was interesting to see my crew of five Highlanders, as, singing a Gaelic song, they rowed the boat in a large semicircle round one of the bays, letting out the net as they went, one end of the rope being held by a man on the shore at the point from which they started.

When they got to the other side of the bay they landed, with the exception of one man, who remained in the boat to right the net if it got fixed in roots or stones. The rest hauled in the net gradually, bringing the two ends together. As it came in a fine trout or pike would be seen making a dart round the enclosed space within the net, or dashing at the net itself, dragging for a moment half the corks under water. The headman of the crew, a little peppery Highlander, invariably got into a state of most savage excitement, which increased as the net approached the shore; and if any stoppage occurred from its being caught by a root or stick, he actually danced with excitement, hallooing and swearing in Gaelic at the net, the men, and the fish.

When all went on smoothly and well, he acted the part of fugleman with no little dignity, perched in the bow of the boat, and keeping the men in proper place and time as they dragged in the net. We generally caught a great number of trout and pike, some of very large size.

By the time we had killed all the fish, and arranged them in rows to admire their beauty and size, the little captain (as the other men called him) subsided into a good-humoured calm; and having offered a pinch of snuff to the gamekeeper, whom he generally fixed upon in particular to shout at in consequence of a kind of rivalry between them, and also in consequence of his measuring some head and shoulders higher than himself, he made a brief apology for what he had said, winding up by saying: 'And after all, that's not so bad, your Honour,' as he pointed to some giant trout: he then would light a pipe, and having taken a few whiffs, he would deliberately shove it alight into his waistcoat pocket, and extracting a netting needle and string, set to work mending any hole that had been made in the net. This done, and a dram of whisky having been passed round, the net was arranged on the stern of the boat, and they rowed round the wooded promontory to the other creek, keeping time to their oars with some wild Gaelic song, with a chorus in which they all joined, and the sound of which, as it came over the still waters of the lake, and died gradually away round the headland, had a most peculiarly romantic effect.

Sometimes we did not commence our fishing till sunset, choosing a night when the full moon gave us sufficient light for the purpose. Our object in selecting this time was to catch the larger pike, who during the day remained in the deep water, coming in at night to the shore, and to the mouth of the burns which run into the lake, where they found small trout and other food brought down by the streams. During the night-time also towards the beginning of autumn, we used to catch quantities of char, which fish then, and then only, approached near enough to the shore to be caught in nets.

In the clear frosty air of a September night the peculiar moaning cry of the wild cats as they answered to each other along the opposite shores, and the hooting of the owls in the pine wood, sounded like the voices of unearthly beings, and I do not think that any of my crew would have passed an hour alone by that loch side for all the fish in it. Indeed, the side which sloped down to the lake itself had the name of being haunted, and the waters of the lake itself had their ghostly inhabitant in the shape of what the Highlander called the water-bull.

There was also the story of some strange mermaid-like monster being sometimes seen, having the appearance of a monstrous fish with long hair.

It was a scene worthy of a painter, as the men with eager gestures scrambled up the fish, glancing like silver in the moon-beams and then, as they rowed round, sometimes lost in the shade of the pine trees which completely darkened the surface of the water immediately below the rocks on which they grew, or came again into full view as they left the shadow of the woods, the water sparkling and glancing from their oars. Frequently they stopped their wild chant, as the strange cries of the different nocturnal animals echoed loudly from the rocks, and we could hear the men say a few words of Gaelic to each other in a low voice, and then recommence their song.

We always caught the largest fish at night-time, both trout and pike, the latter frequently above twenty pounds weight, with the teeth and jaws of a young shark. Sometimes the net brought in a great number of char, which appear to go in large shoals, but these latter only in the autumn.

CHARLES ST. JOHN, *Wild Sports of The Highlands*

Trolling for Ferox

CHOOSE the roughest wind your boat can live in; fish with a good-sized bait not much less than a herring, and do not commence your trolling until after two o'clock in the afternoon, by which time the large fish seem to have digested their last night's supper, and to be again on the move. You may pass over the heads of hundreds of large trout when they are lying at rest and not hungry, and you will not catch one; but as soon as they begin to feed, a fish, although he may have half a dozen small trout in his stomach, will run at your bait. The weight of the sinkers on your line, and the depth at which you fish must, of course, depend on the depth of water in the lake. A patient fisherman should find out how deep every reach and bay of the lake is before he begins to troll. The labour of a day spent in taking soundings is well repaid. The strength and activity of the large trout is immense and he will run out your whole reel line if allowed to do so. Sometimes he will go down perpendicu- larly to the bottom where he remains sulky or attempts to rub off the hooks; get him out of this situation and away he goes, almost towing your boat after him. Then is the time for your boatman to make play to keep up with the fish, and save your line, for a twenty-pounds salmo-ferox is no ignoble foe to contend with when you have him on the end of a common fishing-line, he appears to have the strength of a whale as he rushes away.

I was crossing Loch Ness alone one evening with my rod at the stern of the boat, with my trolling tackle on it trailing behind. Suddenly it was seized by a large trout and before I could do anything but take hold of the rod, he had run out eighty yards of line and bent my stiff trolling rod like a willow, carrying half the rod under water. The loch was too deep for me and he snapped the line in an instant, the rod and the twenty yards of line which remained jerking back into the air, and sending the water in a shower or spray around me. Comparing the strength of this fish with that of others I have killed while trolling, he must have been a perfect water-monster, indeed I have little doubt that the immense depths of Loch Ness contain trout as large, if not larger, than are to be found in any other loch in Scotland.

CHARLES ST. JOHN, *Wild Sports of the Highlands*

LOOKING through a friend's library the other day I came upon a little old book, much tattered and torn, published by David Douglas Ltd., in 1884. The author is an American, John Burroughs, and the title of the book, *Locusts and Wild Honey*. I had not met this author before but he writes with charm, and in some passages he is comparable to Thoreau.

Trout Fishing in Canada

If I were a trout, I should ascend every stream till I found the Rondout. It is the ideal brook. What homes these fish have, what retreats under the rocks, what paved or flagged courts and areas, what crystal depths where no net or snare can reach them! – no mud, no sediment, but here and there in the clefts and seams of the rock, patches of white gravel – spawning beds ready-made. The finishing touch is given by the moss with which the rock is everywhere carpeted. Even in the narrow grooves or channels where the water runs swiftest, the green lining is unbroken. It sweeps down under the stream and up again on the other side like some firmly woven texture. It softens every outline and cushions every stone. At a certain depth in the great basins and wells it, of course, ceases, and only the smooth, swept flagging of the place-rock is visible.

The trees are kept well back from the margin of the stream by the want of soil, and the larger ones unite their branches far above it, forming a high winding gallery along which the fisherman passes and makes his long casts with scarcely an interruption from branch or twig. In a few places he makes no cast, but sees from his rocky perch the water twenty feet below him, and drops his hook into it as into a well.

We made camp at a bend in the creek, where there was a large surface of mossy rock uncovered by the shrunken stream – a clean free place left for us in the wilderness that was faultless as a kitchen and dining-room , and a marvel of beauty as a lounging-room, or an open court, or what you will. An obsolete wood or bark-road connected us to it, and disappeared up the hill in the woods beyond. A loose boulder lay in the middle, and on the edge next the stream were three or four large natural wash-basins scooped out of the rock, ever filled ready for use.

Our lair we carved out of the thick brush under a large birch on the bank. Here we planted our flag of smoke and feathered our nest with balsam and hemlock boughs and ferns, and laughed at your four walls and pillows of down.

Then there is his description of catching a big trout in little *Lake Jacques Cartier* in Canada, and his beautiful word-picture of fishing from a raft, out on the bosom of the lake, and how the life of nature seems to ebb and flow, as the slow hours pass:

The third day, in the afternoon, we had our first and only thorough sensation in the shape of a big trout. It came none too soon. The interest had begun to flag. But one big fish a week will do. It is a pinnacle of delight in the angler's experience that he may well be three days in working up to, and once reached, it is three days down to the old humdrum level again. At least it is with me.

It was a dull, rainy day; the fog rested low upon the mountains, and the time hung heavily on our hands. About three o'clock the rain slackened and we emerged from our den, Joe going to look after his horse, which had eaten but little since coming into the woods, the poor creature was so disturbed by the loneliness and the black flies; I, to make preparations for dinner, while my companion lazily took his rod and stepped to the edge of the big pool in front of camp. At the first introductory cast, and when his fly was not fifteen feet from him on the water, there was a lunge and a strike, and apparently the fisherman had hooked a boulder. I was standing a few yards below engaged in washing out the coffee pail, when I heard him call out:
  'I have got him now!'

'Yes, I see you have,' said I, noticing his bending pole and moveless line. 'When I am through I will help you get loose.'

'No, but I'm not joking,' he said. 'I have got a big fish.'

I looked up again, but saw no reason to change my impression and kept on with my work.

It is proper to say that my companion was a novice at fly-fishing, he never having cast a fly until this trip.

Again he called out to me, but deceived by his coolness and nonchalant tones, and by the lethargy of the fish, I gave little heed. I knew very well that if I had struck a fish that held me down in that way I should have been going through a regular war-dance on that circle of boulder-tips, and should have scared the game into activity, if the hook had failed to wake him up. But as the farce continued I drew nearer.

'Does that look like a stone or a log?' said my friend, pointing to his quivering line, slowly cutting the current up toward the centre of the pool.

My scepticism vanished in an instant, and I could hardly keep my place on the top of the rock.

'I can feel him breathe,' said the now warming fisherman, 'just feel of that pole.'

I put my eager hand upon the butt and could easily imagine I felt the throb or pant of something alive down there in the black depths. But whatever it was it moved like a turtle. My companion was praying to hear his reel spin, but it gave out now and then only a few hesitating clicks. Still the situation was excitingly dramatic, and we were all actors. I rushed for the landing net, but being unable to find it, shouted desperately for Joe, who came hurrying back, excited before he had learned what the matter was.

The net had been left at the lake below, and must be had with the greatest dispatch. In the meantime I skipped from boulder to boulder as the fish worked this way or that about the pool, peering into the water to catch a glimpse of him, for he had begun to yield a little to the steady strain that was kept upon him. Presently I saw a shadowy, unsubstantial something just emerge from the black depths, then vanish. Then I saw it again, and this time the huge proportions of the fish were faintly outlined by the white facings of his fins. The sketch lasted but a twinkling; it was only a flitting shadow upon a darker background, but it gave me the profoundest Ike Walton thrill I ever experienced. I had been a fisher from my earliest boyhood. I came from a race of fishers; trout streams gurgled about the roots of the family tree, and there was a long accumulated and transmitted tendency and desire in me that that sight gratified. I did not wish the pole in my own hands; there was quite enough electricity overflowing from it and filling the air for me. The fish yielded more and more to the relentless pole, till, in about fifteen minutes, from the time he was struck, he came to the surface, then made a little whirlpool when he disappeared again. But presently he was up a second time and lashing the water into foam as the angler led him towards the rock upon which I was perched, net in hand. As I reached towards him, down he went again, and taking another circle of the pool, came up still more exhausted, when, between his paroxysms, I carefully ran the net under him and lifted him ashore, amid, it is needless to say, the wildest enthusiasm of the spectators.

'What does he weigh?' was the natural inquiry of each; and we took it turns 'hefting' him. But gravity was less potent to us then than usual, and the fish seemed astonishingly light.

'Four pounds,' we said, but Joe said more. So we improvised a scale; a long strip of board was balanced across a stick, and our groceries served as weights. A four-pound package of sugar kicked the beam quickly; a pound of coffee was added; still it went up; then a pound of tea, and still the fish had a little of the best of it. But we called it six pounds, not to drive too sharp a bargain with fortune, and were more than satisfied. Such a beautiful creature, marked in every respect like a trout of six inches. We feasted our eyes upon him for half an hour. We stretched him upon the ground and admired him, we laid him across a log and withdrew a few paces to admire him; we hung him against the shanty and turned our heads from side to side as women do when they are selecting dress-goods, the better to take in the full force of the effect.

He graced the board or stump that afternoon, and was the sweetest fish taken. The flesh was a deep salmon colour and very rich. We had before discovered that there were two varieties of trout in these waters, irrespective of size – the red-fleshed and the white-fleshed – and that the former were best.

This success gave an impetus to our sport that carried us through the rest of the week finely. We had demonstrated that there were big trout here, and that they would rise to a fly. We built a raft of logs, and upon it I floated out upon the lake, whipping its waters right and left, morning, noon, and night. Many fine trout came to my hand and were released because they did not fit the bill.

The lake became my favourite resort, while my companions preferred rather the shore or the long, still pool above, where there was a rude makeshift of a boat, made out of common box-boards.

Upon the lake you had the wilderness and solitude at arm's length, and could better take their look and measure. You became something apart from them; you emerged and had a vantage ground like that of a mountain peak, and could contemplate them at your ease. Seated upon my raft, and slowly carried by the current or drifted by the breeze, I had many a long, silent look into the face of the wilderness, and found the communion good. I was alone with the spirit of the forest-bound lakes and felt its presence and magnetism. I played hide-and-seek with it about the nooks and corners, and lay in wait for it with a clump of trees that was moored just to one side of the current near the head of the lake.

Indeed there is no depth of solitude that the mind does not endow with some human interest. As in a dead silence the ear is filled with its own murmur, so amid these aboriginal scenes one's feeling and sympathies become external to him, as it were, and he holds converse with them. Then a lake is the ear as well as the eye of a forest. It is a place to go and listen and ascertain what sounds are abroad in the air. They all run quickly thither and report. If any creature had called in the forest for miles about I should have heard it. At times I could hear the distant roar of water off beyond the outlet of the lake. The sound of the vagrant winds purring here and there in the tops of the spruces reached my ear. A breeze would come slowly down the mountain, then strike the lake, and I could see its footsteps approaching by the changed appearance of the water. How slowly the winds move at times, sauntering like one on a Sunday walk! A breeze always enlivens the fish; a dead calm and all pennants sink; your activity with your fly is ill-timed, and you soon take the hint and stop. Becalmed upon my raft, I observed, as I have often done before, that the life of nature ebbs and flows, comes and departs, in these wilderness scenes; one moment her stage is thronged and the next quite deserted.

Then there is wonderful unity of movement in the two elements, air and water. When there is much going on in one, there is quite sure to be much going on in the other. You have been casting, perhaps, for an hour with scarcely a jump or any sign of life anywhere about you, when presently the breeze freshens and the trout begin to respond. And then, of a sudden, all the performers rush in; ducks come sweeping by, loons laugh and wheel overhead, then approach the water on a long, gentle incline, ploughing deeper and deeper into its surface until their momentum is arrested, or converted into foam; the fish hawk screams, the bald eagle goes flapping by, and your eyes and hands are full. Then the tide ebbs, and both fish and fowl are gone.

JOHN BURROUGHS, *Locusts and Wild Honey*

The Burn in Winter

THE burn in the glen below Cloan was in these winter days no longer a centre of interest to me. It ran cold and shrunken between snow banks and sometimes you could only dimly see it moving in long wriggling bubbles of water and air through the white and grey of the ice. There was no hint of trout, and such was the effect of the changed appearance of the place that during these holidays I believe that I thought little more of them than I thought of the summer green of the bare trees. Once only were we reminded vividly that the trout were still there. One year, after a period of fresh open weather it turned suddenly cold, and for three windless nights it froze very hard. The pond by the keeper's house was frozen over with keen clear black ice, and on the third day we could walk on it and see below us the trout moving among the weeds. I suppose this must often happen, but it is a thing which I had never seen before nor have I ever seen it since.

A. R. B. HALDANE, *The Path by the Water*

Dry Fly on the Earn

FOR several years the Earn trout almost entirely defeated me. Except on rare occasions, the only fish I got were small ones in some of the more rapid streams, the larger ones in the deep pools continuing to disregard the wet flies which I offered them, no matter how carefully I fished, casting the longest line of which I was capable; but the time came when having learned in Hampshire the use of the dry-fly, I came back to Aberuthven to put to the test the growing conviction that now I would have some chance with the big trout in the quiet water.

Morris, the keeper, is one of those who regard trout fishing as a childish but innocent occupation with which those who care, may, on rivers where the salmon run late, pass the time till the real fishing starts. While I do not share his view, I cannot feel surprised at the good-natured contempt with which he regarded my early efforts, and after so many weary fruitless days when he watched me fishing down the Aberuthven streams, he had reason to bless the day I first used a floating fly.

Our first real success came on a day in the middle of May many years ago. Public holidays are not as a rule happy in their coincidence with good fishing conditions, but this one was the exception, a fresh day of late spring following rain in the night which had raised the river a few inches and given it a touch of colour. The air was mild, and a light breeze blew upstream. The Earn has a chronic habit of changing its course, cutting into the sand and clay of the banks first on one side and then on the other. As Morris and I walked down the river that morning we came towards a part where the stream had for the last few seasons been at work eating its way deep into the deep rich soil on the near side. So a steep bank of clay and gravel fell almost sheer to the edge of the water and from the top of the bank great lumps of turf, undercut by the water, had fallen off into the stream. These lay along the edge of the current and some, more recently fallen, lay only half-submerged, making behind them tiny bays of quiet water at the very edge of the fast current. As we came nearer, we saw that the sand martins, which nest in the face of the broken bank were flying backwards and forwards low over the stream, constantly sweeping to the surface as they picked off the water the olive duns which now we could see rising in quantities from the water or blowing from the bank above.

A few small fish out in the stream were taking the flies with eager splashing rises, but what pleased us most was that trout were feeding quietly and steadily in the smoother patches of water close to the foot of the bank. We made a wide and hurried detour, coming back to the water's edge some yards below the lower end of the stream. Lowering myself over the bank I got a precarious footing at the edge of the current and faced upstream, while close at my shoulder the sand martins flashed in and out of their nesting holes. For fifty yards above me, it seemed that each little backwater behind each lump of turf held a trout, and as we watched we would see a nose come quietly up and then a tail appeared as the fish sucked in the olives caught by the eddies and drifted into the quiet water. I had no olives, but a Greenwell did just as well. The light breeze gave all the help one could have wished and if the fly floated even for a few seconds in the smooth water before the current caught the line and dragged it away, it was generally taken. Each trout on being hooked dashed out into the stream and down past me. I could not move back to get below them and some were lost as they were with difficulty brought back against the current; but most were well hooked, and in the end came to the net which Morris, for once reconciled to trout-fishing and as eager as I, handed down from the top of the bank. By the time the top of the stream was reached we had caught nine trout, of which the smallest was not under half a pound, several of them being over one pound.

A. R. B. HALDANE, *The Path by the Water*

The Jealous Miller of the Wandle

AN acquaintance who did not fish himself, asked for leave from one of his intimate friends, a miller, on another piece of water on the Wandle, and a day was fixed for us to go down there together, I to fish and he to walk with and generally assist me. I remember that it was a lovely warm summer day, with a light breeze, and we both looked forward to an afternoon's sport. It was at and below one of the many flour mills in the vicinity, and the water was in perfect condition.

After being welcomed by our host, a benevolent looking and cheery old gentleman, I was putting up my rod and tackle when a very good fish of apparently two pounds rose and took something off the surface.

'That is one of the tame fish I feed,' said our host, and naturally I took the hint and promised not to cast a fly over that part of the stream.

We walked down some two hundred yards when another rise of a fairly good fish under the bank was duly observed. Crouching down in position, and after some bungling attempts, I put a fly to it. A rise, the usual tactics, and the trout was in the net.

At this moment our host arrived on the scene in a breathless state of alarm, and implored me not to hurt this trout as it was one of his special pets. Gently extracting the hook, I dropped a pretty trout of about 1¼ lb. back into the river, and it swam away, to the manifest joy of the old gentleman.

I had noticed a back stream, and inquired whether the fish there were tame fed pets, and on receiving a reply to the negative we all started down this part of the water.

Here again a rising fish was hooked, netted, duly admired, and, in response to an agonising appeal from the miller, also returned unhurt.

Seeing the hooking of one of his trout was so painful to our host, and imagining if by some chance one should get killed he would be in the depths of despair, I then took down my rod, deposited it and my tackle on a bench in his garden, and we had a long and somewhat wearisome conversation until the time arrived for me to catch the train back to London!

F. M. HALFORD, *An Angler's Autobiography*

Kimbridge Days

THE upper part of the back stream at Kimbridge joined the Mottisfont water then rented by our old friends, Foster and Alexander Mortimore.

They asked us to fix a date to come over and have a turn in their water, and the only available day was June 7th. Foster Mortimore wrote us in a day or two that he was afraid we should be full late as there were few fresh flies hatching. However, we decided to go and chance it.

The rods at Mottisfont that day were the two brothers Mortimore, John Day, Marryat, and myself. On our arrival we found the meadows, and even the railway line, covered with spent gnat, and clouds of males were dancing in the air.

There had been very few sub-imagines hatching on the 6th and at our host's suggestion we decided to try all the wide carriers that held fish.

I do not think we saw a single green drake, and these big fish were as shy as possible, having been fished hard for many days, and a large proportion of them hooked and lost.

Occasionally the female imagines would be seen laying their eggs, and at intervals a fall of spent gnat on the water would bring every fish on the rise.

Presently we had a terrific thunderstorm, and we all took shelter in the station booking office. As soon as it cleared off we separated, the two Mortimores going downstream, Marryat walking up, and John Day and I having the central part of the water. Day would not fish; he had been hard at it all through the mayfly, and with his usual unselfishness wanted to see me get a big one.

In one of the carriers we saw the head of a huge trout come up and take a spent gnat. I was on my knees in a moment, crawled up in position and waited for the next rise. This is always a good policy when trout are on spent gnat, as they invariably travel and are dreadfully shy. Up it came again four or five yards higher up, a good underhanded cast landed the fly right at the first attempt, and the fish came with a flop which set my heart beating.

I struck, and upstream went the fish at a great pace. The carrier was full of thick weed beds, and for a time I managed to keep on terms with the trout. At last it plunged into the thickest part of the vegetation, and worked itself round the weeds until at length it stopped.

In those days we knew nothing of the wonders wrought by slacking a hooked fish, and working it out of the weeds by hand, so I held on and did all I could to move the brute. It was of no avail: Day started off, got hold of a pole and went over to the far side of the carrier and tried to move the weeds apart so that we could get at the trout. The usual result ensued – the trout started, and in a moment broke the gut and was free.

Feeling very downhearted, I tried to persuade Day to have a turn at the next rising fish, but he declined and did his best to console me and held out all sorts of alluring prospects of another bigger fish higher up the same carrier, and just below a brick bridge. On our arrival at this place, sure enough, the fish was on the rise, and after another ineffectual attempt to get Day to fish it, I repaired the damage and put up another spent gnat.

The trout was rising in a small open space below the bridge, and above another fearful tangle of weed.

Using all care and keeping well out of sight, another horizontal cast put the fly on the spot, another bold rise, and I found myself again in another big fish.

I then did what I should have done with the first one, jumped up, and without a moment's consideration, skull-dragged the trout over the weed bed and started at full pace downstream. After about thirty yards of this the fish shook its head with a savage jerk and tried to turn upstream. I simply stopped it by brute force, and once more started dragging it down as fast as I could go. This was repeated several times, and at last, when we were quite 150 yards below the bridge, the fish made a roll on the water and was netted by Day before it could recover. It was a splendid female and weighed 4lb. 2oz.

Then we had another heavy storm, and we all forgathered once more in a signalman's hut. The Mortimores had seen few fish, and killed none, and Marryat had killed another beauty, a female like mine, of 3lb. 12oz. A cold, cheerless evening followed, and so ended our mayfly fishing for that season.

F. M. HALFORD, *An Angler's Autobiography*

A Thames Trout

THE usual feeding ground of the big trout was in the black water, between two runs, just above the lower bay of the weir, and a bright bleak about five inches in length having been deftly arranged so as to spin truly on the flight, I took up my place in the punt. Rosewell (his man) meanwhile, was mounted on the beam of the weir prospecting about with live dace, on the chance of coming across another prowling fish. I proceeded to spin steadily backwards and forwards and up and down the two runs and the intervening wedge of black water, and just as a distant church clock struck seven o'clock, as I was drawing my bait up to the apron of the weir, a number of small fry flew in all directions, and a rush through the water indicated the presence of the fish we were trying for. I let my bait gently down, and was drawing it across the stream, when a faint tap made me imagine that a perch or a chub had run at it.

In far less time than it has taken to read these words I struck firmly, my reel was flying round, and a heavy fish plunged at a great rate right down and through the broken white water of the run. It took about forty yards of line in this rush, and then jumped into the air, showing us the outline of a noble trout.

The fish then bored down deep in the water and tore across the runs towards the upper end of the weir. Meanwhile, Rosewell, who had, of course, seen what had occurred, stepped into the punt and quietly worked it along the weir to the bay at the lower end, and then to the bank. I got out, and steadying the fish, found it close under the piles of the weir. On the bank there stood a tree just at the lower end of the weir and I had to lower my rod to pass it round. As I did this the trout made a rush towards me, and although I gathered in the line by hand as rapidly as possible, there was a good deal of slack. To my horror, on recovering this, I found that the line was foul of the willow which, as I described in a previous page, grew in the angle of the bay. The position was a desperate one, but Rosewell proved equal to the occasion. Landing net in hand, he stepped into the water and walked down the slippery slope, over which a strong stream was flowing. I trembled, imagining that he intended to try and net the fish, but his judgment was too good for that. Steadying himself with the handle of the landing net, he took out his knife, opened it, and stooping down, cut away the part of the willow round which the line was foul. As it came clear I raised my rod, and obtaining a good pull at the fish, it started across the weir, and again flung itself into the air.

The rest was easy, the trout kept boring down and plunging heavily, while at every favourable opportunity I reeled in and presented the butt. At last the plucky fish came to the surface, and just as it rolled over on its side the sun peeped out of the clouds and revealed to our eyes as fair a sight as ever appeared to a fisherman.

In a very few moments it was in the net and on the bank and both Rosewell and I fairly fell upon it for fear of its jumping back into the water. A more perfect specimen of a Thames trout I never saw, although I certainly have seen larger ones.

Before Rosewell extracted the hook from the mouth we made an examination of the manner in which the fish was hooked. It may have been purely accidental, or it may have pointed the efficacy of the hanging triangle on the reverse side of the bait, but this had embedded itself deeply in the side of the mouth and the other triangles were all hanging loose.

At this moment the local angler came through the lock in his punt and joined us at the side of the weir. He was naturally sorrowful at our being on the spot before him, but he, in true sportsmanlike spirit, conveyed his warmest congratulations, and insisted on us sampling a curious home-made liquor to drink the health of all good fishermen. After a brief consultation I decided to take the trout down to Halliford in the canoe and get it accurately weighed. On my arrival at the Ship Hotel the landlord put it into the scales and it registered 9¾lb. As it was the largest I had hooked and landed, it was despatched to London the same day, and the work of setting it up in a case entrusted to, and most admirably carried out by Cooper.

This was my last Thames trout, and as the time went on the attractions of fly-fishing, and especially dry-fishing, gradually impelled me to drop all other forms of sport to follow that which may fairly be described as more scientific and more engrossing than any other.

F. M. HALFORD, *An Angler's Autobiography*

A Thames Weir

A Strange Tale

I TELL the tale as it was told to me, I do not vouch for the truth of it, I only say that you will learn, when you fish for a much-fished Thames trout, that he is an exceptional fellow and, like Habakkuk, *capable*, almost, *de tout*.

The eleven-pounder lived, when first I heard of him *above* Marsh Lock. He was a glorious fish, short, thick, and deep, as I know because once in May he followed my spinning-bait almost to the bank. He meant business; like a bullet he came, full speed and wide open. But he came too late. Perforce the bank stopped my minnow's flight. The trout, undeceived, turned aside from the sham with a flounce and a wallop, that, literally, splashed me with Thames water, and was gone. Later in the summer, it was told to me that a young Scotchman, going from Shiplake to Henley, approached the lock in a rowing boat. As he came, he resting upon his oars, sought in his flannel trousers for the three coppers which his lock ticket must, presently, cost him. He found but two pennies and so he must break into a sixpenny bit. In his hand he held the little coin when, to avoid the wash of the steam launch, *Wargrave*, he picked up his oars all of a sudden. The sixpence fell into the water. The young man, like the Scot in the comic papers, looked outboard as his sixpenny piece spun, silverly dropping in the slow current, down into green deeps.

He saw a great fish shoot across the path of his little silver coin and absorb it as though it were a silver dace that wobbled so seductively. That was all.

Next June the Best Thames Angler Ever anchored his fishing punt on the bright shallows below the lock. The bright shallows where the spawned barbel, rolling like cats, roll sidealong in the sun, clean themselves and preen themselves at the tail of the weir. Then, standing up, the angler tossed a spinning-bait hither and yon. Presently, as the blue phantom sped among the piles of the foot-bridge, a yard-long shadow dashed aslant at it. The little rod bent, into a kicking arc, the reel shrieked, and forty yards away – but you've read this sort of thing before, I think?

To make a long tale short then, an hour or so later when the trout was opened in the kitchen, within him was found, and sent upstairs to his captor upon a salver, three coppers and a lock ticket.

As I said, I do not vouch for the exactness of the story, but it is one upon which Father Thames prides himself, and if it isn't true it at least ought to be.

PATRICK CHALMERS, *At the Tail of the Weir*

An Ithan Trout

IN the early spring of 1918 I was living in the NE. of Scotland, and one day I received a letter from a friend saying that he was coming for a day's fishing on the Ithan, provided a ticket was available. On the appointed day I met my friend at the railway station, as I could not go with him I gave him a supply of worms and promised to meet him on the river at one o'clock. My friend had fished all the forenoon with fly and his luck was out, the trout would not rise. I suggested that I would try the worm in a pool often fished by me as a boy, the idea that worming is not sport does not influence me.

The pool was an ideal place, having nice running water and a bottom, the method being to throw across near to the far bank and follow down; tackle being a Stewart tackle, either one large worm or two small ones being used and no sinker. A few trout and finnock were taken and then I hooked something big. It bolted, and sprang out of the river. My friend said: 'You've hooked a brown trout'. My reply was: 'It must be a kelt.'

On my suggestion my friend took the rod and brought the fish to the bank. Having no gaff I placed my fingers behind the gills and lifted it on the bank. The fish was a male brown trout, having lovely red spots; measured 27 inches from point of nose to centre of tail, weight 8lb.; river a dirty brown colour, and weather dull and cold.

The day's fishing ended with eleven trout, including the large one, which my friend considered a good catch. Local experience proved very useful that day, it rid the river of a cannibal trout and gladdened the heart of a visiting angler.

I may add that the eight-pounder was the second largest trout taken in the Ithan, over a period of forty years, a 9-lb trout was landed a few years previously.

JOHN THOMSON

Trout Fishing in Yugoslavia

IN that mountainous corner where Austria, Italy, and Yugoslavia meet, the Yugoslavs were quietly making a sportsman's paradise.

This was chiefly because of the ski-huts they were building in the Dinaric Alps. Even in mid-summer you could climb along the snow-faces for days. You could lose yourself in the snow fog, as I have done, and feel that this time, for a certainty, your number was up – then have a break in the mist and see three chamois staring at you from a landmark of red rocks.

From these snows come streams, the rivers, which hold some of the finest trout in all Europe. And while it may seem a strange statement, the finest consistent trout fishing I ever had was in the mountains of Slovenia.

93

To illustrate what I mean by consistent, I will say that one dusk I took twelve trout out of the Savitica, every one of them over a pound, of which the largest weighed a kilo. The next night I took eleven, all over a pound. The next night I took ten, all over a pound. The number dwindles because I was fishing a restricted spot; I was poaching the Regent's river. This will be no news to him, because he found that out, and refused to give me an interview in consequence. What he does not know is that, after he had come up to his little hunting lodge in the mountains, and discovered me, I still poached his river at night at least once a week.

These rivers came down from a tableland of tumbled mountains, many of whose northern faces were covered with perpetual snow. You could climb with the spring in that part of the world, for when the snows melted away in the lower clearings and the first crocus pushed up through unmelted snow-pockets, the forest was still dark winter. When the beech leaves were glinting along the lake-shore their buds were still closed tight a few thousand feet higher up. The banks of the lower streams became blue with gentians; the big, bell-like gentian, and the little one of the bright hue. The alpine valleys became a carpet of wild flowers, and soon, as you climbed, you came on primulas, pink mauve and yellow, among the higher rocks. Then a climb to reach an eidelweiss became a breathless risk.

In these mountains, where a man had been killed, the peasants painted and put up a little memorial ikon to a rock or tree. If Hans was painted upside down, you knew he had fallen from a cliff. If he was painted lying prone on the ground, with another man standing with an axe or a saw in his hand, then you knew a tree had fallen upon him while they were logging. They were painted with primitive, earnest skill. So were the peasant paintings of the Saints on the white walls of all the little churches. St. Christopher was the favourite, shown carrying Christ across the water on his shoulder. The three inns upon the lake were owned by a Holy Order. Mine was the St. James. Next to it was the little church called the Holy Ghost. And here at a certain Sunday every spring the peasants came to hold a service for the mayfly. I never knew the reason, but for two years I watched them gather there, all of them carrying umbrellas, all praying on the day of the mayfly.

It was a pastoral land, where the valley filled with the tinkling of cow and goat and sheep bells at sunset, as the boys brought them down. Then, one night, you heard the rattle of carts going by; the peasants were taking all their cattle up into the higher alpine meadows.

Up there were seven lakes; one pink, one aquamarine blue, one royal blue, one green. And in the wilderness of rocks that lay around them was another memorial, not quite sympathetic. It was to three Russian soldiers who had escaped from the Germans. They lay in the grave which they had been made to dig before the Germans shot them. The Yugoslav Alpine Club had put up a plaque to them. You could climb Triglav and look down on Italy . . . there were wild strawberries on the sunny slopes.

* * * *

I have never seen such beautiful trout. In the swift, icy, bouldered Savitica their backs were pale mauve. Their spots were vivid scarlet. In the lake itself I once caught a trout weighing over a kilo, which was darker but which must have had a million scarlet spots. He was so beautiful that I wanted to put him back. But he had almost killed himself before he would let me take him. Then there was a golden grayling, which, with its deep sides, rose sharply in the swift runs and almost broke your line before he would let you land him. With his small mouth you would not think him capable of such a fight.

The swift Savitica splayed out into the lake over a shelf of round rocks. It swung against the far bank in its last rush. Standing on the bouldered side you cast into the swift stream pouring down the far bank. When a fish struck he almost pulled your arm down. He was like a fighter who leaps from his chair and fights from the tap of the gong. In such waters there is no time for either fish or man to sulk. In the early spring they are in the river. When the water loses its pace a bit they move out into the lake. Then, when the lake warms, they move up into the river again. But now, in the hot July suns, the snows are melting furiously in the upper mountains, the Savitica is liquid ice. And you dare not fish without waders – or else your legs will swell.

* * * *

We bought a cheap frying-pan at a town about thirty miles below, with this in my rucksack (and a pound of butter) my wife, boy, and I set off on an apparently innocent row up the lake. The Fischer was always hanging around somewhere at first, watching me to see if I took a rod. I could not conceal a trout rod, but it was easy to stick the little four-piece Bristol bait-casting rod up the sleeve of my old tweed coat. So that my first law-breaking was done with Devons.

The Devon, with the little red bead at its tail, was a horrible killer when cast off the mouth of the Savitica. Usually, it only needed half an hour to get us four or five one- or two-pound trout. Then we would row down the lake to a long, rocky peninsular, build a fire, and fry the trout, cut up into chunks in sizzling butter.

I looked up once to find the Fischer standing over my shoulder when I had the frying-pan full of them. 'Nu! Nu! Nu! Herr Farson!' was his admonition. And he shook his finger at me, wagging his head. The next morning the Authority drove up in his pony trap, quite prepared to be nasty about things. But he had a beautiful little German weapon hung on a strap over his shoulder; a sixteen-bore shot-gun, with a small calibre rifle beneath its web – and I was so enchanted about this that he forgave me everything. Over a couple of litres of the resin-like white wine that was grown somewhere in that region he extolled the virtues of his sporting gun: 'You see – I am equipped for either birds or deer . . . or perhaps . . . who knows? . . . it might be a chamois.'

'But, of course!' I said, 'why not? Why not a chamois?' So I broke the gun and peered through its beautifully kept barrels, admired the clean rifling, threw it to my shoulder. And the Authority suggested we might have another litre, and clapped his hands. While the Fischer stood by, near the kitchen gnashing his teeth like the wolf in Red Riding Hood. . . .

But it was in the evening after dinner, when I should have been resting, that I found it the most fascinating time to fish. There was a bridge below the hotel, on the far side, of which stood an ancient little whitewashed Catholic church. On its wall, too, facing the water, was a peasant painting of St. Christopher carrying Christ on his shoulder, wading knee-deep through painted water as miraculously clear as the real water which flowed beneath His feet.

Here every evening was a rise of trout such as I would not have believed possible. You could stand on the bridge in the still spring nights and hear splash, after splash, after splash. And if you waded out from the bushes at the foot of the ancient church, not caring if the water did come over your waders, you had fishing such as you might dream of in heaven.

It was here that I used the unnamed fly tied by the Captain in the English Army of Occupation at Cologne. It was a whitish, hackled arrangement, with a heavy grey body; and I fished it until there was little left of it except the bare hook. Its effectiveness increased with its draggled condition.

Night after night I clumped back to the hotel, almost stupefied by my good luck – the miracle of that fly. And I would slide a bagful of beautiful fish out on the veranda table. In that dim porch light, with the reflection from the green vines, the beauty of those fish had something haunting about them. We loved to touch them, turn them over, pick them up, admire them. The silent shake of the old Austrian

Count's grey head had something of reverence about it. Here was the Adoration of Fish.

I state this solemnly. I have never quite had that hushed feeling about the trout anywhere else. And we all felt it. Then one night there was a terrific strike, my rod bent in the dark, it bent, it bent, it bent . . . for you could not allow the fish to run into the rapids immediately below. And then it straightened out. The line came back empty. The fly was gone. I climbed up the bank by the church with the feeling I was not meant to catch any more fish below the feet of St. Christopher painted on its walls. I never did.

NEGLEY FARSON, *Going Fishing*

My Largest Trout

I CANNOT compete with Mr. Negley Farson. But I have fished in quite a number of countries: in England, Ireland, Wales and Scotland, in France, Belgium, Holland, Germany, Austria, Hungary, and Italy, in Iceland, Denmark, Norway, Sweden and Finland. I have fished in slow rivers and fast mountain streams, in deep lakes and shallow, off rocky shores and mud-lined estuaries, from small boats on the deep sea. I have fished for salmon and for trout, for most of the coarse fish you can think of and for a great variety of sea-going fish. I cannot compete with Mr. Negley Farson in the number of countries fished and I certainly cannot compete with Mr. Farson in the matter of skill, but I have at any rate one thing in common with him: I have never caught a record fish. Indeed, I have never caught a really big fish, or even a big fish, by fair angling. But I have caught a big fish.

There are more ways of taking a fish than by rod and line. I took this one by 'guddling.' Guddling is not regarded in a favourable light by the angling community, which is quite understandable. But it is also looked down upon by the angling community as an unskilful business, which is altogether an inaccurate view. Guddling (you may prefer to call it 'tickling') is anything but an unskilful business. It is every whit as skilful a business as fishing the dry fly, fishing the nymph or any other form of fishing. Indeed I am not at all sure that it is not a very much more skilful business than any of these highly regarded arts . . . and I have tried my hand at all of them. It has one great drawback, of course: it is nearly always illegal. But what is a little thing like that?

Now, you must always start guddling at the downstream end of the water you intend to work. The reason for this is that if you startle your fish and fail to take it, it will be off downstream in a flash, frightening all the other fish and ruining your chances for the day. (You can, by the way, only guddle fish by day: there are other methods of taking fish by night.) You can do this by finding some likely stone and feeling under it for the fish. Once you know your water it is easy to find fish, for there are favourite lies, and if you take a fish from such lie you can be quite certain that there will be another fish in the same place on the following day, and, if you take that one, another the day after, and so on. Having found your fish you rub your fingers gently along its tummy. The first touch of your hand on the fish is the most dangerous moment, for it is more often than not at the first touch that you lose your fish. Once you have started to rub you are fairly safe, provided you are neither clumsy nor too quick, because fish for some unknown reason seem to like having their tummies rubbed. (It is usual to talk of tickling trout, but it is not only trout that like having their tummies tickled. I have lifted many a golden orfe from a garden pond by this method, and I have tried it successfully, on salmon, pike and chub.) Having made contact you must work your hand gradually up the body, with your thumb on one side and your forefinger on the other; until you have reached the point where you can thrust thumb and forefinger into the gills. That accomplished the fish cannot escape. You lift it out and kill it. (If the fish is small you can, of course, lift it out of the water without inserting your fingers in the gills, and the fish will be uninjured. I have lifted many a golden orfe so.) But comparatively few people guddle for fun, they guddle for food. If you are guddling for food it is better to take no chances and to go for the gills, but, of course, I hope you will not be guddling at all, for I am at heart a law-abiding citizen. I have experienced many thrills in my lifetime, but there is no thrill to compare with that which comes when your hand first touches a big fish under a stone.

To return to my big fish. I shall not tell you where I took it. It was taken from a famous river . . . a good many years ago now . . . and it was taken without permission. In fact, it was poached. I was travelling at the time with a party of gypsies, and we needed a little something for supper. One of the men was expert at the art of guddling. He had the gentlest touch combined with the quickest action of any man I have ever met, and I have seen him take many a small and active fish from little mountain burns. But this was not a little mountain burn. It was a big river, well and energetically keepered. It is deep and there are no stones. But in places the bank overhangs little sheltered bays, and it was these places we explored. We made one preliminary reconnaisance, and marked down one or two likely spots. And on the following day we went into action about four o'clock. A hot, still day, the evening rise was not yet and no one was fishing. At my very first bay I found a fish. I nearly lost it at my first contact through surprise. My first touch was sufficient to tell me that it was a big fish, and the further up the body I got the more surprised and more thrilled I became. It *was* a big fish, and thick. But it liked the touch of my hand and remained still. Thumb and forefinger found the gills and out he came, a beauty. I tapped him on the head and stood up. Of my friend there was no sign (this did not surprise me), but upstream, a quarter of a mile or so away, was a man walking towards me. He had not, so far as I could judge, seen me. The fish went into a convenient bush, and I walked upstream. We passed the time of day . . . he rather curtly, for gypsies are seldom greeted pleasantly by the gentry, and I looked gypsy-ish in my ragged clothes . . . and continued our ways. He passed out of sight round a bend. I returned and retrieved my fish, and so to camp. Later that fish was weighed, very roughly, on some kitchen scales and pulled down 4lb. 9oz., a very big fish for that water. And the largest trout, rough weight or not, that I have ever taken. It is not the heaviest fish that I have guddled, nor the heaviest fish that I have taken when angling fair, but it is, even though it was poached, the fish I remember most fondly.

A couple of years later I was on that same water again, this time with permission and rod line. And I confessed. Owner and keeper were disbelieving. They did not, I regret to say, express disbelief that I should have poached (they did not even seem surprised) nor did they express disbelief at the weight. They did not believe that it was possible to guddle a trout from that water. I took them to the selfsame bay and guddled another for them, a beauty of 2lb. 1oz., the while they watched. They were interested.

A year after that I received a postcard from the owner. It read: 'I've done it too. 1lb. 11oz.'

I still get invitations to fish that water.

BRIAN VESEY-FITZGERALD

The Mammoth Sea Trout of the Laerdal

SEA trout on the dry fly . . . the Laerdal in days of peace . . . what a prospect!

That was in 1927, since then there has been no other fishing save an evening rise or two on the Test. But memory is clear, clear as the

A Sea Trout Pool

water of the Laerdal sliding over its granite-bouldered bed. The fish sidle away as only sea trout will if incautious movement shows on the raised banks. Even from a distance of a hundred yards they observe and depart. When new to the river they take freely, but as August ripens, they scatter and become more wary.

Fanny, that unbelievable sea trout, lived in a walled pool and the tiddlers respectfully took up their stations like maids in waiting, in the shallows. The big boys and girls were there too, occasionally rubbing shoulders with the salmon. Sea trout of varying sizes filled the pool; in rippling water one could fish blind up the serried ranks, but it was in the smooth water that the individual quarry was singled out for attack. We had observed Fanny two days previously and her position had been cautiously reconnoitred. She lay in five or six feet of clear water with her slightly caressing tail upstream of a protecting boulder, just about the middle of this huge pool, which was perhaps two hundred yards in length. What Johannes could not see in that clear water with those osprey's eyes of his was not worth worrying about.

The weapon with which I essayed to ensnare Fanny was interesting. Originally an eleven-foot 'Leonard,' one of the famous rods sent over some years ago as a challenge to our makers, it had been cut down to ten feet when Mr. Shea, of Footscray, parted with it to me, on a birthday occasion, together, be it said, with a bottle of '45, (the latter a little weary, perhaps, but nevertheless excellent).

The rod was by no means weary, but alas! in essaying to encompass the snaring of a four-and-a-half pound sea trout the weight of the fish had come upon it and a break had occurred in the middle piece. By glueing and binding, however, a repair was effected just two days before my encounter with Fanny. I had not used it since the operation and my cast on that eventful day had a history also. Not many hours before there had been a picnic by motor-boat up the fjord, and much of the time of voyaging had been spent making up a cast from one discarded by Edward Hewitt (of dry fly for salmon fame) hanks of it, black-stained, which he had abandoned in a slop pail. A tapered cast of nearly fourteen feet was made up (a trick learnt from the same Edward Hewitt). If a fish lies deep in clear water it soon detects the line if one uses only a nine-foot leader.

The sea trout likes to see his fly coming to him afar off, perhaps it gives him time to revolve his grey matter and make up his mind. Then he quits his boulder, swims up to the dancing morsel, and departs downstream with it. Woe betide the too confident angler who tries to strike a large sea trout with undue haste. Johannes knew this. That is why he said no word to me when he saw this monster majestically sweep upon my small red spinner. But I anticipate.

How, you will ask, may one cast fourteen feet of gut? The answer is, my friend, you don't, if there is the faintest zephyr against you. That day was windless and perfect. I might also mention that my cast was attached to 150 yards of line and backing. You sometimes require all that on the Laerdal, even if you have to run, but the big chaps usually make upstream in their first rush before turning their heads to the sea.

I would not go so far as to advise the tactics of one, G. H., who as soon as he had hooked a fish, turned about and ran towards the sea, hoping the sea trout would give pursuit.

My fly, then, was a small red spinner. I had put this on because sea trout, who have been up from the sea a week or so, will not look at a big fly, they flee from it as one who descries a descending bomb.

Johannes takes up his position on the top of the wall with only his head showing, exactly opposite the fish. This was his advanced O.P., to use a military term. The great moment arrives, Johannes gives the signal that all is well, and I creep up to the tail of the pool and then along the bottom of the steeply sloping river wall, and gain position.

There was nothing particular about the cast save that it was a longish one, and directed by my 'F.O.O.' on the wall behind.

'Langer oot,' he said.

A bright glare on the water prevented me from seeing an invisible midget submarine which was rapidly approaching my lure. Perhaps it was just as well. But on the wall-top Johannes sees (with what must have been some excitement for so hardened a hunter) my red spinner being sucked inside a large head, well below where Fanny was known to lie.

'You have him!' he exclaims.

Even then I struck too soon, but luckily, as events proved later, Fanny was hooked far forward in the palate. The reel made a sound like a jet-propelled plane and a hundred yards of line travelled upstream and then a hundred yards travelled down. This was too much for the reel and the line lay listlessly on the wall while the angler retired into the meadow and Johannes supported the line on the wall-top. At last contact was made, and Fanny, having made her first great bid for freedom, seemed winded. Johannes, over-confident, climbed down and showed the gaff. Fanny fled precipitately across the pool and in the process managed to unship the reel from the butt, a reel already loosened by furious winding. However, this was soon replaced. Next, Fanny backed, and I followed after her, wading in the shallow water. The next incident was hair-raising. The over-zealous Johannes again showed steel and had a go at the fish. Once more Fanny showed her paces and the situation was only saved by holding the rod arm high and Johannes with his gaff crouching low, for he was between me and the fish. It was a near thing, but by some miracle the line missed Johannes. After this we gravely proceeded down to the Horse Pool, whose stilly deeps contain stone piers which hold the water for the salmon fishers; a long, quiet pool is the Horse Pool.

The pace was no longer hot, in fact the great fish sulked slowly downstream near the piers. Fanny looked at me, I looked at Fanny all down that pool and we took each other's measure.

Then there came a horrid rasping thrill along the line and I knew the worst. Fanny had retired behind one of the stone piers, the last pier, in fact, in the Horse Pool. She had seen Johannes gesticulating on the island, where he had landed to dissuade her from going down the rapids on the wrong side of the island.

Quick! Jump to the last pier – the fish catches sight of me, and in a flash she doubles back towards the rapids. But in her panic she takes the short route and this mistake costs her her life. Johannes is there, and as the great silver form goes half aground and flapping on the shingles, the sun winks once more on the darting gaff, and the prize is mine . . .

Seventeen years have passed, but those three last seconds are yet remembered.

This sea trout weighed 19 lb. Her length was 37 inches and her girth, nineteen and a quarter. Three-quarters of a mile had been covered in the chase, and three-quarters of an hour of mingled anticipation and despair had ended in triumph.

The Laerdal in days of peace . . . what memories! . . . what a fish!

SIR HAROLD GILLIES

The Sea Trout Wins

BUT even as I have avoided it in this writing there is another picture I have been trying ever since to forget; that was when the 8-lb. sea trout broke my cast. (He might have been 10lb.)

What happened was that the owner of this burn – the local laird – seeing that it was a gin-clear day, with no sign of breeze, had offered me, in his generous way, the chance to fish this stretch of water famous for its unusually large sea trout. And I, seeing that it was a gin-clear day, with no breeze, with no hope whatever of catching a big fish – or even any fish that was old enough to know better – put on an ordinary loch cast and started working quite a way up the burn to reach a loch far above me in the soft peat.

This lovely loch above, with the peat as soft was sponge around it, was one of the most mournful areas of water I have ever encountered. It gave me melancholia just to look at it. Yet it was to this the big sea trout were migrating.

I had picked up a couple of small sea trout and come to a pool. While I was idly casting from side to side of the pool, trying to stir a fairly good fish I had seen in it, and at the same time eat my

A good lie for a sea trout

sandwiches with my other hand; my wife was seated beside me in the hot sun reading a detective story. There was a whoosh! and this huge sea trout, whose presence I never suspected, came clear out of the water at the foot of the pool. I was so startled that I nearly fell in myself.

Then I did everything wrong. I took a few jumps to reach the top of the pool, so as to give me some space to cast, and put my flies over him. On the second cast he took it. I thought he would turn and go downstream. Instead, fast as I stripped in the line to keep it taut, he came right up to me. For an aghast instance he was right below me, his fins and tail working slowly. I could have netted him as easily as you could pick up your hat. Then I stepped quickly backward up along the burn to give some more to that dangerously short line – in case he should jump – and he was off!

I persuaded him not to go through some rocks and up a fast slant of water above me, and he decided himself not to run out of the pool down below. Instead he just went to the bottom of this pool and stayed there. I do not think that either he or I moved a yard in the next hour. I could work him inch by inch to the surface. But every time my dropper appeared, he bored irresistibly down again. So there we were.

As I said, you can see a sheep a mile off anywhere on the skyline in the Shetlands. The bread-van, coming alone to deliver some loaves to the laird, stopped on the granite bridge below me, the driver walked up to me to inquire: 'Why don't you pull him up?' I explained the size of my sea trout, my frayed 3X cast, and so on. He went off shaking his head. The news went about over the Shetlands; two young men appeared from nowhere, leaned over the bridge, watched me silently. An old woman, carrying a creel of peas on her back, knitting as she was walking, also paused on the bridge. They discussed me with each other, I ate the rest of my sandwiches with my free hand, keeping a steady bend on my tip with the other, and my wife poured me out my ration of tea in the top of the thermos flask. I asked her to get some small stones. I threw those down. Nothing stirred him.

'It is a question of patience,' I asserted. 'Which of us tires first.'

Actually I wanted to break the line. The suspense was telling on my nerves. Therefore, when the laird's factor came along and in his gruff way, said: 'Why do you no' pull him up?' I complied. I took the line in my left hand below the first guide, held it firmly, and bent the rod. For that was all I did; the big fish never moved, then the rod straightened out.

'Lost him?' gasped the factor.

I just nodded. There was nothing to say.

As we stood there, staring down into the pool, the huge fish jumped and fell on top of the reeds directly opposite me.

'Whooh!' gasped the factor. 'Yon's a big un, sir!'

He went away, to report to the laird, I suppose, that the foreigner had almost caught one of his famous big sea trout. I trekked wearily home across the island to another laird with whom I was living. For consolation, he at once produced a full whisky bottle.

NEGLEY FARSON, *Going Fishing*

To an Old Friend

The end draws near again, and very near,
The first few fluttered beech leaves fall and gleam –
Light skirmishers that dog the dying year –
But still I see you down below the weir,
A shadow in the stream.

Here have you lurked since spring – in sportive guise,
Rallied the meadows to young April's rout,
Here first I marked the marvel of your size,
Here wooed you with each fleeting season's flies –
O alderman of trout!

Here, when the madcap cuckoo makes his mock,
And the rathe wild-rose blushed in earliest June,
The day the mayfly hatched above the lock –
You nearly had it, didn't you, old cock,
Save that you stopped too soon?

Here have I watched as the dawn spread high
Hoping in vain the prejudice or pique
That makes you – obviously – reject the fly
Would send you hurtling through the startled fry
To grab a proffered bleak!

Here likewise have my steps at eve been drawn
And, as the moon made way behind the wood,
(The same old moon that watched the hunting Faun)
I've found the lobworm garnered from the lawn
Did just as little good!

And now the end is near; we part a space
You to your mud and I to mine – in town;
May Easter find us at the trysting place
There where the dancing bubbles spin and race
To meet the first March Brown!

PATRICK CHALMERS, *Green Days and Blue Days*

106

The Bridge

THERE is mystery about a bridge which spans any water; like a magnet it draws the fisherman and the loafer, and the idler is never idle when he is leaning on the rounded coping-stones. These stones are worn as are the steps to some saint's shrine, not by feet but by worshipping elbows of contemplative men and boys and good-for-nothings. Bridges do not seem to attract women – but then, they are not so affected by water nor have they the time to idle.

Few men can pass over a bridge without looking over it, even if they are in a hurry. Even a fishless stream has magic by a bridge. Upon the under-arch bricks the reflected light plays to and fro, like notes of rare music, and from the high vantage-point above one may see the little minnowlings poised in the current and maybe a lusty chub or trout sliding sideways over spotted stones and bright tins. The tins are there because in an effort to break the spell men must drop things into the tawny current and ragged urchins, freed from the scholastic collar, throw stones.

I remember a bridge where I used to linger as a small boy. It spanned a brooklet not ten feet wide, the water held no fish, not even a miller's thumb or stickleback, yet I could not leave that place.

Terrible penalties were threatened if I should ever attempt to wade, but one day I saw a glittering object just under the rose-red arch where ferns sprouted. It gleamed like a blurred pearl down there and as I gazed I knew I must have it, even at the price of a beating.

In I went, treading delicately on small blue feet, revelling in the exquisite first shock of the crinkling stream. And bending there in the gloom of the archway I put my finger into that magic mirror and drew forth an empty mussel shell. To me that pearly spoon was something of great rareness. Clutching it I hastened up the bank, barefooted still and overcome with triumph. And there was Authority sternly eyeing me and a voice came as of thunder. I had disobeyed!

The pearly treasure trove was snatched away and dashed to pieces on a stone, and I was bidden to put on my stockings and boots. This I did with tears coursing down my cheeks and then, in a silence far more terrible than scoldings, I was led away and punished.

Another bridge I knew was of wood. It spanned a tributary of the Ouse. Under it the deep water had much mystery and sometimes when the sun shone one could see, deep, deep, down among the

The Bridge

waving weeds and snake-like ropes of lily roots, vast fish majestically questing, secret fish in a secret kingdom of which they were the finny kings. I have never seen such chub anywhere as those below the sheep bridge – but then, the youthful mind magnifies.

And lastly there is the high bridge over a northern river, where the water is so deep that the eye cannot penetrate the gloom. A clear river when not in spate, as most Highland rivers are, under the far-flung arch it had the hue of stout, and in sharp contrast, flat and sculptured rocks were pale and ashy.

Once, gazing down into those inscrutable deeps, I beheld a miracle.

Something suddenly became visible, a silvery dimness which, in a moment, resolved itself into a glorious salmon, glittering far more resplendently than my pearl mussel shell. It soared into the air and, curving, hit the water again with a mighty splash which echoed hollowly in the arch. In a second it was gone again and those black deeps had closed over it. I shall never forget that amazing revelation.

'BB', *Fisherman's Folly*

A Warwickshire Trout

I HAVE never captured a record fish but I have caught two 'notable' fish, one a trout and the other a tench. The trout came out of a brook in Warwickshire where no trout were supposed to be, but I afterwards found out this supposition had been cleverly bruited abroad by those whose lands adjoined the brook. The stream was certainly unprepossessing to the uneducated eye. It was very narrow, much overgrown with bushes and the banks patrolled by bulls. The latter, I have no doubt, had been placed there by riparian owners. But what are such trifles to a small boy? Any active and healthy boy is a match for a bull if he keeps his head and as for keepers and farm bailiffs . . .

When I was about thirteen years of age I went to stay one spring with my grandfather, who, in his day, had been a keen fisherman. He had a coachman named Dickon, who wore a glass eye, always an object of morbid fascination to the young. Dickon had lost his eye one winter afternoon when he was chopping wood, a chip flying up had almost gouged it out.

But I digress. One spring morning I was with Dickon in his harness-room watching him polishing the brass fittings to a collar. I remember that harness-room very well, it smelt of saddle soap, leather, horses, and, of course, Dickon. The combination of all four odours was not unpleasing to my juvenile tastes as I sat swinging my legs on a high stool.

The conversation turned to fishing. 'Ah,' said Dickon, polishing away at a buckle, 'there *are* trout if you knows where to look for 'em. Didn't Mr. Free used to get up at five in the morning when he stayed here, and go out and catch them?'

'Trout?' I asked incredulously.

'Aye, trout. Good 'uns too!'

'Where did he go?' I asked.

'Why, Pedder's Mill, of course.'

'But the Commander told me that there were *no* trout there!' I exclaimed. (The Commander being the chief 'riparian owner.')

Dickon smiled and went on polishing. That was enough. I would go to Pedder's Mill as soon as I could get my tackle together.

The next day I developed a roaring cold in the head. But despite this, and managing to conceal my malady from adult eyes, I set off soon after breakfast with my trout rod neatly dodging my grand-father who was talking to Dickon by the coach-house.

It was a wild April morning, grey and blowing hard, with occasional showers. Though the wind was cold it was one of those days when you feel the spring everywhere, you hear it too, and smell it.

I reached Pedder's Mill and had barely rigged up my tackle in the shelter of the hawthorns by the old mill pool (they were speckled all over with bursting green buds and a thrush had built a very new emerald nest in the heart of one of them) when the miller up at the mill opened the hatch and the still water at my feet became alive with thundering turmoil, dead leaves appeared and drowned sticks turned over and over in the muddy maelstrom.

Then came the miller and ordered me off. I went out on the road, walked down it for a quarter of a mile and rejoined the brook.

I lay low under a willow stump until I saw the Commander come down the drive in his neat trap, complete with cockaded coachman, and then began to fish. Soon a man appeared up by the Dower House kitchen garden fence, and bawled at me at intervals. I took no notice for a time until he began to purposefully climb the fence. Bailiffs and bulls are best left to themselves. He meant business so I stood not upon the order of my going.

These interruptions were tiresome and this latest interference made me impatient. I made another détour and came upon the stream again. Here, under a pallisade of alder trees I at last got my fly on the water and fished the brook down for some two hundred yards without the sign of a rise. Then the stream took a sharp turn to the left in a sort of elbow.

Under the far bank, the current was swift and the fly tittupped round on the ripples and was engulfed. The reel sang as a big fish made upstream and I had to follow. He made for a biggish pool some twenty yards above and there we fought it out for twenty minutes. I had no net (the very young do not carry nets) and I had to play my fish right out and beach him on the shingles at the pool head.

He was a beauty and I took no chance with him, he was practically drowned when I towed him ashore and fell upon him, a trout of three and a half pounds.

The battle won I wrapped it up in dock leaves and put it in my pocket, though the tail flapped under my right arm. I regained the road and almost at once heard the sound of a fast-trotting horse. It was as I had feared, the Commander was returning.

I raised my cap respectfully, and then I heard the clatter of hooves mingle and stop as the trap was pulled up. The Commander was a red-faced man, clean-shaven, of course. He glowered at my rod. I endeavoured to keep my right side turned from him lest he should see the 'tell-tale tail'. I wished the ground would open and engulf me but at that moment Providence took a hand. There came again the sound of trotting hooves and just as the Commander was about to cast aside his carriage rug and descend upon me, no doubt with the object of searching my small person, there swept round the corner my Grandfather, likewise in his trap, with Dickon beside him. Under the confusion of the meeting I bolted through the hedge and ran all the way home.

Now, by hook or crook, I had made up my mind to have that fish 'set up.' As bad luck would have it my grandmother met me in the drive and I foolishly showed her my trout, telling her I was going to have it stuffed.

She said nothing, probably because she knew I was a determined young devil, but when my grandfather returned, having calmed the Commander, she told him I was going to have my big trout 'stuffed.'

'That trout will be eaten here!' he thundered, and, as I was afraid of my grandfather, I said no word. Next day I was due to leave for home and without saying anything to anyone I raided the larder, procured my trout and wrapped it up in paper, posting it off from the post office 'ere I left for the train.

In the queer way grown-ups have, the trout was forgotten in the business of seeing me off to the station and on the way thither I confided in Dickon what I had done, and he gave his unqualified approval. That is why that three-and-a-half pound brook trout still surveys me as I write these lines, superbly mounted in an ebony framed case, a pleasant reminder of boyhood's triumphant victory over elders and betters, and an aldermanic fish.

'BB', *Fisherman's Folly*

Memories of Early Days

VERY wonderful is the perspective of childhood, which can make a small burn seem greater than rivers in after life. There was one burn which I knew intimately from its source to the sea. Much of the upper part was wooded, and it was stony and shallow, till within two miles of its mouth. Here there was for a child another world. There were no trees, the bottom of the burn was of mud or sand, and the channel was full of rustling reeds, with open pools of some depth at intervals. These pools had a fascination for me, there was something about them which kept me excited with expectation of great events, as I lay behind the reeds, peering through them, and watching the line intently. The result of much waiting was generally an eel, or a small flat fish up from the sea; or now and then a small trout, but never for many years one of the monsters which I was sure must inhabit such mysterious pools. At last one evening, something heavy really did take the worm. The fish kept deep, played round and round the pool and could not be seen, but I remember shouting to a companion at a little distance, that I had hooked a trout of one pound, and being conscious from the tone of his reply that he didn't in the least believe me, for a trout of one pound was in those days our very utmost limit of legitimate expectation.

There was a mill pond higher up in which a weight had been attained and we who fished the burn could talk of trout of that size, and yet feel that we were speaking like anglers of this world. But this fish turned out to be heavier than one pound, and when at last he came up from the depth into my view, I felt the great moment had come which was to make or mar my happiness for ever. I got on to the shallow water below the fish, and after great anxieties secured, with the help of my hand a fresh-run sea trout of three pounds. Never was a dead fish treated with more care and honour. It had swallowed the hooks and rather than risk spoiling its appearance in getting them out, the gut was cut and they were left inside. The small trout and eels and flounders were turned out of my basket and put in my companion's so that the great sea trout might lie in state. It was felt that the expectation of years was justified, that the marvellous had become real, that the glory which had been unseen was revealed, and that after the present moment the hope of great things in the future would live for ever.

LORD GREY OF FALLODEN, *Fly Fishing*

The End of the Houghton Club

TRULY Houghton was a pleasant place to live near. Words fail to express adequately the feeling of delight those never-to-be-forgotten days and evenings at glorious Test side created. Grim winter had vanished, the month of April, all smiles and some tears, reigned. Lovely was the walk through the Marsh Court water meadows by the riverside.

Moorhens flitted in and out of the brown sedges on the banks, jerkily flirting their little white tails. Later on the birds would be followed by their tiny broods, which, not having as yet learnt to dive, could easily be dipped out with the landing net. Snipe, far overhead, floated rapidly down from the sky in a wide graceful curve, bleating loudly during the descent, while somewhere in the distance a cuckoo now and again heralded the birth of spring.

On the water a sleek water-vole enjoyed a personally conducted tour, a lump of weed being his P. & O. liner. There were martins in the sky fly-hawking, and for the matter of that, picking the duns off the water, which the swift never does, the latter merely opening wide his mouth and down go the unlucky Ephemeridae one after the other, the bird never slackening his speed for a moment. But those mayfly murderers are late in coming to the river. One met fishermen here and there with whom to exchange greetings for the first time since last summer. Many of these anglers owned to names well known to dry fly disciples, and they assembled from all parts, one enthusiast coming every season from far-off India, but all drawn together by the irresistible magnetism of the grand river Test.

Down the river somewhere would be met the old head keeper H. He was quite a character, totally destitute of the smallest modicum of suavity, but what was more to the purpose, of thorough rightness. He was not to be 'had,' even by the most insinuating member of the poaching fraternity, whom he thoroughly hated, the more so that when keeper on the Itchen he had received a very hard hammering at their hands. The old man's peculiarity was that he hated to see the trout caught. On one occasion an angler found six trout lying at intervals behind each other, and all feeding on the Grannom as it floated down under the opposite bank. Of course, he began with the lowest fish, which old H. landed for him. The next trout shared the same fate. H. again operating with the landing net. So it continued until five trout would never swim again. The sixth just touched the fly, and thereafter lay low.

The fisherman, knowing the old fellow's weakness, got up from his knee saying: 'I think that's about enough, H., isn't it?'

'I think it be, sir,' was all the poor old chap managed to get out, but the tone of his rugged voice, and the look on his weather-worn face was quite pathetic; even a prompt *douceur* for his assistance seemed not to atone for the death of five of his pets.

Those who live near a river, and are constantly on its banks, see many interesting things, and some very strange ones. Kingsley truthfully said the ordinary wayfarer in the country saw but the outside of Nature, whereas the angler saw the inside as well. Below the place, some little way, where these trout were caught, was the charming and well-known mill, at which one of the members had quarters and dispensed lavish hospitalities to his friends, in fact, it may be said to have kept open house. The big waste water pool was noted for its numerous and heavy grayling, and many a goodly trout lived there as well.

A very strange and unusual sight was witnessed in it one day. Some thoughtless bucolic had slain a full-sized grass snake, a most harmless and inoffensive reptile, but to Hodge all snakes are adders – and cast the writhing body into the pool. The current from the hatches gave a lifelike movement to the poor thing as it lay on the surface. Suddenly from the depths dashed up with a mighty splash a huge trout, which, seizing the dead body commenced worrying it on top of the water, then, catching sight of the spectator standing above, plunged down into the black depths again, taking the snake with it.

But our pleasant times on the beloved Test were coming to an end. Happily we did not know it. Eighteen halcyon seasons had flitted by all too rapidly, and then, without warning, the blow fell! The Houghton Club died suddenly. If one could, on December 31st 1892, have seen what was passing in the mind of him, who homeward bound with the fish-bag half-full of grayling, as he crossed the bridge at Boot Island for the last time – a blended picture of present sorrow and past pleasure would have presented itself. Even as he stepped on the Island and closed the wicket – from force of habit – the destruction of the bridge had already commenced on the far side.

The Houghton Club died when in full vigour. At the time of its dissolution the list was full and with four names down for any occurring vacancies.

F. M. HALFORD, *An Angler's Autobiography*

Making the Loch at Foswell

A SHORT way back into the hills behind our house was a piece of soft boggy ground where mallard nested in early spring and snipe were often shot in autumn. It lay in a saddle, on one side whins sloping up to heather and on the other, a grassy hill with old Scots firs growing on its top. The bog covered the watershed, and from one end the water drained north-west straight down to Strethearn, while from the other it flowed south to feed the small burn which ran near the keeper's house, finally reaching the valley of the Earn rather farther to the east.

In 1908 my father and my brothers had the idea of making the bog into a small loch, and I remember watching them taking rough measurements with the aid of a spirit-level laid on the barrel of a shot-gun to determine where the banks would require to be placed and the approximate area of water which would be enclosed. The site seemed a curious one, the ground falling at both ends, and the supply of spring water from the bog itself being insufficient, it was necessary to provide for water being led in a ditch round the hillside from the small burn nearby. But all these difficulties were found to be capable of solution and eventually a local contractor set to work to construct the banks.

All that summer and autumn the work went on, and by early spring the loch was complete and filling gradually while we remained happily ignorant of the fact that owing to the use by the contractor of an inaccurate level, one bank was in the centre appreciably lower than the other. It so happened that as the water-level neared its highest point, a big snowfall occurred followed by sudden heavy rain, with the result that such surface water was added to the normal intake to the filling loch. The water rose suddenly, reached and overflowed the top of the low bank, while a strong east wind added to the danger. Early one morning we were roused by the news that the loch had burst, pouring down into the valley and sweeping away trees and bridges, but mercifully hurting no one.

Later that day we gazed on the ruin of six months' work. A clean-cut gap thirty feet wide had broken in the bank of the loch, and through this the water had burst. From the nature of the damage done, it seemed that the column of water had not spread out sideways but had largely retained its initial shape, with the result that the damage was restricted to a narrow belt within which the water had cut far into the ground, tearing and gouging long trough-like holes many feet deep. The worst of the damage was on our own land, so serious complications were avoided.

The bank was securely rebuilt, the loch refilled, and the damaged ground planted with young trees in narrow strips which in their early years formed admirable nesting ground for partridge. Now after thirty years these have developed into belts of well-grown trees, almost the only place on the estate where one has a reasonable chance of cornering a cock pheasant. The day came at last when the loch was full again and the young trout were transferred in cans and pails up the hill to their new home. We knew that the flooding of the ground and the subsequent rotting of the surface vegetation would produce ample food supply for the trout for several years, during which periods we could look for their rapid growth. To improve the position further and to provide food later on after the richness of the early years had passed we sank at various shallow points in the loch, round baskets containing roots of lakewort, a useful food-producing water plant which covers the bottom in the shallows like a great lawn of lush grass, giving, when the light strikes it, a lovely tint of green gleaming through the golden brown of sunlit water. We made small piles of stones in the shallows, too, and among them we put hundreds of little freshwater snails, while in the ditch bringing water to the loch we placed watercress from the burn and other water weeds among which live the freshwater shrimps which form an important part of a trout's food . . .

During the loch's existence, there can be few circumstances of time, of season, or of weather in which I have not seen it. I have seen it in late March when a hard cold wind blew from the east, bringing the smell of burning grass from the hill behind Dunning, when the young larches on the hill above showed as yet no speck of green and only the frogs croaking in the shallows and the plover calling over their nesting ground told one that 'the hounds of spring are on winter's traces'; on long summer evenings when it seemed that if one climbed the hill above the loch one would see the sun barely dipped behind the Grampians; on autumn days of wind and rain from the south-west, or winter evenings when the smoky orange and pink of the sky was reflected in patches of smooth grey ice which the wind had swept clear of the snow lying powdered and crusted on the frozen surface.

A. R. B. HALDANE, *The Path by the Water*

By the Exe

THE whortleberry bushes are almost as thick as heather in places on the steep, rocky hills that overlook the Exe. Feeding on these berries when half-ripe is said to make the heath poults thin (they are acid) so that a good crop of whortleberries is not advantageous to the black game. Deep in the hollow the Exe winds and bends, finding a crooked way among the ruddy rocks. Sometimes an almost inaccessible precipice rises on one shore, covered with firs and ferns, which no one can gather; while on the other is a narrow but verdant strip of mead. Coming down in flood from the moors the Exe will not wait to run round in curves, but rushes across the intervening corner, and leaves behind, as it subsides, a mass of stones, flat as slates or scales, destroying the grass. But the fly fisherman seeks the spot because the water is swift at the angle of the stream and broken by a ledge of rock. He can throw up the stream – the line falls soft as silk on the slow eddy below the rock, and the fly is drawn gently towards him across the current.

When a natural fly approaches the surface of running water, and flutters along just above it, it encounters a light air, which flows in the same direction as the stream. Facing this surface breeze the fly cannot progress straight up the river, but is carried sideways across it. This motion the artificial fly imitates; a trout takes it, and is landed on the stones. He is not half a pound, yet in the sunshine has all the beauty of a larger fish. Spots of cochineal and gold dust, finely mixed together, dot his sides; they are not red nor yellow exactly, as if gold dust were mixed with some bright red. A line is drawn along his glistening greenish side, and across this there are faintly marked lozenges of darker colour, so that in swimming past he would appear barred. There are dark spots on the head between the eyes, the tail at its lower and upper edges is pinkish; his gills are bright scarlet. Proportioned and exquisitely shaped, he looks like a living arrow, formed to shoot through the water. The delicate little creature is finished in every detail, painted to the utmost minutiae, and carries a wonderful store of force, enabling him easily to surmount the rapids.

RICHARD JEFFERIES, *Life of the Fields*

COARSE FISH

Don't Forget

DON'T forget that . . .

To dry waders it is a good plan to stuff them tightly with newspaper. A pad of newspaper cut roughly in the shape of the boot will keep the feet dry. This pad is placed in the sole of the boot and will soon conform to your foot. Also it may be removed when damp and a fresh pad inserted.

However watertight rubber waders may be, sweat condenses on the inside and after wearing them a few times the boots may become very damp, causing the most acute rheumatics. By using the paper sole this can be guarded against.

It is inadvisable to place rubber waders too near a fire as the rubber will perish. Keep them in a warm dry room, such as a kitchen, but keep them away from direct heat.

A child's boat, either clockwork steamer or sailing boat, is useful for carrying out your baited line to a tantalising area of water which is out of reach by casting from the bank.

When your offspring is out of the way raid the toy cupboard. On reaching the waterside coil the line twice on the decking with the bait hanging over the side. Wind up the clockwork ship, adjust the rudder, or, in the case of a sailing boat trim the sails correctly, and with a fervent prayer, speed the craft upon its way. When the vessel has reached the exact spot – gently pull your fishing line. The bait will then drop into the water and the ship (we hope) sails on, its mission completed. The rightful owner may then be sent to the other side of the pond to retrieve it.

If the boat goes aground afar off, or becomes marooned in a lily bed, then that's just too bad – you will have to buy him (or her) another one.

Toy balloons, leaves, and logs, also make good 'carriers' but unless there is a wind they are, of course, useless.

In every pond there always seems to be one enchanted area which by normal methods you can never reach. It is always there the big fish lie, basking in security. Hence the above suggestion, which I have tried myself, and found most effective. Whether it is a strictly sporting method I leave for you to decide for yourself.

The devil may suggest attaching spinners to the stern and a fine line to the bow, but don't listen to him. I know a keeper's son who caught a large trout in a forbidden water by swimming across it with a spinner attached to one of his legs. This method is chilly and tedious.

Another method of casting out a bait such as floating crust (for carp) is to attach a heavy pike float to the line. But carp are suspicious fish, and unless you can design a gadget for releasing and retrieving the float once the crust is out, they will keep a respectful distance and the bait will be laboriously devoured by innumerable roachlings.

An old-fashioned bicycle brake will make a good rod-rest. I refer to the type where the brake shaft enters a sleeve and is adjusted by a screw. The fork for the rod may be made of an old bicycle clip, soldered or fastened in some other way to the top of the smaller shaft.

Another type of rod-rest may be made out of a short length of garden cane in the top of which you may place two six-inch nails bent into a V.

Rod-rests are invaluable to the coarse fisherman. Many fruitless hours have been spent searching for forked sticks in a country where few bushes or trees are visible. Some farmers and landowners dislike the booted stranger disturbing their hedgerows and woods in search of forked sticks.

A running float is useful for fishing deep water. If a fixed float is used and the depth of water is great it is almost impossible to cast out any distance. Any ordinary float will make a running float. A quill is the best. Weight the end by a piece of lead placed inside the quill or wrapped about its lower extremity, so that it will cock of its own accord. Splice two fairly large rings or eyelets at the top and bottom of the float so that they protrude at right angles. Your line is threaded

The Old Lock Gates

through the rings so that it runs easily. When you cast forth your bait, the float will slide down to the single shot above the hook. The float will disappear but in a moment it will bob to the top, having run up the line.

A small piece of green weed (silkweed) such as grows on riverside piles (beneath the water) is sometimes a deadly bait for roach and perch.

To make a line or gut cast sink rub it with mud or clay.

When casting a fly against a strong wind use a short cast, when the wind is behind you use a long cast.

Spinning baits may be preserved in formalin solution, a mixture of 1 per cent formalin to 99 per cent water.

When a fish seeks refuge in thick weed do not apply pressure from the rod tip. Take the line in the left hand and apply a steady gentle pressure with the rod held nearly horizontally. After a few seconds release the pressure for a moment, and continue the process. If this fails to achieve your purpose you will, if a hardy and determined angler, have to divest yourself of your clothing and seek to grapple with your victim in his own element. Some risk is attached to this. A friend of mine was weeded by a salmon in the Test. He stripped and went in and was about to come to terms with his opponent when he observed, a field away, that his host *and hostess* were approaching, I leave the rest to the reader's imagination.

In the winter and early spring, when your energies are, I hope, diverted to the garden and the tilling of the soil, save the most appetising worms that your spade reveals to the light of day and place them in a shallow tub full of earth. You will be glad of them in the hot days when every worm is beyond your reach. In drought only a bulldozer or excavator will reach them.

Worms may be induced to come up for air by soaking an area of grass or earth with a mixture of mustard and water. They also come out at night but you will have to become as deft as a thrush to catch them and your wife will raise objections if you arise in the small hours to catch worms in the garden.

I know a man who practised this method and used to put the captured worms in his pyjama pocket. The inevitable happened – he omitted to take all the worms out of his pocket when he came back to bed. He is now divorced. There are some things which even a fisherman's wife will not stand for.

Wasp grubs, if lightly baked in the oven, will keep for a considerable time. If you do not bake them the chances are that on lifting the lid one day you will be reminded of Pandora's Box. The grubs will have hatched, or they will have died – which is worse.

Dried beans such as can be bought at the grocer's, make a good bait for carp when lightly cooked. French fishermen use them a good deal.

When going to fish a new pool or river for any particular species of fish try and find out beforehand to what bait they have been 'educated.' Potato is useless for carp in a pool where they have learnt to appreciate the flavour of wasp grub or wheat.

Bulls and wasps wait upon the unwary angler with evil intent.

Bulls, even the most savage, can be halted and even put to flight. Roll about on the ground and make uncouth noises. It takes nerve to do this but is effective. Wasps, if you should happen to unwittingly trespass on their nesting site, can be very vindictive, even dangerous. Little can save you if you have the whole swarm after you unless you emulate the moorhen, diving into the water and coming up to breathe under a lily pad. Bees may be baffled by seeking refuge in a dense thorn bush but not so wasps. Wasps will thread a dense thicket once they get their blood up.

Live bait are best secured in the winter. If put in a roomy tank fed by rainwater they will live a long time provided you feed them and shield them from the direct rays of the sun. If you catch them in the heats of summer 90 per cent will die. Church fonts make good bait tanks as at least one sporting parson has discovered.

A gudgeon of three inches long is the best possible bait for a big perch. The very big perch are almost entirely predatory. The next best bait is a minnow, and these cannibals will also take their own fry with avidity. You need not bother to cut off the spines – the perch knows how to deal with them as he wears them himself.

An old rubber tobacco pouch makes an excellent cast damper.

Fish lose weight after being caught, so carry pocket scales with you and if possible, a witness! A carp of 10lb. weight was found to lose 10 oz. in three hours. Such phenomena give rise to the absurd and libellous notion that fishermen are untruthful.

If you catch a very big fish in a free water keep it under your hat (if your hat is big enough). The trouble will be that your head will swell and once the secret is out your fellow anglers will be queueing up to fish that particular place.

To avoid midge bites, don't go fishing. I have tried many supposedly infallible recipes and have found them useless. Strong shag, puffed in dense clouds, is as effective as any, but you have to work hard and you will smoke a lot of tobacco.

Don't go fishing without the gaff or net.

Fish by yourself. If you must have a gillie secrete him afar off until you hook your fish.

A stream may be stalked from behind a cow. Horses are not so placid as cows, they have a habit of suddenly taking thunderous flight.

It is amazing how fish can distinguish between the tread of a man and that of stock. The latter they do not mind, but any quick movement overhead, such as a swiftly flying bird or a swishing rod will put fish down.

Learn to make your own landing nets. It's very simple. Any

professional fisherman will teach you. Most of the Thames fishermen make quite a tidy income from this easily acquired art. A hand-netting needle is required. This can be very easily made out of wood and its size varies with the size of the mesh. For a mesh measuring one inch from knot to knot a spool of two inches in circumference is required. Most deep-sea fishermen have spare spools and will show how it should be done.

Sticking ferrules may be remedied by heating the metal part in the flame of a candle, taking care not to heat the wood. Or a drop of paraffin applied to the junction of the male and female ferrules will often loosen them, but time should be given for the paraffin to soak in. Sticking may always be prevented by greasing the female ferrule, either with grease, soap, or blacklead.

To keep fish fresh wrap them in a layer or two of newspaper.

If your hook fouls some underwater object keep your temper and try pulling gently from various angles. It's surprising how a seemingly hopeless 'foul' can be cleared in this way.

Don't forget to keep a cork on the end of your gaff. If the cork has a small slit in one side this can be used for straightening kinked gut. In desperate emergencies it can be transformed into a float.

If you find you have come without your split shot, tie a small stone to the line, the fish will be less suspicious. Air-gun pellets (the hollow-backed) make excellent shot and you don't have the agonising experience of cracking your last remaining good tooth. All you have to do is to make a small slit in the thin part of the lead and squeeze the lead on to the cast.

Don't be tempted to set forth (after a hearty breakfast) for a day's fishing without taking a well-packed lunch and something to drink as well. It's worth the extra weight.

In gaffing a fish don't attempt to do so if the fish is too deep. Wait until it is near the surface, certainly no deeper than a foot. The best way is to extend the gaff swiftly but firmly over the fish and *beyond* it and give him the steel with a sharp jerk of the wrist and elbow. Your movements should be always under complete control, don't lose your head or attempt a risky stroke, you will only scare the fish and he will be scared enough already. Besides, you may gaff the line.

If you have no gaff with you then you don't deserve your salmon, but if you *do* find yourself in this predicament you will have to 'tail' him. Grasp him firmly just above the root of the tail and haul him ashore. It sounds easy and looks easy with a beaten fish but you will be a lucky man if you grass your fish at your first attempt. I advise you not to forget that gaff.

You can land a pike by grasping him by the eye sockets but the chances are you will find your hand inside his mouth if he is a big fish and then you will realise how difficult it must be for a roach to escape once it is seized by a pike. You will certainly bear honourable scars as a memento for many days to come.

Don't poach. I know many fishermen, and shooting men too, who have no qualms about trespassing on forbidden ground. Make sure of the limits of your beat beforehand.

If you are caught by an irate keeper and you have no loose change, speak rapidly in a foreign tongue. It works sometimes. If the owner catches you this ruse will not avail you and you deserve to feel uncomfortable. Remember there are two things which are guaranteed to make an Englishman very angry: 1, if you abuse or threaten his dog; 2, if you are trespassing in pursuit of game on his ground.

'BB', *Fisherman's Folly*

Coarse Fishing

THERE are coarse fish everywhere, except in those places where men have been allowed to save their private pockets by poisoning the public water. But there are some counties in which, when men speak of fishing, coarse fishing is meant, counties in which roach and bream, carp and tench, perch and pike are not the tolerated second cousins, the poor relations of the trout and salmon, but have things all their own way and yield precedence to none. We have pike and perch in plenty in the Lake Country, but few fish for them who can fish, for trout are there also. Neither Shropshire nor the Lake Country, nor any of the land that lies between them, can be considered the exclusive domain of those fish which, having no adipose fins submit, disdainfully, to being called 'coarse,' even by those who prize them at their proper worth. That exclusive realm of theirs is the country south of the Humber and east of the last hills.

They flourish in sluggish water and do not love the stony-bottomed rivers which hurry down the steep valleys where the rocks are near the surface of the soil. The trout and salmon fisher thinks of Scotland and the north as his own country. The coarse fisher thinks of a land so unlike this that it is difficult to believe that they can both be parts of the same island. I came to that country by way of Leeds, leaving the great trout rivers, Lune, Ribble, and Wharfe, in flood and working eastwards to the valley of the Trent. The Trent is not what it used to be, though, if the polluters will give it a chance, it may again become what it was in the days when J.W. Martin wrote his delightful books about its barbel, chub, and pike. After crossing the

A Quiet Reach of the Severn

Trent it was almost as if I had crossed the North Sea. There were the square sails of barges moving before the wind among the rain-soaked crops. Here and there were windmills. The road ran along the top of a dyke above a canal where the ripples of fish turning on the surface continually invited me to stop. And so on to Brigg and the Ancholme, where the Sheffield men ply the little rods, the 'toothpick' floats, and the lightly-shotted casts that are so strange a contrast to the heavy shotting and the cork-covered floats of the men of

Nottingham, a contrast strange only to those who have not compared the waters where these styles developed. Who that has read it can forget old Martin's description of the great float that was made for him, to carry a dozen shot and two big pike leads? But that float was for the fishing of a swim twenty-five and thirty feet deep, in water where less lead would have failed to keep the bait to the bottom. Here in the Ancholme a single shot is enough, and that is carried near the float, so that the bait, instead of being forced downwards, sinks slowly at its own speed, the only solid mouthful in a cloud of rapidly evanescent ground bait. The Ancholme was in flood, and, though it was possible to take fish in it in the Trent style, I saw some Sheffield men turn from it in dudgeon, to ply their special craft in some ponds near by.

From the Ancholme, where, just before the flood, a local angler landed a golden tench of 4lb. 10oz., I turned south to the Witham and the Welland, through a country absolutely flat, where the highest mountains are the dykes, where the sky is as wide and the horizon as level as on the plains of Russia. In this country, except in the towns, are no large houses, the cowsheds are the biggest buildings. Travelling hither and thither about it, from one famous drain or river to another, I saw in many days outside the towns no single building that would be described by an auctioneer as a 'gentleman's residence.' The houses are small, as if those who built them feared that they might drop through into the mud if they were a brick or two heavier. They are small boxes built of brick, often with a weatherproof coating of black tar. They are in keeping with the tradition of the country, the descendants of the huts of the fenmen, hidden here and there with their eel traps among the reeds of the swamp. The swamps have been drained, dykes built, and the fenmen live now on the edges of the drains, no longer in impregnable fastnesses of swamp and water. But this was never a country where it was worth while to own much land. A man wanted room for a hut, a landing place for his boat, and the whole wilderness of reeds and water was as much his as anybody else's. The great drains cutting the map in a series of parallel straight lines, the neat roads following the drains for miles along the tops of the imprisoned dykes, give the country now an orderliness that makes it easy to forget how long it survived in wilderness parts of England that we still think not wholly tamed.

Here are no rivers with babbling shallow, narrow gorge, deep pool, and restful eddy, but streams between banks almost as regular as those of the drains, and with scarcely more motion in them, hundreds of miles of still water, and in it the finest coarse fishing in

England. There is no strong water, except at flood times, and very little deep. Wind, not current, dictates the shotting of the cast. Except in a very few places you fish always with mile upon mile of water stretching on either side of you, in appearance exactly like the water before you, between banks exactly like the bank on which you sit. Here is nothing to distract the mind. Here, indeed, is the rigour of the game. Canal fishing, if you like, but canal fishing of superlative quality. The Middle Level Drain, near King's Lynn, where I saw those big bream pulled out a week ago, is like a railway cutting filled with water. So is the Forty Foot. So, in miniature, are the North and South Drove, the Counter Drain, the Hobhole, the Bell Water, and all these other famous places. From all parts of England men come to fish these waters, and those who have come once come year after year. Nor are the fenmen themselves without great pride in their posses-sion. In Boston, in Spalding, in Surfleet, men talk with hushed voices of great tench and bream. In Spalding the local anglers not only return all small ones to the waters, but bring their large ones carefully wrapped in wet cloths, to their secretary, who, if they are not to go in glass cases, turns them into a pond in some gardens belonging to the town, where the fishermen can call upon them and watching them grow to yet greater weights, recall the glory of their capture. Coarse fish indeed. There is no place in England where the captured trout can look forward to a pension and such honour in his old age.

ARTHUR RANSOME, *Rod and Line*

CARP

Carp

AUGUST and September are the best months in the year for carp fishing, and it is pleasant to turn to the carp from such fish as trout and salmon which put a less insistent strain upon the nerves. But not too often. A man who fishes habitually for carp has a strange look in his eyes. I have known and have shaken hands respectfully with the man who caught the biggest carp ever landed in England. He looked as if he had been in heaven and in hell and had nothing to hope from life, though he survived, and after six years caught an eighteen-pounder to set beside the first.

Carp fishing combines enforced placidity with extreme excitement. You may, day after day, for weeks watch your rod fishing on your behalf (for you do not hold it in your hand), and then, at last, you see your float rise and move off and, striking with proper delay, are suddenly connected to the fastest fish that swims. A salmon keeps it up longer, but I doubt if even he has the carp's appalling pace. Trout are slow, dogged creatures in comparison. Further, carp are immensely strong. To hold them safely you need stout gut, but to use stout gut is to throw away most chances of having a carp to hold. There is something terrifying about the fish. To hook a big one is like being jerked out of bed by a grapnel from an aeroplane. Their speed, size and momentum are enhanced, in their effect upon the mind, by the smallness and stillness of the ponds in which they are to be found. The pleasantest such place I know is the lake in front of a tower that Cromwell burnt, a placid pool where frogs spawn in spring, with ancient trees on the still more ancient dam that holds it up. These trees have, during the storms of several centuries, dropped branch after branch into the lake and the bottom there is rich with decaying leaves and fortresses for fish.

You cast out and pray (1) that you may not hook an oak bough, and (2) that if you hook a carp he may neglect the snags on either side of him and give you just a slightly better chance of catching him by burying himself in the water-lilies in the middle of the lake. You cast out, I say. Alas, there is no longer anything to cast for. The lake was drained for its fish during the war, and the men who took them, took even fingerlings, and left nothing alive that they could see. The carp in that lake, however, did not run very large. There were a few big ones killed when it was drained, but nothing of the size I saw at the week-end in a duck-pond that could scarcely have covered two acres. This pond was square and used for washing sheep. There was a little wooded island in it and a sunken willow tree. Its banks were almost without bushes. It was simply a shallow bath-tub of a pond. It had not even water-lilies. It looked as if it had no fish. When I came to the pond side, I believed I had been misled and was consoled by watching a flock of wild Canadian Geese resting beside it. For some minutes they took no notice of me, then, all together twelve or thirteen of them, they raised their long black necks and a moment later, they rose into the air, cleared the hedge, and lifting slowly, flew away. I was still watching them when I heard something like a cartwheel fall into the pond. Huge rings showed, even on the wind-swept surface. I watched for a particularly clumsy diving-bird to come up again. None came, but, just as a gleam of sunshine opened the racing clouds, there was another vast splash and a huge, pale gold fish rose into the air, shook himself in a cloud of spray, gilded by the sunshine and his own colour in the midst of it, and fell heavily back into the water.

In a few minutes after that, the rods were up and the baits cast out (with the helping wind it was easy to get them well out towards the middle of the pond). The floats were adjusted so as to lie on the surface, held by the resting shot, while the bait with a couple of feet of fine gut lay on the bottom. The placidity of floats so adjusted is like that of anchored ships. Life has left them. They lie dead, on the top of the water. They do not drift. There is no feeling that they may be approaching a fish. All that can be hoped is that down below, on the mud, a fish is approaching them. The fisherman can do no more. A yard or two of line lies on the ground beside his reel. Until that line is drawn out he must do nothing. He is immobilised, while tremendous events impend. Chained hand and foot, he waits on destiny. And destiny, rumbling here and there, with terrific splashes of golden leviathans, makes havoc of his nerves. He cannot, like the trout fisher, find expression and relief in lengthening his line and casting over a rise. He must steel himself to leave his rod alone and this enforced inaction in the exciting presence of huge fish, visibly splashing, produces a sort of drugged madness in the fisherman. I could not keep my hands still, nor could I reply sanely to questions. A true record of the life of an habitual carp fisher would be a book to set beside De Quincey's *Confessions of an Opium Eater*, a book of taut nerves, of hallucinations, of a hypnotic state (it is possible to stare a float into invisibility) of visions, Japanese in character, of great blunt headed, golden fish, in golden spray, curving in the air under sprays of weeping willow, and then rare moments when this long-drawn-out tautness of expectation is resolved into a frenzy of action. When, at last, I hooked one of these fish, I could not keep in touch with him, though I was using an American multiplying reel with which, on a trout rod, I have kept easily in touch with a salmon. Again and again he won yards of slack and yet, when he was landed he was no glass-case fish, but quite an ordinary carp, which at the end of the day I put back into the pond. For carp fishing, it was a lucky day. Four times the baits were taken by eels, landed amid anathemas, tempered by the thought of next day's breakfast. Four times they were taken by carp. One fish was landed. Twice the carp shot off with such speed that the reel overran, checked and gave him warning. On the fourth occasion one of the monsters made a direct run of thirty yards and then broke me, the fine gut cast parting above the float. There then occurred an incident that illustrates the uncanny nature of these fish. My float, lying out in the middle of the pond, turned and sailed slowly in again to my very feet, towed by the monster who then in some manner freed himself, thus returning me my tackle with a sardonic invitation to try again. No other fish is capable of putting so fine a point on irony.

ARTHUR RANSOME, *Rod and Line*

Mr. Evans' Carp from Boye's Sandpit

THE uncertainty of fishing is one of its chief attractions. Big carp and tench, for instance, should, by all normal rules, be tucked up in a nice warm bed of mud when winter approaches. We associate these giant 'cyprinidae' with the slumberous twilight of summer and brooding heats, cattle under willows, and the 'dog-days.'

When Mr. H. Evans set out to fish his Club Water (Boye's Sand Pit) on Wednesday, the 27th of October 1943, I can guarantee that the possibility of catching 'carp' was far from his mind. True, the morning was not cold, but a fine rain was falling backed by a light south-westerly breeze, and the rain looked like keeping on. Thoughts of summer days were far away, leaves floated down from the fast thinning trees, the swallows had gone.

Yet such a morning might yield a good roach. Therefore Mr. Evans baited up his ledger with a large knob of paste and the weighted line curved out to fall gracefully in the water thirty-five yards distant. Then he settled down to wait. It was not yet eight o'clock. Many other less fortunate and less imaginative folk were just sitting down to breakfast, the city men were perhaps at that moment kissing their wives and putting on their mackintoshes in preparation for the walk to the station. I can imagine them saying: 'Rotten old morning, dear, regular autumn morning . . . I'll be back on the six-ten.'

Mr. Evans was more happily engaged, watching his line. All at once it quivered and began to pay out, something had taken the ledger bait on his number nine hook, a good roach without a doubt. Mr. Evans's hand stole to the butt of his rod. He had eighty yards on his Allcock's Aerial reel. It was a silk line with a seven-pound breaking strain, his cast was a 5X. He had no cause for anxiety.

And then he knew that this was no mere roachling that had taken his lump of paste, it was something very different that pulled like a runaway bull.

The rain freckling the still water was unheeded, something very big was at the other end of his tackle, something which did not show itself for a considerable time.

When at last he *did* see a bronze gleam out there in front he gave a gasp and took one sidelong peep at his landing net, a fourteen-inch net. Such a net would never enfold that massive breadth, for the fish was a monster carp, a carp of a lifetime. There was only one thing to do – to play that fish until it had not the ghost of a flip left in him; to attempt any other course with so puny a net was folly. And so, playing for safety, Mr. Evans began a long struggle. Ten minutes passed, fifteen . . . twenty . . . twenty-five . . . and then he saw the great fish was done, it allowed itself to be towed like a sunken log.

In it came, but how to land it? Mr. Evans decided to grasp it with both hands and heave it on the bank. It was a terrible risk to take, but he is a man of spirit. Dropping his rod he fell upon that inert bronze beauty and dragged his ashore. He had a spring balance with him and when he saw the needle rise and rise he must have felt a glow of triumph, for that carp weighed no less than 16lb. 2oz. A fine catch indeed for a rainy autumn morning!

And now – I take my hat off to Mr. Evans and make him a respectful bow. Not only had he landed that fish without a net, not only had he heaved it to terra firma with his naked hands, but now, his triumph complete, he was going *to return it to the water*! What a gesture! What a sportsman! I must confess that here and now I would have done no such thing, it would have been despatched with feverish haste to the nearest taxidermist. But as I say, Mr Evans is a true sportsman and one which the Beacontree Angling Society might well be proud to number in its ranks. And the weighing completed and the battle won he gently replaced that grandfather in his native element and watched him swim drunkenly away and down into the rain-freckled depths of Boye's Sand Pit. It was not the first carp he had had from this water – a nine-pounder was his previous best fish caught from a punt and which had given him a lively time by going under the craft.

'BB'

Mr. H. T. Sheringham's Carp Classic

FOR practical purposes there are big carp and small carp. The latter you may sometimes hope to catch without too great a strain on your capabilities. The former – well, men *have* been known to catch them, and there are just a few anglers who have caught a good many. I myself have caught one, and I will make bold to repeat the tale of the adventure as it was told in *The Field* of July 1, 1911.

The narrative contains most of what I know concerning the capture of big carp. The most important thing in it is the value which it shows to reside in a modicum of good luck.

So far as my experience goes, it is certain that good luck is the most vital part of the equipment of him who would seek to slay big carp . . .

And so to my story. I had intended to begin it in a much more subtle fashion, and only by slow degrees to divulge the purport of it, delaying the finale as long as possible, until it should burst upon a bewildered world like the last crashing bars of the 1812 Overture.

But I find that, like Ennius (though without his justification for a somewhat assured proceeding) *volito vivus per ora virum*. Now that a considerable section of the daily press has taken cognisance of the event, it is no good my delaying the modest confession that I have caught a large carp. It is true. But it is a slight exaggeration to state that the said carp was decorated with a golden ring bearing the words '*Me valde dilexit atque ornavit propter immensitatem meam Issachius Walton, anno Domini MDCIII.*'

Nor was it the weightiest carp ever taken. Nor was it the weightiest carp of the present season. Nor was it the weightiest carp of June 24. Nor did I deserve it. But enough of negation. Let me to the story which will explain the whole of it.

To begin with, I very nearly did not go at all because it rained furiously most of the morning. To continue, towards noon the face of the heavens showed signs of clearness and my mind swiftly made itself up that I would go after all. I carefully disentangled the sturdy rod and the strong line, the triangle hooks, and the other matters which had been prepared the evening before, and started armed with roach tackle. The loss of half a day had told me that it was vain to think of big carp. You cannot of course fish for big carp in half a day. It takes a month . . .

I mention these things by way of explaining why I had never before caught a really big carp, and also why I do not deserve one now. As I have said, I took with me to Cheshunt Lower Reservoir roach tackle, a tin of small worms, and intention to try for perch, with just a faint hope of tench. The natural condition of the water is weed, the accumulated growth of long years. When I visited it for the first time some eight years ago I could see nothing but weed, and that was in mid-winter. Now, however, the Highbury Anglers, who have rented the reservoir, have done wonders towards making it fishable. A good part of the upper end is clear, and elsewhere there are pitches cut out which make excellent feeding grounds for fish and angling grounds for men. Prospecting, I soon came to the forked sticks, which have a satisfying significance to the ground-baitless angler. Someone else had been there before, and the newcomer may perchance reap the benefit of another man's sowing. So I sat me down on an empty box thoughtfully and began to angle. It is curious how great, in enclosed water especially, is the affinity between small worms and small perch. For two hours I struggled to teach a shoal of small perch that hooks pull them distressfully out of the water.

It was in vain. Walton must have based his 'wicked of the world' illustration on the ways of small perch.

I had returned about twenty and was gloomily observing my float begin to bob again when a cheery choice, that of Mr. R. G. Woodruff, behind me, observed that I ought to catch something in that swim. I had certainly fulfilled the obligation; and it dawned on me that he was not speaking of small perch, and then that my rod was resting on the forked stick and myself on the wood box of the Hon. Secretary of the Anglers' Association. He almost used force to make me stay where I was, but who was I to occupy a place so carefully baited for carp, and what were my insufficient rod and flimsy line that they should offer battle to 10-pounders? Besides, there was tea waiting for me, and I had had enough of small perch.

So I made way for the rightful owner of the pitch, but not before he had given me good store of big lobworms, and also earnest advice to try for carp with them, roach rod or no roach rod. He told me of a terrible battle of the evening before when a monster took his worm in the dark and also his cast and hook. Whether it travelled north or south he could hardly tell in the gloom but it travelled far and successfully. He hoped that after the rain there might be a chance of a fish that evening.

Finally, I was so far persuaded that during tea I looked out a strong cast and a perch hook on fairly stout gut, and soaked them in the teapot till they were stained a light brown. Then, acquiring a loaf of bread by good fortune, I set out to fish. There were plenty of other forked sticks here and there which showed where other members had been fishing, and I finally decided on a pitch at the lower end, which I remembered from the winter as having been the scene of an encounter with a biggish pike that got off after a considerable fight. There, with a background of trees and bushes, some of whose branches made handling a 14-foot rod rather difficult, it is possible to sit quietly and fairly inconspicuous. And there accordingly I sat for three hours and a quarter, watching a float which only moved two or three times when a small perch pulled the tail of the lobworm, and occupying myself otherwise by making pellets of paste and throwing them out as ground bait.

Though fine it was a decidedly cold evening, with a high wind; but this hardly affected the water, which is entirely surrounded by a high bank and a belt of trees. Nor was there much to occupy the attention except when some great fish would roll over in the weeds far out, obviously one of the big carp, but a hundred yards away. An occasional moorhen and a few rings made by small roach were the only signs of life. The black tip of my float about eight yards away, in the dearth of other interests began to have an almost hypnotising influence. A little after half-past eight this tip trembled and then disappeared and so intent was I on looking at it that my first thought was a mild wonder as to why it did that. Then the coiled line began to go through the rings, and I realised that here was a bite.

Rod in hand, I waited until the line drew taut, and struck gently. Then things became confused. It was as though some submarine suddenly shot out into the lake. The water was about six feet deep, and the fish must have been near the bottom, but he made a most impressive wave as he dashed straight into the weeds about twenty yards away, and buried himself in them. And so home, I murmured to myself, or words to that effect, for I saw not the slightest chance of getting a big fish out with a roach rod and fine line. After a little thought, I decided to try hand-lining, as one does for trout, and getting hold of the line – with some difficulty because the trees prevented the rod point going far back – I proceeded to feel for the fish with my hand.

At first there was no response; the anchorage seemed immovable. Then I thrilled to a movement at the other end of the line which gradually increased until the fish was on the run again, pushing the weeds aside as he went, but carrying a great streamer or two with him on the line. His run ended, as had the first, in another weed patch, and twice after he seemed to have found safety in the same way. Yet each time hand-lining was efficacious, and eventually I got him into the strip of clear water; here the fight was an easier affair, though by no means won. It took, I suppose, some fifteen or twenty minutes before I saw a big bronze side turn over, and was able to get about half the fish into my absurdly small net. Luckily by this time he had no fight left in him, and I dragged him safely up the bank and fell upon him. What he weighed I had no idea, but I put him at about twelve pounds, with a humble hope that he might be more.

At any rate, he had made a fight that would have been considered very fair in a twelve-pound salmon, the power of his runs being certainly no less and the pace of them quite as great. On the tackle I was using, however, a salmon would have fought longer.

The fish knocked on the head, I was satisfied, packed up my tackle, and went off to see what the other angler had done. So far he had not had a bite, but he meant to go on as long as he could see, and hoped to meet me at the train. He did not do so, for a very good reason; he was at that moment engaged in a grim battle in the darkness with a fish that proved ultimately to be one ounce heavier than mine, which, weighed on the scales at the keeper's cottage, was sixteen pounds five ounces. As I owe him my fish, because it was his advice that I put on the strong cast, and the bait was one of his lobworms, he might fairly claim the brace. And he would deserve them, because he is a real carp fisher and has taken great pains to bring about his success. For myself – well, luck attends the undeserving now and then. One of them has the grace to be thankful.

H. T. SHERINGHAM, Coarse Fishing

So ends Mr. Sheringham's account of how he caught his big carp, surely a classic in all the annals of angling.

Swancoote Pool

WE now come to Mr. Frank Barker's account of how he and a friend did battle with a tremendous carp in a Warwickshire pool, which, for the purpose of this narrative, I will call Swancoote Pool. That is not its proper name but the identity must be disguised.

This story of his perhaps stirs me more than most because, after reading it, I made a pilgrimage to this historic water on the last day of July of this year, 1944.

The impression it made upon me was so great that it would be well to set it down.

Burdened with basket and rods I journeyed thither through an early morning mist and a lifeless close atmosphere. It was one of those days so typical of late summer. The cottage gardens were gay with phlox and hollyhock, the hay smelt richly, bird song was stilled. I was soon in a remote and magic countryside, where the roads were gated and the farms amidst their orchards were in the old rose-red half-timbered Warwickshire style, and ancient men plied their scythes among the roadside weeds.

The lane became more rutty and sequestered, dipping down into a bowl of heavy elms and elder, and suddenly, there was Swancoote Pool, differing a good deal from the place I had in my mind.

It was very large, almost completely embowered with willows, elms, and oaks. It was square, its edges fringed with a wide carpet of yellow water-lilies. But the centre, a very large area, was clear. The water was black, black as ink, and by the sluice gate which figures in Mr. Barker's narrative, and on which he rested his rod, it was very deep. Indeed it looked bottomless until I plumbed it and found it to be eight or nine feet close into the dam wall.

I must confess that I was spellbound by the beauty of this pool, never have I seen such an 'exciting' place. Moorhens and coots tripped or preened upon the lily leaves and over all was that smell of

Swancoote Pool

ancient lily-girt water, some would call it a miasma, but to me it was a fruity yet thrilling smell.

One solitary man was regarding his float as it swung at anchor by a lily bed. His eyes had the unmistakable dreamy gaze of the carp fisher or, shall I say, the carp addict.

I asked him, in lowered tones, whether he had heard of any big carp taken from this place. (I knew of one eighteen-pounder at least.)

'There are carp in here, mister, as big as a man – ah, as big as a man. I've seed 'em, I'm afeared to 'ook one on 'em.' His voice was husky with emotion.

'Have you ever caught one?' I asked.

He shook his head. 'No, I've fished here for years and never had a smell.' (He was wrong there, Swancoote Pool fairly *reeks* of the terrifying creatures.)

There the pool lay, pearly now in the sunlight which was breaking through the mist. Waterfowl chased each other about the lily beds and as the sun grew in power many sleepy-eyed brown cows came

138

trooping gravely down to wade into the shallows where they ruminated hour after hour, whisking innumerable tails.

But no vast mail-clad shape leapt from those inscrutable waters, only countless small roach jostled and played water polo with a crust, far out.

I fished as intently and as silently as a heron, right through that steamy noon and on to dusk. But my float never stirred nor did the float of my fellow sufferer. And when at last night came and the wild duck circled over the trees we both packed up our tackle.

I have not got rid of the smell of that place yet, it haunts me. I know that I shall return again and yet again and I may never have even a small carp, but I shall return.

The carplings were much in evidence, the sound of their suckings filled the air. Whenever the sun shone forth from the hazy clouds the 'kissings' increased all over the pond, just as the seed-pods of broom crack audibly in the fierce heats of summer. And then as the shadows began to lengthen and the wood pigeons came back to the willows, lulling the whole valley with their drowsy cooings, the 'kissing' of the carp died away. Incidentally, this sound is caused by the fish feeding on the undersides of the lily leaves on minute transparent worms.

Such a place is Swancoote Pool and now to hear how two more fortunate anglers fared here on just such another summer's evening in the long ago.

'BB'

A Warwickshire Carp Pool

SWANCOOTE pool is a much lily-covered water of some few acres situated near an old Warwickshire village which, in my boyhood days had given me many hours of good fun with small roach, but that was all.

Many anglers have wended their way there when better places have been inaccessible to them, and lying as it does, in the lap of lovely leafy country, who could blame them paying sixpence to old Mr. Thomas at the Farm and then watching their porcupine or quill for the whole of a summer's evening, while a pipe kept away the midges and gave consolation to the smoker?

Bites were frequent enough but seldom were the roach more than three ounces and never half a pound, yet the water looked so clear and deep it enchanted those who besought it and almost instilled hopes of better things.

Each summer, for these ever-so-many seasons, I have taken a few nice tench here, some good fish in the four-pound region, but apart from these, the small roach, and an odd eel, nothing else could be expected.

Going back more years than I care to remember brings me to a sultry July afternoon when Arthur called and suggested we tried the tench at Swancoote Pool, and to it (with desire for its peace rather than the fishing) we slowly cycled.

Of the many baits with which tench can be caught we found lightly ledgering with wasp grub usually gave the best results and so in accordance with usual practice we soon got going opposite our favourite lily beds.

The small roach trouble us less on wasp grub but several were taken before Arthur's rod refused to straighten and this was the first tench; two pounds or a little more.

The sun had dipped behind the hills now but the sultry atmosphere was almost oppressive; just the night for tench.

I rebaited and lightly cast again, drawing in a little to allow the grub to lie nicely, but for half an hour or so the old porcupine lay slantwise and was troubled not.

Arthur was into another fish but could not get it up, for a few moments it was held, but very slowly and more surely went out for the lily roots and bang! the hook had gone.

My reel was now spinning as the rod lay on the floodgate and exactly the same thing happened, out went the line without my ever retrieving an inch and I was broken too.

It should be explained here that any fish had to be checked before it reached the lily roots – some twelve yards distant – or disaster was certain; we usually stopped our biggest tench in half this distance but not these fellows biting now.

Arthur retackled with a stronger hook and gut but I put on another number twelve and we began again.

Hardly had my wasp gone down when history repeated itself and in came another slack line.

'Rare sport this,' said my friend, as his float slid gently along the top towards the weeds. 'Must be big eels.'

With his newly attached number eight hook he was a better match for his quarry this time, but even so he never got his float above the water again and the line shot back into the sycamore under which he was sitting.

My friend changed his line for one of nine pounds breaking strain and in the meantime tench number two came to my net.

It was not long, however, before the big goose quill on my right was sailing out again and my friend's light Spanish reed rod was a half-circle. But this time the fish was stopped; it bored deep and turned very slowly, took a yard or two and gave a yard back, now it was under the rod tip, then away again towards the lilies, but nicely checked with a few yards of the safety margin to spare. Ten minutes, twenty minutes, and then we saw the fish for the first time – a carp – which later weighed eleven and a half pounds.

The roach were playing me up now and Arthur had settled under the sycamore again and as sure as before out went his old quill.

Since that distant incident the writer has lost many a big salmon but never has he hoped to see a fish landed more than he did this old carp.

Like the others it went away very slow but strong and forty-five minutes packed with thrills still found the fish as game as ever.

Almost in the lily roots then away again and oh! so many times this happened.

When at last the fish became more reasonable we saw its huge bulk lying ten feet below us, nearly a foot wide across the back and eyes larger than those of a dog.

He rested and then away again towards the roots, then very slowly back bankwards. The landing net was useless, an outsize one was required, and after much fumbling, trying tail first, out he went once more, this time a little quieter.

Arthur stopped him and he came to the surface where his huge dorsal moved about the top like the sail of a boy's yacht, leaving a wake like that of a duck.

He submerged and took a yard of line, then another, a foot more then a few inches, got perilously near the lily roots then, with tip of the rod well up, Arthur held on.

There was a slow creaking, a 'zip' and the line flew back into the sycamore tree and the carp – the biggest I have ever seen – went back to his home in the lily roots.

FRANK J. BARKER

There is a strange story concerning carp to be found in Isaak Walton's *Compleat Angler*. It has been advanced by several fish culturists as an explanation for the disappearance of carp from ponds. Whether or not there is any truth in the story I do not know: it is certainly not so fantastic as that of shrewmice catching fish. Frogs, at spawning time, grip one another with a vice-like grip, and it is quite impossible to separate one from another. The forefeet of the male frogs are fastened on to their 'ladies' like the points of sharp pliers. They cannot be prised apart without injuring either party.

Carp and Frogs

I HAVE both read it, and been told by a gentleman of tried honesty, that he has known sixty or more large carps put into several ponds near to a house, where, by reason of the stakes in the ponds, and the owner's constant being near to them, it was impossible they should be stole from him; and that when he has, after three or four years, emptied the pond, and expected an increase from them by breeding young ones (for that they might do so, he had, as a rule, put in three melters for one spawner), he has, I say, after three or four years, found neither a young nor an old carp remaining. And the like I have known of one that had almost watched the pond, found of seventy or eighty large carps, not above five or six; and that he had foreborne longer to fish the said pond, but that he saw in a hot summer, a large carp swim near the top of the water with a frog upon his head; and that he, upon that occasion, caused his pond to be let dry; and I say, of seventy or eighty carps, only found five or six in the said pond, and those very sick and lean, and with every one a frog sticking so fast on the head of the said carps, that the frog would not be got off without extreme force or killing.

ISAAK WALTON, *Compleat Angler*

Here is Albert Buckley's account of how he caught his big carp from Mapperley. In the last few years the Carp Catcher's Club – which is limited to twelve members – have investigated Mapperley and have caught large mirror carp there but (to date) none as big as Buckley's. It is a difficult carp water because of its great size, but by careful preparation and fishing at night, Berth Jones, one of the members of the Carp Catcher's Club, accounted for a good fish in the sixteen pound class in 1953.

That there are others far larger in Mapperley there can be no doubt whatever and I myself have seen a fish well into the thirties swimming at the top end of the reservoir. But Mapperley will always present a problem and is, I should say, a very 'exacting' water to fish. Here is Buckley's story.

Mapperley Reservoir

Mr. Buckley's Record Carp Story

A N angler all my life and the son of an equally keen fisherman, my opportunities of indulging in my favourite sport have been restricted almost entirely to the canals and reservoirs of the border country of Notts and Derbyshire, that is, the waters within reasonable distance of my home.

During recent years the form of angling which has proved most attractive to me has been pike fishing, and it was this branch of the sport, which, in fact, introduced me to the Mapperley carp.

During several recent years my father and I have fished for pike in the waters on the Shipley Estate, and from one or another we have secured some fine fish, including one specimen weighing over twenty-two pounds.

A fortnight or so after the opening of the coarse fish season in 1930, I was trying for pike in the Mapperley Lake, in which a small group of friends and I have secured the privilege of angling, when a companion, who was fishing for roach nearby, hooked a fish of unknown species which promptly broke him and sailed away with a considerable portion of his line and tackle. He reported the happening to me who, aware of the legend of the carp which the water contained, watched carefully what happened when my friend had renewed his gear and recommenced his efforts.

Sure enough, in a very few minutes, off went the float again and for over a hour a great fish was played but was ultimately lost.

Up to that time I had never seen a carp caught, but like a wise angler I commenced my campaign against them by reading up all I could on the subject of carp fishing, and at my very first attempt, which I made a few days later, I was successful to an extent far beyond my wildest dreams, for on that occasion I secured a brace which weighed fourteen and sixteen pounds respectively.

Encouraged by this success, on the morning of my great good fortune, I reached the lake, unaccompanied, just after 9 a.m. on 24th July 1930.

Mapperley Lake, covering an area of twenty-nine acres, is a beautiful spot just inside the borders of Derbyshire. It lies in a valley with Mapperley village on one side and the old Shipley Hall and grounds on the other. Its waters are used for the colleries nearby and there are two more reservoirs close together on the road to Heanor, a town about two miles away. On the same estate which was once owned by the late Squire Munday, of Shipley, there are rhododendron bushes which grow profusely all over the woods and grounds, making a gorgeous sight in the summer-time.

There had been heavy rain on the previous day, and the water which normally is very clear, was slightly muddy. I fixed up a rod, a common roach rod, and fished from my favourite place, the margin of the road which passes along the crest of the embankment, at the lower end of the lake.

My tackle was light and fine, 250 yards of No. 1 gauge line, the breaking strain of which would not be more than 3½lb., while the gut of the bottom tackle was 4X gauge and No. 10 hook, just ordinary roach strength, and no more. The tackle was weighted with one small shot, just sufficient to 'tip' the crow-quill float to a vertical position. The bait was a small pellet of home-made paste of brown bread and honey, almost as big as a swelled pea. Owing to the gale with the wind blowing straight towards me down the lake I could only fish about two yards from the embankment. At the foot of the embankment the depth of the water is great, thirty feet or so, and the slope of the wall is so steep that within a few feet of the margin a fishing depth of fourteen or fifteen feet can be found. At this depth the bait rested and before it had been in position more than five minutes the first bite was registered by a trembling lift of the float and its drift in towards the foot of the wall. That fish was 15½lb. and it took about an hour to bring to the net. Within another five minutes or so of the new bait being cast out there followed another tussle with a smaller fish of 11½lb. Following this was the least of the four carp taken during this wonderful morning, a 'midget' of 9½lb.

Then came the fish of the day. Once again, almost immediately after the bait had sunk to the depths, the float indicated the interest

of a fish, and on striking gently I realised that I had hooked a carp far larger than any of my captures on previous occasions.

Being determined to secure the prize I played it with the greatest possible care, but there were many anxious moments during the following hour and a half, for it fought magnificently. There was great similarity in the fighting tactics of all the carp. As soon as they felt the prick of the hook they tore away through the water parallel with the bank at a great pace and almost immediately turned sharply up the middle of the lake, keeping well down on the bottom. The line was torn off the reel at an amazing rate. The first dash took off a good hundred yards and a check affixed on the reel made a screeching noise as the fish made for the shallow waters. The giant carp gave me an anxious time and though I supposed I ought to have changed the gut and hook which had stood so much I had not done so.

Fortunately that stretch of the bank is clear of bushes or other obstacles, otherwise it would have been impossible to retain control of the fish. On each occasion, and particularly in the case of the twenty-six-pounder, after the first wild run alongside the wall they made mad dashes out towards the centre of the water and it was only by the exercise of the greatest skill that it was possible to turn them in their course before they reached a wooden platform from which the main pen-stock of the lake is worked, and which projects from the surface at a distance of sixty yards or more from the embankment. After just over an hour the fish showed signs of weakening. His wild rushes covered less distance, and he began to move in circles deep down for nearly half an hour. As I was using very fine tackle I dare not put much strain on to get him to the top. At last he came to the surface near the bank where he swam around for several minutes. On the wall side there were some stones which formed an inlet pool about a yard square, but not deep enough to draw the fish into. Although I used the net on the others I could not on this one owing to his size. At last he came to the bank side where he lay inert under the straining rod point, and, with hands which I confess trembled greatly, unhitched from my coat buttonhole the point of the gaff, which fortunately I had snatched up as the fish made its first wild dash, and, taking advantage of an opportunity which the fish offered as it rolled quietly just beneath the surface, I lifted the point of the sharp hook into its shoulder.

For some curious reason the fish hardly moved even then, but to my horror, as I dropped the rod and took both hands to the gaff, the shaft broke and the fish slid back into this small inlet pool, and lay motionless! There was nothing for it but emergency measures, and regardless of all but the fear that my prize might even then ultimately jump back into the lake and escape me, I grasped the slippery bulk with both hands, and working my fingers into the gills commenced to heave it on to the bank. It was then that he struggled violently, lashing out with his great tail, drenching me from head to foot. The other fish had been securely tied up in a large bag, but without troubling about them or the risk of damage to my rod which lay where it had fallen, I ran to the keeper's cottage nearby with my dripping prize. There it was put on the scales, but as their capacity was only 25½lb. the register bumped to its limit and I knew that the fish exceeded that weight.

Greatly (and very naturally) excited over my trophy I was undecided whether to recommence fishing or not because there was in my mind the problem of getting my prize home. Fortunately at this juncture there appeared on the road an old man from the village who remarked it was the best catch of fish he'd ever seen in his life. On telling him of my difficulty in carrying the weight of fish (which was 62½lb.) to Heanor, two miles away, this good Samaritan offered to go up to the village and see whether it was possible to find some means of transport.

While waiting I packed up and went to the keeper's house from one o'clock till about four p.m. Shortly afterwards there appeared coming down the hill the desired transport in the guise of a small boy pushing a little home-made two-wheeled handcart. I packed the fish into this and we commenced our two-mile tramp over the hill to the tram at Heanor. I helped the lad over the worst part of the journey by taking the hand-cart which contained two records for the British Isles (though I did not know that till later on) one, for the biggest weight of carp caught in a day, and the other for the biggest fish. I gave the lad, who was about ten or eleven years of age, a shilling, and bought him some sweets, and off he went back home with his wagon, happy in himself, little knowing how much he had meant to me for the lift.

Upon arriving home from the tram I decided to take the big carp to Nottingham, about nine miles away, where I knew a taxidermist who would set it up for me. About eight o'clock at night I arrived at his house and showed him my capture. He weighed the fish, which was caught about one o'clock, and it scaled 26lb. When I told him about the other carp at home he asked me what I was going to do with them. I said I didn't know, so he asked me if I would mind if I gave them him to set up for the Nottingham Natural History Museum at Wollaton Hall. I said he could have them, so he came back with me the same night for me. They are now all preserved in their natural forms, except the large one, which is a plaster cast, the original specimen I now have at home.

This is the story of my great red-letter day, a day well worth remembering and equally well worth recording, and one which would satisfy most of us. But not so me! I am sure Mapperley Lake contains carp of far greater size than any of my recent captures, and one day, with the best of luck, I hope to beat my own record.

ALBERT BUCKLEY

The Mighty Mahseer

NO account of battles with big carp and barbel would be complete without some reference to their relatives in the East, the best known of which is the mighty mahseer.

The writer has had the good fortune to fish for them in many of the rivers of India, and for the kindred species in Iraq. Fierce battles have occurred when many big fish have been killed. Unfortunately I can lay claim to no personal records on rod and line, but I have been able to measure a number of these fish. The characteristic of the mahseer is to seize the bait with a terrific initial rush which may take out well over two hundred yards of line, so the fish must be followed. He will fight gamely to the end, when the best method of landing him is by beaching, for the gaff does not easily penetrate his thick-armoured scales. To quote a few authentic cases:

Colonel J.S. Rivett-Carnac, on the 28th December 1919, fishing with rod and line (using 'ragi' paste bait) on the river Cauvery, South India, killed a mahseer (*Barbus Torassullab*) and succeeded in landing it in thirty minutes. The fish was a spent female decidedly out of condition, weight 119lb. This is the biggest authentic record for India, caught on rod and line.

Another mahseer of 110lb. was killed on the river Cubbany (South India) on the 22nd of October 1938, by Mr. A.E. Lobb, using a similar bait, but it took him three hours and fifty-five minutes to land it – a hen fish in good condition. Still larger fish have been caught on rod and line in Iraq. Major H.L. Colan killed one on the Diala River (a tributary of the Tigris) in September 1918, which weighed 125lb. Major Colan was using a 14-ft. rod, bait *ata* paste, and it took one and a half hours to land.

One yet bigger was caught by Major F.B. Lane on the Tigris at Samarra on the 21st of September 1915. This fish weighed 140lb. and was killed on a rod, the bait being a two-inch spoon. Both the above varieties have been identified as *Barbus Seich*.

The writer has also been fortunate in witnessing many battles with big fish of this type which have broken him (an all too common occurrence.)

Far bigger fish than any of these mentioned have been caught by the troops but *not* on rod and line. In some cases I have been able to take measurements and photographs.

The normal battles took place as follows: During the war 1914–18, a lot of stout telephone cable, abandoned by the Turks, was salvaged by the men. This made excellent line, all that was required being a mighty hook, usually fashioned by the unit's armourer, the bait used being meat, or more frequently, a large pear-shaped blob of *ata* paste. Once a big fish took this bait the unfortunate angler was sometimes seen rapidly disappearing into the water. His friends, rushing to his assistance, joined in the tug-of-war until the monster was dragged on to the bank and despatched with a crack on the head. Cases of the angler being drowned did occur when, in his excitement, he hung on too long until he was swept away in the dangerous currents.

One of these fish (photographed) weighed 167lb., and another from the Euphrates at Massiriyah scaled 213lb. This weight was vouched for by some staff officers of the 15th Indian Division, 1918.

Still bigger fish lie in the rivers of Iraq and also in India, Burma and Malaya, but it is difficult to get accurate weights for very heavy scales are rarely carried when in camp. Most anglers who have done much mahseer fishing will be able to record first-hand experiences of battles with these monsters, which, incidentally, are usually hen fish.

Unfortunately, the rivers are so large and the currents so strong that it is often impossible to follow up your fish owing to bad ground. The battle has probably lasted for hours until the angler is completely exhausted.

So it is not surprising that sooner or later a break will occur, rendering an authentic record impossible, although the thrill of the fight will remain for ever in the mind of the angler.

LT.-COL. R. B. PHAYRE, M.C.

The Record Carp Story

ON 12th September, 1952, Peter Thomas and I went to Redmire. We left home in a downpour, but by the time we had reached our destination the sky had cleared and the stars were shining brightly. It was very cold indeed, but we fished until about 2 a.m., when we noticed a bank of black cloud coming from the north-west, and decided to pitch our tent before it began to rain again.

We chose a spot on the west side of the lake, in deference to a theory I have that when carp have been driven into deep water at night by lowering temperature, they usually move out of it again in the early morning on the side which first catches the morning sunshine. Here we camped, pitching the tent with its open end about three yards from the water and directly facing it. Between the tent and the water's edge a large ground-sheet was spread.

Looking across the lake, about a hundred yards wide at this point, we could see a line of trees, which appeared as black shadows. To the left, ten yards along the bank, was a clump of weeping willows, whose branches trailed in the water, and beyond them was the tough pond-weed of which I spoke when describing the capture of Maurice Ingham's fish. This extended about twenty yards out into the lake, as did another bed of the same stuff on the right of our position. Beyond that, forty yards away, was the dam at the end of the lake, which runs at right-angles to the bank from which we were fishing. Half-way along the dam were once some chestnut trees, which have long since been felled, but their stumps still live and a tangled mass of writhing roots trail in the water. Immediately to our right, on the bank from which we were fishing, was a mass of brambles hanging in the water and extending to the bottom, concealing an undercut bank hollowed-out to a depth of between three and four feet, a favourite haunt of moorhens and rats.

Having arranged our week-end home, we baited our hooks and cast out to the edge of the deep water, a few yards beyond the pond-weed; Peter's to the left and mine only a few yards to the right of where his bait landed. Both baits consisted of balanced paste and breadcrust on No. 2 hooks which had been carefully sharpened beforehand; mine was whipped direct to a 12lb. B.S. plaited nylon line, of which I had 100 yards on a fixed-spool reel. Rods were the usual Mk. IV carp-rods, which have never failed us yet – ten ounces of hardened split-bamboo can be made to do surprising things. Electric buzzers were clipped to the lines between butt-rings and reels, and all was ready for the carp to bite; to attract them, mashed bread ground-bait was thrown out. By this time, the sky had clouded over completely, and instead of rain there was a decided increase in temperature, but the darkness was intense. I cannot remember ever being out on a blacker night. It was so dark that even the rats were less active than usual, and all I could see were the silhouettes of the trees opposite. The lake was completely still, its surface unbroken by either wind or the movements of fish; and so it remained, except for one heavy splash far out, and a brief spell of 'flipping' by very small fish on the surface, until some time between 4.30 a.m. and 5 a.m. About that time one of the buzzers sounded, and we were both at the rods at once.

'It's yours,' said Peter. I raised the back of my hand under the rod to feel if the line was being taken, and felt it creep slowly over the hairs, an eerie but satisfactory sensation. In went the pick-up; a pause to make sure the line had been picked up properly, and then I struck hard and far back. I encountered a solid but living resistance, and Peter, needing no telling that a fish was hooked, reeled up his line out of the way. I crouched so that I could see the curve of the rod against the sky – even that was difficult in the extreme darkness – and waited on events. I did not want a fresh lively fish brought too soon into the fifteen-yard wide channel between the weed-beds, and I determined that if possible the battle should be fought in the deep water beyond.

The fish moved slowly and solidly towards the dam. Every few seconds came a tremendous tug; it felt as if the rod had been struck by a sandbag. As the fish neared the dam, I remembered those chestnut roots. Four pounds or forty, it must not get among them, or all would be lost, so I increased pressure. At first it had no effect; then as I bent the rod more, the efforts of the fish became intensified. I knew only a few yards separated it from disaster, and hung on grimly. The rod bent as never before – I could feel the curve under the corks in my hand; but everything held for the two or three minutes that the fish continued to fight his way towards his refuge. Then, suddenly, he gave it up. He turned and forged into the weed-bed between me and the roots, and I was only just able to keep the line taut. Presently he stopped, and all was solid and immovable.

Peter said, 'Take it easy. Wait and see if he'll move.' I did. Nothing happened. I said, 'I'll try hand-lining.' Peter said, 'All right, but *take it easy*. That's a big fish, you don't want to lose it.'

I had no idea how big a fish it was. I knew it was a good one, but all I could think of then was: 'Maybe another twenty-pounder – I hope!' I pulled off a couple of yards of line, so as to be able to get the rod up quickly if the fish bolted suddenly; then I pointed the rod straight at the fish and began tugging. The first few tugs made no impression; then came a frantic pull, up went the rod, and out went the fish into the deep water again. I let him go well out, and then tightened up firmly again, praying for him to move *left*; and he did. When he was opposite I gave him the butt and crammed on pressure to the limit; and in he came, grudgingly, pulling and boring every inch of the way, but always losing ground, until at last he came to the surface and rolled three or four yards out.

Peter was ready with the net, and as I drew the fish towards it, he switched on the electric lamp. We saw a great expanse of golden flank as the fish rolled. 'Common carp,' said Peter. The fish rolled again, then righted itself, and suddenly, with a last effort, shot towards me, and to the right. I could do nothing to stop it, and to my horror it crashed through the fringe of trailing brambles; in the light of the lamp I could see the swirls as the fish tried to thrust even farther under; but though I put the rod-point under water and strained it as hard as I dare, nothing would shift the fish, which eventually settled down into an immovable sulk.

Peter climbed out to the edge of the overhang and put the big net, thong down, over the hole in the brambles where the fish had gone in. Then, feeling carefully down the line with his free hand, he reached the fish's nose and pulled it round, steering it into the net. I saw vaguely a commotion; then Peter began to lift. He stuck half-way and called for me to take his lamp. I slackened line, put down the rod, and went to his assistance. Once I had the lamp, he could grasp the mesh of the net, and with a tremendous heave he swung net and fish up and over the brambles and on to the bank.

We knelt side-by-side looking at it. I knew it was big, and suddenly it dawned on me it was more than that. It was tremendous! I cut a stick, notched its end, and with this Peter extracted the hook which was only lightly lodged in the roof of the mouth. Then we put the fish in a sack and lifted it on my spring balance, which goes up to 32lb. The pointer came up against the stop with such a thump that we both knew at once that here was a new record; but we could tell no more; so we tied up the mouth of the sack and lowered it into the water.

Then we re-baited our hooks and cast out again. Peter went into the tent; but I knew I could never sleep, and sat smoking and thinking till dawn. It was then that I resolved that, record or no record, that fish should not be killed. Many, many times I had wondered what I should do if ever I caught a record carp; now I had to decide, and kill it I could not.

At about ten-thirty, I was able to telephone Mr. H.F. Vinall, curator of the aquarium at the London Zoo. To cut a long story short, a van containing a vast tub, and two good fellows, who gave up their Saturday afternoon for the purpose, came and fetched it; and it arrived alive and well. I asked that it should be accurately weighed on arrival, which was done, and the weight recorded at 44lb. I thought the sack must have been included at first, but the matter was investigated, and it has now been established that the weight really was 44lb. to the dot, without the sack or anything else.

It is now living in a large tank at the Zoo aquarium.

R. WALKER, *Still Water Angling*

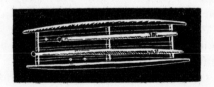

TENCH

A Little Pond in Hampshire

THE tench is a very curious fish in its habits. You may see a pond which is stocked with good tench, and look over it narrowly, and even do so many times, without having the slightest idea there is a fish in it. I have known ponds which have been supposed to be fishless for years, by the merest accident to be discovered to contain large numbers of fine tench in them. In many places tench are very peculiar also in their times of feeding; on some days they will feed well, while at other times you will not manage to get a fish in a week; and though this is not *always* the case, they are yet usually more or less capricious. As an illustration of the above, I may state that I once knew a little pond in Hampshire, which was not perhaps more than about twenty yards square. I had many times seen it, but never saw a fish in it, when one day the person to whom it belonged, knowing that I was fond of fishing, asked me if I would not like to catch some of the tench in the pond. I had no idea there were any in it, but as he assured me there were, and as I had nothing else to do one afternoon, I got a bag of worms and walked down the pond with my rod.

I put up a small light cork float, and a couple of hooks, one four or five inches above the other, baited with red worms, threw in some

153

broken worms, and waited. Presently I caught a little eel; then another, then a little tench of less than half a pound weight; then one or two more eels; and, although I kept on throwing in the broken worms I did no more, and finally threw in the rest of my worms and went away disgusted, not having seen another fish move.

Still the proprietor assured me that there were good tench in the pond, and urged me to try again; and the next afternoon, being inclined for a lazy hour or two, I took my rod, a book, and my pipe, and walked down to the pond. I pitched my float as usual, and sat down behind a bush, lighted my pipe, and began to read, when, on looking up I found that my float had disappeared, and was making tracks for the middle of the pond. Thinking it was only a small eel, I got up lazily, took up the rod and struck, when to my surprise, I found that I had hold of something a good deal larger than I bargained for, and after a tolerable tussle, I got out a fine tench of a pound and a half. The book was at once consigned to oblivion, and I set to work carefully, and barely was my float settled, when 'wriggle, wriggle, wriggle,' it went, and after the usual preliminary gyrations and bobs which the tench usually communicates to it, off it went; I struck again and got another fine tench of nearly two pounds; after this the fun grew fast and furious. Unfortunately, I did not keep a score of the fish I caught, as, finding I was having such great sport, I was afraid of clearing the pond out, so I put most of them in again, merely keeping three brace of two-pounders; but I should imagine that I must have captured about thirty fine tench, not one of which would be under a pound and a quarter, and many of them topped two pounds and a half. Where all these large fish could have packed themselves in this mite of a pond without ever attracting notice, I could not imagine.

Tired of pulling them out, I left off in the evening while the fish were yet biting fiercely. I went there again the next day, and caught *one* tench of three-quarters of a pound; but though I fished there many times afterwards, *I never caught another tench*.

Tench at times feed freely enough all day; but the favourite feeding time is at dusk, and when you can barely see your float – then they will take if they take at all.

FRANCIS FRANCIS, A Book on Angling

I wrote to Mr. Alston to get the story of how he caught his record fish and here is his reply which I consider to be of outstanding interest to all fishermen:

Rev. Alston's Record Tench

A S I expect you know, any water in which the level alters usually contains big fish. In the mere where I caught my record tench and rudd this was the case. The mere is at Wretham, Norfolk, and is called Ring Mere, and this water goes dry every twenty years or so. When I first went to Wretham there were no fish in the mere. I restocked it with fish from Standford Water, a few miles away. I put in rudd, tench, and a few pike and an odd roach or two. I suppose I put in about fifty rudd and fifteen tench. The rudd were about ¾ to 1lb. in weight, the tench 2½ to 3lb.

After putting the fish in I did not bother about them at all and the first intimation I had of the success of my experiment was when a village lad caught a rudd of 3¼lb.

I at once went over to the mere and I think I must have had about the best catch of rudd on record. I do not exactly remember the number I caught, but it was in the neighbourhood of thirty fish, ranging from 2¼ to 4¼lb., the largest weighing 4½lb., which I had mounted by Cooper.

I paid a village lad to carry the rest to a small mere close by but when I went to look at it I found the stupid fool had thrown most of them on the mud and they were all dead. The fishing remained good at Ring Mere until it was 'found out.' People came from all quarters, some from great distances, towing boats behind their cars. I do not think these visitors did much, as I fear I had taken the cream of the fishing and the fish soon became very shy. I stocked many places round with them and I think that some people had some fun with the tench. They gave great accounts of being broken by large fish, probably tench.

I used to see some monster tench in Ring Mere when I was fishing for rudd, some were very big, from 7lb. to 10lb. I caught one of them, a seven-pounder, which was also mounted for me by Cooper, and this fish was one of the *smaller* ones that I saw. I used to see them turning over in the weeds when I was fishing.

The following summer Ring Mere went dry, and I went down with a landing net to see what I could save. The tench were there but thin as rakes, I saved as many as I could. They were very thin and gaunt and weighed from 5¼lb. to 5½lb. I forget how many I rescued. There were also a lot of rudd up to 2½lb. and I saved all I could. The pike did not grow to any size, the largest I had was 11lb.

REV. ALSTON

The Rev. Alston's record rudd weighed 4½lb., and his tench, which weight he shares with Mr. Stacey's big Weston-super-Mare fish (caught 1882) weighed 7lb. What, in my opinion, is so interesting is that Mr. Alston says he saw tench up to 10lb. weight among the reeds. It is curious no tench of this size has yet been caught by rod and line in these islands.

There is, of course, the famous *Thornville Royal Tench*, which weighed upwards of 11½lb., but this was found when the lake at Thornville Royal was drained. A plate of this magnificent tench is shown in the early edition of Daniels's *Rural Sports*, and I give a copy of it in this work.

A Singular Tench

A PIECE of water which had been ordered to be filled up and into which wood and rubbish had been thrown for years was directed to be cleaned out. Labourers were accordingly employed and, almost choked up by weeds and mud, so little water remained that nobody expected to see any fish, except a few eels, yet nearly two hundred brace of tench of all sizes, and as many perch, were found. After the pond was thought to be quite free, under some roots there seemed to be some animal which was conjectured to be an otter; the

The Thornville Tench, weight 11 lb. 9¼ oz.

place was surrounded, and on opening an entrance amongst the roots, a tench was found of singular form, having literally assumed the shape of the hole in which he had of course for many years been confined. His length from eye to caudal fork was twenty-three inches, his circumference almost to the tail was twenty-seven inches, his weight eleven pounds nine and a quarter ounces; the colour was also most singular, his belly being that of a char or vermilion. This extraordinary fish, after having been inspected by many gentlemen was carefully put into a pond, and at the time this account was written, twelve months afterwards, was alive and well.

The tench is most tenacious to life of any freshwater fish except the eel. Such is the perfection of the organs of the species that they have been proved by experiment to be able to breathe when the quantity of oxygen is reduced to 5,000th part of the bulk of the water – river water containing about one part of oxygen in a hundred.

DANIELS Rural Sports

BARBEL

A Barbel on a Single Hair

FISHING for barbel with fine roach tackle is ... certainly
productive of the most sport, though it is not the way to make a
large bag; for, if the angler be using fine roach tackle and hooks a
good fish, he may waste an hour and a half over him, and then lose
him after all, as I have done scores of times.

I always fished with a single hair formerly, when float-fishing from
punt, and have killed very many barbel of four and five pounds
weight with it; but so much time and so many fish were lost at it that
I have long discontinued it.

I once remember, many years since, hooking an apparently large
fish on a single hair, about five o'clock one November afternoon, I
played him for a long time until my arm grew tired, when I handed
the rod to a friend who was with me. He tired and gave the rod to
Wisdom, who in turn, gave it back to me. They both despaired of
ever killing the fish and set his weight at a dozen pounds at least.
'He'll take you all night, sir,' said Wisdom. 'Then I'll stop with him all
night if he does not break me, for I never have been able to kill one of
these big ones with a single hair,' was my reply.

I had often on the same spot hooked three or four of these monsters in a morning, but I never could kill one of them. They always got away, for not far below us was a large deep hole, full of snags, old roots, and rubbish; and sooner or later they always remembered their hole there, and dashed into it headlong. Even stout ledger tackle would hardly have held them, and that they were very shy at, preferring the single hair greatly. This hole was about fifty yards below us, and I constantly expected the fish would make for it.

However, though he made constant runs, he never cared to go above half the distance, but sheered about, now out in the stream, and now in towards the campshot.

It had long been dark, and he showed no symptoms of tiring, though he had in turn tired all of us. Playing a fish in the dark is awkward work, so we hailed some men, several of whom, attracted by the report of our having hooked 'a big 'un,' were standing on the bank, to bring us a couple of lanthorns and some hot brandy and water, for it was bitterly cold; and with the aid of the lanthorns we at length managed to get the net under the fish and lifted him out. It was half-past eight when he was landed, so that I had him on three and a half hours. And now what does the reader think he weighed? I was disgusted to find that he was only a six-and-a-half-pound fish; had I known it I would have broken from him hours before; but it turned out that he was hooked by the back fin, and his head being perfectly free, he of course played as heavily as fish of double the size; and even now, remembering what the stream was, I wonder how I did succeed in landing him, as a fish so hooked, having his broadside opposed to the water, has great powers of resistance. Indeed I consider that the accomplishment was equal to killing a fish of double the weight if *fairly hooked.*

The feat may sound incredible – three and a half hours with only a single horse hair, a fin-hooked fish, and a heavy stream – nevertheless it is strictly true. Had the hold been in the mouth instead of the hard tough fin, it would probably have cut out in half the time.

FRANCIS FRANCIS, *A Book on Angling*

The following notes on baiting for barbel have been sent to me by Mr. Webb, Thames Registered Fisherman. I include them because they are the fruits of a lifetime's study of the habits of the fish and are the methods Mr. Webb himself employs. It is followed by Mr. Webb's true story of a battle with a giant barbel.

Baiting up for Barbel in the River Kennet

BARBEL inhabit this river in great numbers as far up as Newbury. Anywhere in the river between Reading and Newbury is good. Much of the river fishing is private property let to Angling Associations. There are still stretches of the river where permits may be obtained.

Method of baiting: I choose a spot where the water is deep and full of eddies. I fish late and early, using number eight Sowerbutt hooks to 6X drawn gut, four-pound breaking strain, fifty yards of undressed silk line six to ten pounds breaking strain. I use a fifteen-foot roach rod with an Alcock's Peeke, or Hardy reel.

Great patience is required. As to baiting-up, it is a great help if you know the whereabouts of the fish and it is always wise to gain first-hand information on this point from the local professional fisherman. Best baits are lobworms. These can be obtained direct from Nottingham or by the aid of a lamp at night. A closely mown lawn is the best place to look for them, especially after rain. The number of worms required depends on the time one has to fish but I need at least 2,000.

Having selected my spot, where as I say the water must be deep, I place three or four hundred worms in a large clay lump, after having made a number of holes in the clay. I pass through the clay cake a line or cord which may be twenty feet long or more, it all depends on the depth of the water to be fished. This is lowered into the depths and to my end of the line I attach a cork.

This ball of worms embedded in the clay is left in place for about two days. It is then pulled up and the process repeated, and again two days later, though this time the worms should be thrown in loose.

It is readily understood that the worms inside the clay find their way out through the holes, emerging gradually. This attracts any barbel in the vicinity.

Mill streams, weir pools, under clay banks, and in mid-stream are all good places. An half-ounce coffin lead is necessary on your gut, but this should be painted the colour of a stone. When fishing from a punt the punt should be at least forty yards from your fish.

Not many anglers will go to all this trouble, but those who do will, if they have patience, enjoy one of the greatest and most exciting forms of coarse fishing.

J. L. WEBB

A Midnight Battle with a Monster Barbel

I HAVE taken many barbel, both from the Kennet at Reading, at Burghfield, and at various posts on the river Thames. I am a professional fisherman and my boats are moored at Moulsford Grange, Berkshire. For barbel fishing I use number eight hooks and five or six X drawn gut. Barbel are the fish I simply live for, it means a lot to me to be a barbel fisher, sir, one has to go without many things, including sleep, and you must possess great patience, both in waiting for the fish to take hold and in baiting up.

When roach fishers are catching roach the barbel fisher never gets a full basket. Well, it was an evening in September 1943. For some days previous I had been fishing a spot opposite the third meadow below the French Horn Hotel at Sonning, and had been baiting this spot for some time, though I had caught nothing but fish up to 7 lb., and few at that.

Well, this particular evening I had caught nothing and had no bites; not even an eel, roach, or perch, came to break the monotony. In fact my father had said to me before I came out that it wasn't worth going as it wasn't the right sort of evening. But I told him that I was going to catch a big barbel there. You see, I have been a barbel fisher for forty years.

So I began to fish. I was using a fourteen-footer bank rod with a split cane top, an Alcock's reel with 150 yards of undressed silk line on it. I had gone over it carefully to see there was no faulty place and it seemed all right.

Somehow I thought I was going to get a two-figure fish that evening, I don't know quite why; on the other hand I might be going to have a blank. It was a dead flat calm. I had plenty of lobs and a nice place to sit and wait. I baited up my eight-hook with a big lob through the head and threw it out, well out, into the river. For the next hour nothing happened save once a small perch pulled at the bait. I had ground baited with chopped worms, but nothing moved save a chub or two under some bushes and a few roach. Now the light was going fast and night was all but come. An owl got up out of a nearby wood and passed by me. I rebaited once more and cast out again. A friend came along and I had a cigarette from him which I lit. A few plover passed overhead otherwise there was nothing to break the solitude. I couldn't see no farther than the end of my rod. A moorhen was moving about not far away and some rats splashed in some rushes.

161

Suddenly I feels a steady pull on the line and holding firmly for half a minute (for that is as long as you will 'hold' with a barbel) I struck, and felt a fast movement down-river which sent me to my feet. It was surely a pretty big fish. The line was running freely through the rings. There are some who say that a barbel does not move much, but that first mad rush was more like a devil from hell. After his first plunge he seemed to go broadside on to me, then his nose went down and he seemed to be trying to hit the line with his tail. What a time that was! I brought pressure to bear on him and that is more or less the supreme moment in barbel fishing, unless it is when he is coming to the net. The pressure I put on him was steady, but the fish was now at least fifty yards from me and still heading down-river. Then he changed his tactics. Downstream from me was a fair-sized hedge and at all costs he must not go down there or he would get me smashed up in the roots which go into the river at that spot. You must remember by now it was nearly dark and my watch showed it was ten minutes to nine which meant I had had him on for twenty minutes and he was still heading downstream as fast as he could go. More pressure was urgent. I must turn him, so I applied more pressure. I prayed the gut would hold. Well, at that the fish slowed and little by little I brought him back, though he was trying to turn all the time. Then he turned again and headed downstream as hard as he could go and I thought the line must break. Still he hadn't showed himself. Then I coaxed him back again. How my heart beat! getting tired he was, no doubt of that, so the fight went on. At long last he strikes surface and showed me his snout. At that off he went again downstream, but he was tiring. After a time I began to look around me for a landing-place. God was good to me that night, for just then the moon peeped out and I saw two concrete slabs a foot or so from the bank. I unhooked my landing net. The time was just one hour and twenty minutes since he first broke surface. But he was not yet mine for he was still trying to get away downstream. But the pressure I brought to bear was burning him up and he surfaced this time close by and just quietly swam away. I got him in again coming broadside, I sees his mighty tail give a flap and he was swimming in again to me as I stood on those concrete slabs. I could see his yellowy white belly there in the half dark. Then he made a last bid for freedom. It was no use, his strength was near spent, and next time he comes in, I thought, you will be mine, either that or the battle would be lost. I steadily bore him towards the net, waiting for the right moment. Then I had the net ring under him, twelve pound he was. He was mine at last.

J. L. WEBB

PERCH

Mr. H. Green's Record Perch

ON the ninth of November 1936, Mr. H. Green, of St. Germans, King's Lynn, set out for Stradsett Lake in Norfolk. It was a calm day with scanty wind; what there was was southerly. How little he must have guessed, as he and his friend started out on that gentle November morning, that he was going to capture the largest perch ever caught on rod and line in the British Isles, the best perch since 1889! I have no doubt that his mind was more busy with the possibilities of pike, for he tells me that when he reached the lake he began to try for 'esox,' putting on a six-inch roach as live bait. It was not long before his pike float went under. It was undoubtedly a run. He struck, but the tackle came in; he had missed. He had other runs, each time he failed to hook a fish. This was puzzling. Perhaps he guessed then that big perch were on the prowl, at any rate something prompted him to alter his tactics. He changed his bait, putting on a very small roach of barely three inches in length. He used a number six hook to gut, hooking the minute fish through the back. It was not long before he had a run and a moment or two later he had upon the bank a fine perch of one pounds twelve ounces – no mean fish.

Those first unproductive runs seemed now explained. Big perch frequently swim in shoals, the smaller ones likewise, they seem to 'shoal' according to size.

Quickly he rebaited and then his float went down again. This time there was definitely something bigger on his line, indeed, I will wager he thought it must be a pike by the power of its runs and the fight it gave. It was not until fifteen minutes had passed that he had the fish ashore and then he saw that it was a truly monster perch, the biggest he had ever seen. It is no mean feat to land a fish of five pounds four-and-three quarter ounces on a number six roach hook and a silk line with a ten-pounds breaking strain. He must have played it well; a big perch is a game fish.

He tells me he was fishing at a depth of three feet. He had one more perch on that memorable day which weighed one pound eight ounces. In addition he caught 247 roach, 68 rudd, and 3 bream. Evidently his lucky day! And I should image that it will be many years before his record perch is beaten and certainly, by all the laws of averages, he will never catch another of such noble dimensions.

He tells me that his record catch, for one season is 6,106 fish, (in 1938). Stradsett Lake may hold even bigger perch, a six-pounder is not an impossibility. Instances are on record of a seven-pounder from the Lee at Ballincollig in 1899, and Mr. Tate Regan in his classic work, *British Freshwater Fishes*, mentions a perch of eight pounds caught from the Wiltshire Avon on a night line and another ten pounds from Bala Lake in Wales. So keep fishing, Mr. Green, the big fellows seem to like you, and you may yet beat all records, including your own, despite the laws of average.

'BB'

THE following account has been given to me by a naturalist, the Rev. Victor James, of Sibbertoft, Market Harboro'.

It is such a noteworthy experience and (knowing Mr. James) so obviously true, that it deserves setting down on record. I have been unable to find any reference to it in any work on natural history, though Mr. James tells me he has found a note on the subject in a public library:

Fishing Shrews

THERE was an abundance of permanent springs around the rectory where I was spending some months, two of which figure prominently in the experience I relate.

One of them ran under the house itself, emerging on lower ground into a five-foot high water-butt through a circular pipe. The other had cut a channel for itself across the middle of the lawn.

My brother and I deepened this latter, putting into it several score of perch, roach, ruffe and gudgeon. We completed its population with a small shoal of minnows.

It time our little guests became, as we had hoped, reasonably tame, feeding freely in our presence.

But it soon became plain that their numbers were decreasing. Suspicion naturally rested first on the wild waterfowl so numerous in the neighbourhood. To guard against this supposed menace we covered the whole of the short reach with close mesh wire-netting. Yet still the fish disappeared more and more quickly.

The solution of the problem offered itself most unexpectedly in the following manner: One afternoon I was looking into the water-butt mentioned before, where we had stocked a reserve of roach and gudgeon, when I saw a quick movement opposite. A shrewmouse appeared from inside the inlet pipe, poised itself on the edge, sniffing the water delicately, then dived, using its large forefeet with extraordinary rapidity to assist its downward progress. For a matter of seconds it swam at the bottom, then rose, and, evidently alarmed by some slight movement of surprise on my part, it disappeared into the pipe whence it had previously emerged.

I had a long net near at hand and used it at once. After one or two dips the net brought up a gudgeon newly severed in two!

Following such a revolutionary discovery we kept close watch on the small stream and were rewarded by seeing a shrew find an easy prey in the shallower water. It seized a gudgeon and severed it in half as before.

Subsequently we found the remains of minnows, roach, and even perch that had been similarly treated. Needless to say, we removed the rest of our defenceless friends from danger.

One day, however, long after the little stretch of water had been deemed uninhabited, I espied one survivor in the person of a quarter-pound perch. He was a cunning warrior! His method was obvious. He had found a hole in the bank which protected his entire body, revealing only his nose – and teeth – to a hostile world.

REV. VICTOR JAMES

ROACH

The Subtlety of Roach Fishing

IT is our business now to talk about catching roach. We shall assume that the angler is in possession of rod and tackle, and that he knows how to put them together, that he has ground bait in his bag and hook bait in his tins, worms or maggots, and probably paste and bread. If he can get down to the water an hour or two before he intends to fish, he is advised to do so and to throw in his ground bait. Its purpose is to clear the way and to make the path of the angler easy.

If he cannot go himself it is not a bad idea to entrust a friend with the job, but the friend should be an angler and not a novice. Rather than let this important work be done by a bungler, I would forgo the advantage of having it done in advance and do it myself as soon as I arrived. If the water is a river you look out for a fishable swim. The experienced angler can tell at a glance whether a water looks 'roachy' or not. A nice, gentle, swishing, gliding current, with a bottom of gravel and occasional trailing weed, that is my favourite pitch. If the water is clear enough, there is a joy in peering into it and trying to make out the dark shapes of the fish as they move about, and now and then your senses are quickened by the vision of a silvery flash as a sizeable fish turns half over as he alters his course and sails across or down.

Having found such a pitch, you put in your ground bait, throwing it in gently and with as little splash as possible. You do this above the swim so that the current carries it down to where you think it will be most effective. Keep out of sight as much as possible. Don't wave your arms about. Above all, don't run up and down the bank and stamp your feet and thus make a concussion which will communicate itself to the delicate senses of the fish. I am no believer in the theory that fish can hear. On the contrary, I have conducted experiments which have satisfied me that they cannot hear. You may sing and shout as much as you like and it is certain the fish will never hear it. They live in a soundless world. Nothing is more certain than that. But they have remarkably keen vision. They see the angler long before he sees them unless he stalks them like a Red Indian. And they certainly feel the vibration or concussion produced by heavy footfalls on the bank. You may test this by keeping out of their sight and kicking the ground. If you can observe the fish it is ten to one they will vanish in a flash. They have not heard it, but they have felt it, and that is good enough. Therefore, play no pranks at the waterside. At the expense of being regarded as faddy, you may fall prone on your stomach, to reduce the chance of the fish seeing you between the water and skyline, and so throw in your ground bait. In a heavy water, coloured by rain, or in the deep water of a pond or lake, these precautions may not be as imperative, but under all circumstances it is better to be over careful rather than to take risks which may wreck your day's fishing.

In ground baiting a lake, of course, the idea of throwing it in where you do not intend to fish would be absurd. If feasible, it is not a bad plan to fix upon one or two pitches of ground and bait them both. Your sportsmanship will be called upon to stand a rather severe test if, while fishing at one pitch, you see a strange angler come along the bank and calmly take possession of your second pitch. The intensity of the situation will be increased if you see him pulling out a succession of good fat roach whilst you are doing next to nothing at your own station. Favourite pitches on waters that are more or less regularly fished acquire a reputation and are eagerly sought for. To go by train to a popular riverside resort means, when you leave the station a rapid trek to the river, and the latecomer finds that all the best swims are appropriated. You can tell them by the fact that the bank is worn by footmarks, and a cleft stick projecting above the earth will prove to you that somebody has been before and has left his rod rest for the next comer. Now we put up the rod. We fix the reel and run the line through it. Then we put on the float big or little, according to the depth and strength of the stream, white-tipped or red-tipped according to the light and hue of the surroundings. The tiny hook on its yard of fine gut is last of all attached. You can tell almost by instinct the number and weight of shot you require and in any case it is easy to regulate this matter after a few casts have shown whether you are too light or too heavy. If the swim is a five-footer, you place the float just that length above the hook. You intend to fish on the bottom, or as near the bottom as may be, and the float must be so placed as to make this possible. Whatever your bait, you place it on the hook, and then you are ready to make your first cast.

Now it may be said at once that casting is an art. It is not everybody who acquires it. Some men, otherwise good anglers, are poor casters. Either they cannot throw out any great distance, or if they can, they chuck the tackle on to the water in a splashy sort of a mess. Other men can manipulate ten and twenty yards of line with ease. The line sweeps behind them, then it is recovered and sent forward again with a gentle swish, and when it is fully extended over the water, the action of the rod is stopped, and float and hook simply fall on the surface by their own weight. That is the perfection of casting. Like everything else, it may be acquired by practice. My advice is to learn how to cast away from the waterside. At one period in my angling career I gave lessons in fly-casting. Nobody seems to think lessons in float-casting are necessary. Yet this latter art is quite as difficult as fly-fishing. Get out into a field, or a spacious yard, place an opened newspaper on the ground, and then cast at it. As you become proficient increase the distance, so that your casts become longer, and at the same time keep on doubling the newspaper and reducing its size. When at twenty or thirty feet with the newspaper folded the size and shape you get it from the bookstall, you can drop your tackle on it every time, so softly that you can hardly hear it, you may begin to think you are acquiring the art of casting.

At the waterside, things may be a bit more difficult. There may be a breeze in your face or blowing sideways, and it may take the line out of your control. Pull off a few yards of line from the reel, swing it in the air, sweep it behind you and then project it forward. Do not begin with long casts. Make them as short as possible at first. In time the beginner may have sufficient confidence to make long casts. He may take a yard or two of slack line in his left hand, and then, when the line is over the water the impetus will take out this extra slack and give him a longer cast. A light and easy-running reel will enable

him to make long casts, as we call it, 'from the reel.' That is to say, the impetus of the throw will cause the reel to revolve and the line will be unwound. In this case the angler keeps his finger on the edge of the reel and uses it as a brake. Thus, when he sees that his float is pretty near where he wishes it to alight, he brakes his reel with his finger, the line stops running, and by gently lowering the rod the tackle just drops on the surface of the water by its own weight. Casting looks simple and so it is when you have mastered it, but it requires care and skill, otherwise the shotted line and float will make a splash when they touch the water, and this is never conducive to good fishing. Nor should the angler, when his outfit is in the water and the float is nicely cocked be pulling it out every few minutes to see if the bait is all right. This again is apt to scare the fish. On the other hand it is not advisable to let it remain in the water too long, particulary if the float has moved ever so little and given the impression that a fish has been paying attention to the hook. Roach are crafty creatures. It is amazing how they can strip a hook and leave it bare of bait. Therefore, if there have been a nibble or two, and then there follows a period of inaction, it is advisable to pull out and see if all is right. It is exasperating to find the bait gone but it is better to learn the fact early than to continue fishing with a stripped hook.

In fishing a swim the float travels down the stream. As near as possible the bait is at the bottom, tripping along, as it were, but as the bed of a river is never as flat as a table, and there are stones and weeds to interrupt it, the hook occasionally will be held up for the fraction of a second. The novice will probably take this to be a bite, and strike. When he has done this a few times without result he will gain the wisdom that comes from experience. A real bite is very different. It can be described only with difficulty. The great difference is this, that if the hook is held up for a second by an obstruction, it sort of stops and hangs dead, it looks lifeless, whereas in the case of a bite it is lively and decisive in its action. It stops, quivers, probably moves from side to side and then goes down, either straight or in a slant. The experienced angler rarely makes a mistake. There is a fishing sense, as there is a golf or any other sporting sense, and the angler who knows his business is seldom tempted to strike at a false moment. At the same time, for the novice it is better to strike at the first symptom of a movement rather than miss a fish. Keep your eye on the float and strike every time it stops till you acquire the instinct to decide between a real bite and a mere holding up due to obstruction. So the float travels down to the end of the swim. When it has reached its limit you draw it out and cast again. Do not pull it out with a rush. Lift it gently. Hold the rod well up and draw the baited hook out of the water as near the perpendicular as you may. Do it slowly. Many a good fish has been caught at this moment. It has seen the bait come into its line of vision. It refused to take it on the bottom. But as soon as it saw the bait making a slow upward movement it leapt after it and made a grab.

This applies more to perch perhaps than to roach, but roach will sometimes behave on these lines, and by lifting the hook out of the water with care and quietude many a roach has been lured to its doom. Never make the mistake of some novices who, on reaching the end of the swim, do not take the hook out of the water, but draw it near the surface and then trail it to the top of the swim for the next cast. This is about as foolish a trick as can be imagined. By taking it out carefully and causing no disturbance and making all your changes of position when the bait is out of the water, you give the fish no cause for alarm.

ERNEST PHILLIPS, *Float Fishing*

BREAM

Breaming in the Midlands

IN July and August there are almost miraculous draughts of fishes amongst the bream in the Ouse. Not a hundred yards from Bedford Bridge there is at least one bream hole out of which sixty pounds of fish have been taken in a morning, and you hear of bream of six pounds. That, however, is a very unusual weight, but a three-pound fish is not at all uncommon in any part of the river. I must confess to no great respect for the *Cyprinnus Brama*. A fish that is shaped like a bellows, that is as thin as a John Dory, that is as uneatable as the John Dory is delicious, that is capricious in its habits, and that rarely rises at a fly, cannot be termed beautiful or useful to either cook or sportsman.

In the Ouse country, nothwithstanding its bones and general insipidity, the poorer people do eat the bream and like it passing well. At Huntingdon on one of my outings by the Ouse, the landlady of a small inn served up a breakfast dish which I relished to the extent of absolute consumption. It was a thin fillet of white fish, from which the bones had been extracted, and which was served up yellowish brown with some description of savoury herb sauce. Having eaten every flake, upon inquiry I found it was the bream I had on the previous night so execrated. But frequent trials since have utterly failed to make the bream a decent edible.

Yet I do not forget that the French proverb says: 'He who hath bream in his ponds may bid his friends welcome,' and that Chaucer, who may be said to have known a thing or two, wrote:

'Full many fair partrich hadde in mewe,
And many a breme, and many a luce in stewe.'

A recital of a little personal experience of bream fishing will give some insight into the habits of the bream. Having at odd visits to John Bunyan's pretty and interesting old country town seen Howard's workpeople returning home staggering beneath burdens of fish taken from the bank in the meadows near Cardington Mill, I resolved to lay myself out seriously for rivalry; but unfortunately it was October before I could carry out my intention.

This I did not require to be told was fully a month or six weeks too late, but a celebrated professional bream catcher, at Bedford, nevertheless got his boat ready and took me a couple of miles down the river. We tied ourselves to the reeds with fourteen feet of sluggish water beneath us, and to our dismay found the surface smooth and clear as glass. The bream angler in July should be at his post on the river and quiet as a mouse by daybreak, for the chances are that he will have finished all his work by breakfast-time. But later in the season it is necessary to let the morning chills evaporate. Seven o'clock had struck before we began.

Balls of mingled slime and brewer's grains the size of bomb-shells were first cast into the water five yards from the boat, the boatman observing: 'You'll see a lark presently, guv'nor.' He then began to make ready his tackle, long, heavy, rudely made rods, coarse lines without winches, clumsily leaded guy hooks, and seven or eight nasty little worms affixed *en masse* to each hook, of which there were two to each line.

'Why don't you throw out?' I said, all being ready, and looking out upon the dreadfully unruffuled surface of the broad river.

'You hold hard, guv'nor, there'll be a lark presently,' he still replied, looking down the stream with a patient, wistful gaze.

'There they are,' he said, by and by, 'don't move guv'nor, I know the beggars, bless you, I told you so. You keep still guv'nor.'

He now made a monster cigarette from a leaf of Bradshaw's railway guide (having forgotten to bring out his pipe and tobacco) and watched what he had termed a 'lark,' with a benign expression of countenance. It was certainly amusing. Quite fifty yards down the river, large dark somethings splashed, twisted, and plunged upon the surface of the water in hundreds, all advancing towards the point where we were stationed. This, the boatman said, was a favourite winter home of the bream, and his theory was that they had scuttled away in shoals at our approach and were now slowly returning in good skirmishing order. Steadily the host advanced, the splashes and backs of the fish appearing at intervals of four or five yards. The signs ceased, when they should have appeared opposite our boat and this led the bream master to remark: 'The darned skunks! They've winded us!'

Be that as it may, in a few moments the hubbub recommenced many yards above us, and then all was silent as before. After a decent pause, the bream having evidently retreated upon their former position below, the plunges began again, and another cautious upward movement commenced; and to our delight this time there were no indications that the fish had passed us.

The boatman then deftly threw out his baits and fixed his rods under the thwarts, and I followed his example with my lighter implements. Five minutes elapsed, when down went both of his floats. They came up, went down, came up, and again went down, while the fisherman grimly sucked his Brobdingnagian cigarette. Soon a decisive slanting movement of the long float led him to strike sharply, and his great rod bent to the encounter. Two or three struggles appeared to exhaust the bream, and they were netted in succession without much finessing or trouble. My companion thus caught seven fish in the course of an hour. Then my turn arrived. To my chagrin I had been wholly unable to throw my delicate tackle out to the baited ground, but now the porcupine quill went clear away at a shoot; to be brief, the drawn gut parted at the sullen resistance to the too-eager strike, and the boatman, emitting a great oath, said we should get no more sport.

'If it had been summer,' he said, 'it would not have mattered so much, we should have whacked 'em out like a shot, but it's all up now.' And even so it proved. The processes necessary to successful bream fishing, like those insisted upon by barbel fishers, are not nice. Ground baiting, hours before you fish, is a necessity. Great fat lobworms, or unsavoury brandlings, are the orthodox bait, and the fish himself is covered with slime that is not pleasant to handle. No angler would care to fish often for bream if there were other fish within his reach, but in Bedfordshire, Huntingdonshire, men of the artisan type manifest a rooted affection for the sport; and wherever bream exist, having found the same predilection, I always look upon the fork-tailed, light brown bottom grubber as a kind of working-man's candidate.

Hard by a village I once visited in Yorkshire there ran a canal in which there were a good many breams. Amongst the men who, at about six-feet intervals lined the banks on a summer's evening, was a quaint, shrewd Barnsley pitman with whom I became very familiar. He would think nothing of a fourteen-mile walk, for the sake of three hours with his pet bream, than which, he firmly believed, no nobler game swam the water. He was a consummate coarse fish angler, and a hero amongst the Yorkshire Waltonians. Poor fellow! Years passed and I had forgotten him. Then I saw him, blackened and dead, one of a ghastly row of unfortunate colliers just brought up from a pit, laid out on benches, and ticketed, till the coroner should inquire into the miserable circumstances which without warning cut them off from the land of the living.

'RED SPINNER', *Waterside Sketches*

PIKE

Record-breaker

IF you live in Ireland and fish for pike, you will sniff at our pike. If you live in the Gaeltacht and fish for pike you will not sniff at our pike, you will snort; for fish that provide an English angler with after-dinner stories to last him the rest of his life are regarded as pretty ordinary thereabouts. Did not the *Limerick Chronicle* of 9th May 1862, report the capture in Lough Derg, on rod and line, too, of a pike that weighed 90½lb., and measured 5 feet 8 inches in length? That (no one accepts it as a record by the way) remains the master pike. And then there are two Irish pike of over 70lb., both caught on rod and line: the County Clare pike of 78lb., taken in 1830, and the Kenmure pike of 72lb., which was taken on a fly. Neither of these fish find acceptance in the record books. The record Irish pike, rod caught, weighed 53lb. and was taken in Lough Conn in 1920 (a 60-pounder was reported to have been taken in the same lough in 1942) by Mr. John Garvin. These are exceptional fish, but pike of over 30lb., fish that would instantly find their way into English record books, are common enough in the Irish Lakes, and there have been more than a few of over 40lb. taken in recent years. So, if you live in Ireland and fish for pike, you will sniff at our pike, and small blame on you.

You will sniff, too, if you set store by the Cheltenham pike or the Whittlesea pike. But you should not do so. The Cheltenham pike did undoubtedly weigh 60lb., but it was not caught. It gave itself up. It was seen floating on the surface by the caretaker of the reservoir, who put out in a boat and hauled it aboard by the tail. It was very, very old, and quite blind, and it was dying of old age and starvation. The Whittlesea pike did undoubtedly weigh 52lb. But the poor thing was not caught. It was stranded when the mere was drained. No, you should not sniff at our pike in relation to either of these fish. Our pike at least was caught. It did not weigh 60lb. nor even 52lb., but it was caught and it remains the heaviest English pike that was caught. You will not find it in the record book, because it was not caught by fair angling. And you can sniff at that if you like.

Caught by fair angling or not, the fish was caught. And it is more than just the heaviest pike to be caught in England. It *is* the heaviest yet caught in England, but it holds two further records, records that are, I imagine, extremely unlikely to be broken. It is the only pike, so far as I am aware, to be caught on a croquet mallet. And it is the only record fish, so far as I am aware, to be hooked by a child three years of age. Our pike, you see, holds three records. It occupies a position of honour in the study now, looking very fierce in its glass case. Below it, in letters of gold, are its measurements: weight 40lb., length 4 feet 1 inch, girth 25 inches; a noble fish.

It was caught in 1865 in the big pond in the grounds of Upton House, Edgehill, in Warwickshire. It was actually caught by the late Colonel R. Purefoy Fitzgerald, but it was 'hooked' by his son, then aged three, and later a famous admiral. And it came about in this wise. The little boy, as befitted a future Admiral of His Majesty's Navy, was playing boats. His boat was a child's croquet mallet, and to the handle was attached a length of stout string in order that he might not lose control of his fleet. The pike took the croquet mallet and made at full speed for the centre of the pond. The small boy, showing already signs of that tenacity for which he later became famous, did not immediately relinquish hold of the string, and so followed the pike into the water. He then let go of the string, and the pike made off. Now the water in the pond was low (1865 was a very dry year) and the fish, no doubt rather upset by the strange feel of the prey it had seized, grounded itself at high speed on a mudbank. It was not itself visible, but floating on the surface was the tell-tale string. Colonel FitzGerald waded out, took hold of the string, and after a short but severe tug-of-war, hauled the pike ashore. It was weighed almost immediately, and it was weighed again within a few hours by no less an authority than Frank Buckland, a friend of the family. The weight he found is inscribed on the glass case. He found also that the fish was starving. But he was very excited about it, and exhibited it in London on several occasions shortly afterwards.

Not a fish to be proud of, you say?

BRIAN VESEY-FITZGERALD

Mr. Grief's Pike

YOU might be interested in a 25½-lb. pike I was fortunate enough to catch on 21st December 1941.

Imagine a couple of semi-optimistic anglers setting out on a cold Saturday morning, to have a go at the pike, armed only with a selection of home-made spinners fashioned with odd pieces of white metal we were able to find (being unable to purchase any from tackle dealers) and arriving at our pond furtively concealing our efforts from the gaze of fellow members, who, we knew from past experience, would welcome an opportunity to pull our legs to further orders. However, we put our tackle together.

I was using a light spinning rod, with an Alcock's Aerialite reel, and a seven-pound B.S. 'Jagut' line attached to a thin wire trace, with my home-made kidney spoon and one small treble hook. My friend, S. Holland, was using similar tackle, with what we hoped might successfully pass for a Norwich spoon. So away we started round the lake, and soon had the satisfaction of seeing our spinners revolving in the water. I don't remember whether we were surprised that they actually spun, but as you might guess they most certainly did. After spinning for about four hours, we decided that there were no darn pike feeding that day, and anyhow what can we expect from home-made spoons, plus an easterly wind and the coffee all gone? Nothing to stay for, we might as well pack up and dump the old spinners in a ditch on the way home, and nobody in the club would be any the wiser. However, we did none of those things, but decided to have a final run round the lake, in case a 'Johnny' might take pity on us; half-frozen with cold, no fish, no coffee, no hope, and so we recommenced our efforts and, about the third cast, my friend 'hit' a fish and, from the curve in his rod, it was a good one, but whether it was the shock of hooking a pike on a home-made spoon, or whether he was frozen stiff, we never knew, however, he lost it the very next minute, polluting the air with typical angler's language. Anyhow, we thought, there was at least one pike in the lake that was blind enough

177

to take a home-made spinner, so we kept on, and shortly after 3.30 p.m. it was my turn to receive a shock, for I hooked a fish, and I knew it was a good 'un for it soon bored away like fury, taking about twenty yards off my reel in the first rush down, and then came the usual anxiety, will my light line take the strain? Was the treble securely affixed? etc. etc., advice being freely given by my well-meaning fellow members, who had gathered round to see the fun.

Meanwhile the shocks increased, as the fish bore out towards the middle of the lake and redoubled back, causing a lot of slack line which I reeled in furiously. Fortunately, he was still on, and so it went on for thirty-five minutes, until I could bring him into reach of the gaff, and what a sight greeted our eyes. A truly magnificently proportioned, and beautifully coloured specimen, as the size of girth justified this later, so at long last, after missing him with the gaff the first time, and causing him to rush out again, he was firmly gaffed, and the most amazing part of all, as soon as he was being lifted out of the water, the hook came out, and we had to scramble up a four-foot bank with him! You can imagine my feelings if that gaff had came out during the scramble up the bank. I think I should have dived in after him. However, it was my lucky day, everything held, and it was triumphantly carried to the club-house, but not having sufficient weights to weigh it (nobody ever imagined a fish of that weight ever being in our water) it was weighed at the local railway station, and the result: weight, 25lb. 8oz.; length, 42 inches; girth, 22 inches; nape to kneb, 11 inches.

J. H. GRIEF

The Monster of Powder Mill Pond

IN the summer of 1944 a Charterhouse School boy, Alan John Anscombe, went a-fishing in the Powder Mill Pond, Battle Abbey. His lucky star was in the ascendant.

Spinning with an American plug bait he connected with the monster of the Powder Mill Pond, a pike which had for 30 years been the terror of all fishers, and fishes.

It took him half an hour to land it, or rather to 'empunt', with the aid of his father.

It weighed 33lb., was 46½inches in length, and its girth measured 21½inches.

'BB'

Curiosities

ON Tuesday last, at Lillieshall Lime Works, near Newport, a pool about nine yards deep, that had not been drained for ages was let off by means of a level brought up to drain the works, when an enormous pike was found. He was drawn out by the gills, amidst hundreds of spectators, in which service a great many men were employed; he weighed upwards of 170lb., and is thought to be the largest ever seen.

Some time ago the clerk of the parish was trolling in the above pool, when his bait was seized by this furious creature, which, by a sudden jerk pulled him in, and doubtless would have devoured him also had he not by wonderful agility and dexterous swimming escaped the dreadful jaws of this voracious animal.

From a newspaper dated 1765

In the year 1610 a pike was taken from the Meuse bearing a copper ring on which was engraved the name of the city of Stavern and the date was 1448.

In June 1855, Richard Briscoe, Esq., whilst fishing in Melbourne Pool, Derbyshire, caught a pike which weighed 20lb. This fact is interesting as being one step towards solving the question of the progressive growth of pike. The pool was emptied of water, cleaned out, and stocked with pike and other fish on 16 December 1847. So that this pike had grown to that weight in rather more than eight years and five months. This pike was three feet three inches long and eighteen inches in girth round the shoulders. His head was small in proportion, his body in prime condition, beautifully marked, bright and symmetrical in shape, and the fish was evidently in the prime of life.

'BB'

Poaching

ON the subject of my poaching experiences let me make a clean breast of it and relate how, when a young man reading at a tutor's on the banks of the Thames, my finer perceptions were on one occasion blunted and my better feelings done violence to, by the sight of a splendid specimen of *Esox Lucius* in one of the stew ponds of Mr. Williams of Temple, the then member for Great Marlow.

That morning I had seen him (the pike) lying basking, and in the afternoon (to this day I cannot tell how it happened) I found myself, for some unexplained reason, standing by the side of the aforesaid stew pond, and wondering whether anyone would see through the surrounding withy beds, topped by a notice board threatening legal pains and penalties against trespassers.

What is still more inexplicable I carried in my hand an extra long sort of walking stick – or shall I say it at once – ? hop-pole – and in my pocket a coil of what certainly bore an external resemblance to copper wire. A couple of feet of this wire had somehow got on to the end of the hop-pole whence it dangled in such a manner as almost to deceive the eye into the notion that it was not altogether unlike the abomination known as a noose or 'sniggle'.

Hop-pole in hand I bent carefully over the water and reconnoitred the position of my best esox, merely in order of course the better to admire his majestic proportions as he supported his huge body on his ventral pinnae and feathered the water with pectoris and caudal fins.

'A delicate monster truly,' I observed, 'quite an ichthyological study.' And simultaneously an uninitiated spectator might have imagined that the appearance of the noose aforesaid passed gently but quickly over his head and shoulders. There was a curious sudden commotion in the water, and at the same moment a rustling in the withies behind and then a well-known voice! being, in fact, that of Mr. Edwards, head water bailiff and fisherman, was heard in accents sarcastic which I shall never forget: 'Well, Mr. Pennell, this 'ere be a pretty go!'

'Confound you,' I said, furious with conflicting emotion, 'you've made me miss him – a twenty-pounder if he was an ounce!'

'Well, what's to be done, sir?' was the remark.

By this time my wrath had cooled down a little and I instinctively felt in my waistcoat pocket. It was empty.

'Unluckily, Edwards,' I said, 'I have left my purse behind.'

''O, never mind,' was the reply, 'everyone knows your *credit's good at the Bull*!'

CHOLMONDELEY PENNELL, *Coarse Fishing* (Badminton Library)

CHUB

Two Chub

SOME three years ago I was spending a few days holiday fishing a small river in Sussex. It was towards the end of September and at the time summer was having its last fling with quite a powerful heat-wave. Sport, as was to be expected, was very slow during the daytime but towards evening a few average-sized roach and dace found their way to my keep-net. It was the last day but one of my stay, that I was having a little refresher at the local inn, when a fellow angler, considerably older than myself, inquired as to my luck. I duly related my small successes with roach and dace. He seemed quite interested and was only too pleased to tell me something about himself.

It appeared that he lived quite close to the river and spent most of his time either fishing or making flies, and as if to convince me that he was genuine he produced a case of his home-made flies for my inspection. He had a name for all of them but I am sure they were far from standard patterns, both in colour and size. As the river has a run of sea trout, most of his creations were intended to deceive those fine sporting fish, but how many ever did is quite another matter. His discourse on fly-tying seeming to have no end, I began to feel that it was time to get back to the river, so handing back the fly-case and rising from my chair, the hint was taken and he suggested that before I went I would accept one of his flies, to which I agreed, thinking it would be very unlikely that it would ever get used. He picked out a weird-looking specimen with a large white body that he called 'The Woolly Bear' and said that it would tempt the biggest chub in the river. With the usual best wishes we parted and I made my way back to the river to enjoy the many attractions of the waterside and await the cool of the evening to bag a few nice roach.

The following day the heat-wave continued and with a cloudless sky any hopes of any sport during the day seemed at a discount, but as it was my last day I felt that the unexpected might happen, so taking some light refreshment with me, I made my way downstream until I came to a nice shady spot on a bend in the river where I decided to settle down and enjoy the peaceful surroundings. Not a bite rewarded two hours roach fishing with the lightest of tackle, so placing my rod at one side I was about to take some refreshment when straight in front of me, as I was sitting and a few yards downstream, I noticed, almost with a start, a brace of fish, undoubtedly the best fish I had actually seen during my stay. They were almost stationary and close to the surface. At first glance I thought they were trout. Were they roach or dace? and then it dawned on me, they were chub and good ones at that. The bigger must have been 3lb. and the other slightly less. Slowly they turned with the stream and quickly dropped back about a dozen yards and keeping close together they slowly made their way upstream again, every now and again breaking the surface of the water as if sucking down a small fly or insect. I was sitting in full view, almost afraid to move for fear of frightening the two beauties, but I began to feel that something had to be done, surely this was not a chance to be missed.

Now I had never caught a chub. The first thing seemed to be to get out of sight, so slowly and quietly I drew myself away from the bank, taking my rod and tackle with me. Now came the query. What bait? I decided to try a single maggot on a number twelve hook and a fine, two-yard length of gut floating on the surface. Selecting a lively fat maggot I carefully impaled it on the hook and now with landing net in one hand and rod in the other, I was ready for action. Working my way slowly and as quietly as possible towards the river I reached a point a yard from the bank from which I had a clear view of the water. The chub were still there, almost stationary, half a dozen or so yards downstream. Branches of trees made casting almost impossible, the only way of getting the bait well into the stream away from the weeds at the sides, was to use a sideway flick. Drawing the line from the reel and crouching low out of sight of the fish, I made an

The Haunt of Chub

attempt but failed to obtain momentum to carry out the line, with the
result that the hook caught in the side of the bank. With the use of
the landing net I managed to release it, but in doing so I had cast a
shadow on the water and my friends the chub immediately dropped
back out of sight. Taking up my old position I made a few practice
flicks before settling down to await the return of the chub. To my
great surprise I had but a very short time to wait before they

reappeared, slowly working their way upstream. Taking every possible care I again made that sideway flick and this time the bait sailed
beautifully into mid-stream and started gliding down in the direction of the chub. I held my breath as the great moment arrived.
Would they take the bait? The next moment the larger fish spotted it,
made straight for it . . . now! No, he hasn't taken it! but drops back to
the other fish and the bait sails past! After two more swims down
without any reponse the chub turned, almost in front of me, and
again dropped downstream out of sight.

I now realised that some fresh method of enticement must be
adopted if I was to bring about the downfall of one of these fine fish.
I had read of bluebottles or cow-dung flies being successful if
presented in the right manner, so bringing my rod away from the
bank, I started searching round the field, but although mosquitoes
were present in their thousands, not a bluebottle or a cow-dung fly
could I find. Wondering what I should do I suddenly remembered
the day before at the inn and the fly I had given me, the fly that
would catch the biggest chub in the river. Now was the chance to put
it to the test.

Without more ado I soon had 'The Woolly Bear' mounted to a
length of fine gut and again carefully prepared for action. This time I
had to wait quite a long time and was, in fact, just beginning to think
of moving downstream, when they once more came into sight,
moving in that slow and graceful manner that is most fascinating to
watch. Lying almost flat I flicked 'The Woolly Bear' out and by good
fortune it settled nicely in mid-stream and started to drift in a
straight line to the two chub. My thoughts during the seconds that
followed were many; should I be able to hold him from that big bed
of weeds near the opposite bank? Had I tied a proper fly knot? Would
my roach line stand the strain? But now my fly was about a yard from
the fish. Which one would take it? Ah! they had seen it, now both are
rising to it, which would reach it first? Suddenly they both stopped
right under the fly, then, splash! Instantly I gripped my rod expecting
the line to run out but alas! the fly remained on the surface and the
fish had disappeared from sight.

'The Woolly Bear' had not proved irresistible after all and I have
still to catch my first big chub.

MR. D. BATEMAN

184

The Chavender or Chub

I WENT into the Plough Inn at Long Wittenham in mid-November to arrange about sending some game to London. The landlord, after inquiring about our shooting luck, went out and came back into the parlour, saying: 'Now, sir, will you look at my sport?'

He carried on a tray two large chub weighing about 2½lb. each which he had caught in the river just behind the house. Their colour, olive and silver, scarlet and grey, was simply splendid. Laid on the table with one or two hares and cock pheasants and a few brace of partridges they made a fine sporting group in still life – a regular Thames valley yield of flesh and fowl. The landlord is a quiet enthusiast in this Thames fishing.

It is a pleasure to watch him at work, whether being rowed down on a hot summer day by one of his men, and casting a long line under the willows for chub, or hauling out big perch or barbel. All his tackle is exquisitely kept, as well kept as the yeoman arrows and bow in the *Canterbury Tales*. His baits are arranged on the hook as neatly as a good cook sends up a boned quail. He gets all his worms from Nottingham. I notice that among anglers the man who gets his worms from Nottingham is as much a connoisseur as the man who imported his own wine used to be among dinner-givers.

Drifting against a willow bush one day, the branches of which came right down over the water like a crinoline, I saw inside, under the branches, a number of fair-sized chub of about 1lb. or 1½lb. It struck me that they felt themselves absolutely safe there, and if in any way I could get a bait over them they might take it. The entry under which I find this chronicled is August 24. Next morning when the sun was hot I got a still rod and caught a few grasshoppers. Overnight I had cut out a bough or two at the back of the willow bush, and there was just a chance that I might be able to poke my rod in and drop my grasshopper on the water. After that I must trust to the strength of the gut, for the fish would be unplayable. It was almost like fishing in a faggot stack. Peering through the willow leaves I could just see down into the water where a path of sunlight about a yard square struck the surface. Under this skylight I saw the backs of several chub pass as they cruised slowly up and down.

I twisted the last two feet of my line round the rod top, poked this into the bush with infinite bother and pluckings at my line between the rings, and managed to drop the hopper on to the little bit of sunny water. What a commotion there was! The chub thought they were all in a sanctuary and that no one was looking. I could see six or seven of them, evidently all cronies and old acquaintances, the sort of fish that have known one another for years and would call each other by their Christian names. They were as cocky and consequential as possible, cruising up and down with an air, and staring at each other and out through the screen of leaves between them and the river, and every now and then taking something off a leaf and spitting it out again in a very independent and connoisseur-like way. The moment the grasshopper fell there was a rush to the place, very different from what their behaviour would have been outside the bush. There was a hustle and jostle to look at it, and then to get it. They almost fought one another to get a place. Flop! Splash! Wallop! 'My grasshopper, I think' – 'I saw it first' – 'Where are you shoving to?' 'O-oh – what is the matter with William?'

I called him William because he had a mark like a W on his back. But he was hooked fast and flopping, and held quite tight by a very strong gut and hook, like a bull with a ring fastened to his nose. I got him out too – not a big fish, but about 1½lb.

This showed pretty clearly that where chub can be fished for 'silently,' 'invisibly,' they can still be caught, even though steam launches or row-boats are passing every ten minutes.

This was mid-August; my next venture nearly realised the highest ambitions of a chub feature. It also showed the sad limitations of mere instinctive fishing aptitudes in the human being, as contrasted with the mental and bodily resources of a fish with a deplorably low facial angle and a very poor morale.

There was just one place on the river where it seemed possible to remain unseen yet to be able to drop a bait over a chub. A willow tree had fallen, and smashed through a willow bush. Its head stuck out like a feather brush in front and made a good screen. On either side were the boughs of the bush, high, but not too high to get a rod over them, if I walked along the horizontal stem of the tree. It was only a small tree, and a most unpleasant platform. But I had caught a most appetising young frog, rather larger than a domino, which I fastened to the hook, and after much manoeuvring I dropped this where I knew some large chub lay. As the tree had only been blown down the day before, I was certain that they had never been fished for at that spot.

I was right; hardly had the frog touched the water when I saw a monster chub rise like a dark salamander out of the depths. Slowly he rose and eyed the frog, moving his white lips as if the very sight imparted a gusto to the natural excellence of young frogs. I nearly dropped from the tree stem in a fear of suspense, when he made up his mind, put on steam, and took it! He was fast in a minute, and kindly rushed out into the river where I played him. Then I wound my line and hauled him up till his head and mouth were out of the water. As there was an impenetrable screen of bushes between him and me I laid the rod down, trusting to the tackle, and ran round to where close by was a farm punt made fast. It had been used during harvest time and was full of what in the classics they call the 'implements of ceres.' All of these that do not seem made to cut your leg off are designed to run into and spike you. Besides scythes and reap hooks, there were iron rakes (sharp end upwards) wooden rakes, pitchforks, and garden forks, and the difficulty was to move in the punt without getting cut or spiked. The last users of the punt had also taken peculiar care to fasten it up. It was anchored by a grapnel, and by an iron pin on a chain, the pin eighteen inches long and driven hard into the bank. In a desperate hurry I hauled up the grapnel, did a regular Sandow feat, in pulling up the iron peg, seized the punt pole apparently weighted with lead, but made out of an ash sapling, and started the punt. It would not move. I found there was another mooring, so picking my way among the scythes, spike, rakes, etc., I hauled this in. It was infernally heavy and turned out to be a cast-iron wheel of a steam plough or other farming implement. Then I was under way and got round to the fish. It was still there. I could see his expressionless eye (about as big as a sixpence) out of the water and its mouth wide open, when I remembered I had forgotten the landing net in my hurry.

Then came the period of mental aberration common to the amateur. The fish was certainly four pounds in weight yet I tried to get him in with my hands. Of course he gave one bit flop, slipped out and disappeared – the biggest chub I ever shall not catch.

J. C. CORNISH, A Naturalist on the Thames

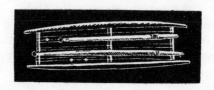

SEA FISHING

A Fishing Dog

ONE day I witnessed a very strange thing, the action of a dog by the waterside. It was evening and the beach was forsaken; cartmen, boatmen, fishermen, all gone, and I was the only idler left on the rocks; but the tide was coming in, rolling quite big waves on to the rocks, and the novel sight of the waves, the freshness, the joy of it, kept me at that spot, standing on one of the outermost rocks not yet washed over by the water.

By and by a gentleman, followed by a big dog, came down to the beach and stood at a distance of forty or fifty yards from me, while the dog bounded forward over the flat, slippery rocks and through pools of water until he came to my side, and sitting on the edge of the rock began gazing intently down at the water.

He was a big, shaggy, round-headed animal, with a greyish coat with some patches of light reddish colour on it; what his breed was I cannot say, but he looked somewhat like a sheepdog or an otter hound. Suddenly he plunged in, quite vanishing from sight, but quickly reappeared with a big shad of about three and a half to four pounds weight in his jaws.

Climbing on to the rock he dropped the fish, which he had not appeared to have injured much, as it began floundering about in an exceedingly lively manner. I was astonished and looked back at the dog's master; but there he stood in the same place, smoking and paying no attention to what his animal was doing.

Again the dog plunged in and brought out a second big fish and dropped it on the flat rock, and again and again he dived, until there were five big shads all floundering about on the wet rock and likely soon to be washed back into the water.

The shad is a common fish in the Plata and the best to eat of all its fishes, resembling the salmon in its rich flavour, and is eagerly watched for when it comes up from the sea by the Buenos Aires fishermen, just as our fishermen watch for mackerel on our coasts. But on this evening the beach was deserted by everyone, watcher included, and the fish came and swarmed along the rocks, and there was no one to catch them – not even some poor hungry idler to pounce and carry off the five fishes the dog had captured. One by one I saw them washed back into the water, and presently the dog, hearing his master whistling him, bounded away.

W. H. HUDSON, Far Away and Long Ago

Sea Fishing with George

AT last the weather became favourable. We therefore at once determined to go fishing, and see whether, after their long holiday from hook and line the fish would not be in a biting humour.

'How long shall we be out?' said the friend who went with me.

'As long as the fish bite,' said I, 'therefore we had better take some food with us, for there are no bakers' shops by the Spit Buoy, and they don't sell cheese at the "Boyne".'

'Morning, sir,' said Barney, the civil and obliging provider of boats on the beach, and whose name was once Barnabas, but who never will be called anything but Barney again. 'Better have the *Laughing Jackass*, sir, she's all ready.'

I have an unfortunate habit of looking after little matters, and knowing that there is a hole, which ought to be stopped up by a cork in the bottom of every boat, I examined it to see if the cork was in its place; of course it was not. We soon got a cork and fastened it in tight, one of our party telling us that he once knew a young man who went out a little way to sea, and who, finding that there was a little water in the bottom of the boat, actually took the cork out of the hole to *let the water out*, quite forgetting that the water would rush in; it did rush in to his great surprise, and the boat was pretty nearly full before he could get ashore again.

We were soon out on the marks Robinson Crusoe had indicated,

and were wondering whether the old man would keep his appoint-
ment. At last we were delighted to see him paddling away out off the
harbour. He was soon alongside, his brave old face radiant with
smiles, for he had taken a great fancy to me, though he does not to
everybody.

'Are we on the marks, George?'

'Not by a long ways, sir.'

'Then just put us right like a good fellow, will you? Better come
into our boat; we will tow your old tub astern.'

'Don't you go to insult my old boat, sir, or I won't show you the
wrack.'

'Never mind, George, it's only a joke.'

'Let go the anchor, boy,' said George.

The boy picked it up and spat on it.

'What's that for?' said I.

'That's for luck,' said George. 'And to make the fish bite; but it
don't always, for a chap the other day spit on his anchor (and it was a
brannew one, too) he heaved it overboard; but there was no cable on
it so he lost it right off, and was obliged to go home to fetch another,
so he lost his anchor and his tide of fish too.'

'When do you go out fishing most, George?'

'I don't fish much of a day, sir; I fishes at night most and almost
every night too when it's anyways like weather. I got no clock nor yet
watch; but I've got the stars, as will let me know the time to a quarter
of an hour. There's one star in particular as serves me, and in a
month's time I noticed there was never a quarter of an hour's
difference in her time.'

'Do you ever go to sleep, George?'

'No, sir. I don't go to sleep; but I tell you what, sir, I thinks the fish
sleep of nights that's my experience of them. I've been out thousands
of nights and I've always observed as one particular hour is different
from any other hour of a night, and that's between twelve and one.
The fish never bites at that time, and after that hour is over they
begins again and keeps on till daylight; but before that hour they
always fishes slack, and I can sleep between twelve and one if I likes,
for it's no use heaving the line overboard; but after the clock strikes
one the fish won't let me go to sleep and I've always found it so.
That's what makes me think the fish sleep; if they don't sleep they
rises to the top of the water. When the water is thick and it's a
moonlight night, that's the time to catch 'em if the water is thick and
it's dark too, the fish can't see the bait. They are on the bite, too, of
frosty nights. I puts my sail over my head, and it gets as white as a
sheet. I often prays for it not to come daylight, for I never feels cold as

long as the fish bites, the night is the best time to catch the congers, sir. The congers is as taffety fish as is; ther's not a delicater fish as swims, and they are very nice in their feeding. If a whelk was to get on the bait the conger would never touch it, not if you was to bide all night; they are regular bait robbers them whelks. But when the congers gets on to the hook they lets you know it, and when you pulls them up, they curls their tails and holds a powerful sight of water; it's ten to one you don't lose them if you have not got strong gear. But you must have nice fresh bait.

'If there's a bone in the bait they won't touch it; Master Conger will have the first grab, or none at all. I've cut up a dozen pouts, and seen the conger whack at them all, and then he never takes them if they don't quite suit his taste. The biggest conger as ever I catched was in 'the Grass' at the back of the Gosport Hospital. Just as the sun goes down I hooks my gentleman, and says I to the man who was fishing near me: 'Joe, I've got him this time and no mistake, and a beautiful fish he is!'

'He towed me and my little boat round my anchor six times, and I got a good Dutch line, so strong that three men could not break it, for we tried it afterwards. Master Conger had got hooked outside of his teeth, still the hook had a good strong hold, but yet it gave him the chance of chawing the line; and he kept on chawing it a good one, so I played him till at last I got him alongside, and tried to gaff him, and then he flew right at me out of the water. It was a terrible dark night, and I could hardly see, but I hit him a rap over the head with my stump, and then I was obliged to let him run again, or he would have slewed my arm right off, and pulled me out of the boat as well, for I could not slip my cable. At last I got terribly tired, and so did Master Conger, for he let me haul him up alongside; Joe then came up with his boat, and we both whipped our gaffs into him amidships, and jerked him into the boat. When he got aboard I thought he would have knocked my old boat all to pieces, for he was fore and aft in a minute, and sent everything flying. I was only afraid he would get his tail on the gunwale (for congers is terribly strong in the tail) and then he would have hauled himself overboard; so I watched my chance, and hit him a crack just where his life lay, and then he was quiet at last.

'He was all six foot long and sixteen inches round the thickest part. His great head was like a sheep's, and his jaws was awful. I sold over four shillings worth of him, besides what I ate myself; and all along his back bone was fat, as fine and white as suet.

'He was a fish he was.'

FRANK BUCKLAND, *Curiosities of Natural History*

191

The Capture of a Big Skate off Looe, Cornwall, 1936

IT was a beautiful August day in 1936 and my father and I were fishing from *Paula*, a motor-boat owned and run by Bill Butters of Looe.

We had anchored about seven miles out from Looe and our baits were just on the edge of a rock about twenty fathoms down. I had been doing rather well with conger up to 20lb. on a handline, but my father had not had much sport when he seemed to have his tackle hung up. We were using the usual tackle for that part of the world – two longer hooks on whipcord laying on the bottom, and we assumed that one hook was caught in the rock.

Bill Butters told my father to leave it there as the other hook should be in a good spot and a bite might clear the jam.

After quarter of an hour my father tried again to free the hook and found that the weight would move a few inches after the line had stretched fully. He lifted it clear of the bottom and asked Butters to feel his line. We decided that it was a fish and Butters said: 'It's either a shark, a skate, or a submarine!' (My personal opinion favoured the sanguinary submarine!)

The fish came up fairly peacefully until he saw the light, then he just put his nose down and went straight to the bottom.

By this time there was a strong ebb-tide running down Channel and the fish took full advantage of this. My father slowly worked him up until we saw something flat and white shining in the water and said: 'Skate.' A couple of other boats fishing near by and a motor cruiser on its way to Plymouth had seen something of the struggle and gathered around to watch the *coup de grâce*.

The fish grew slowly bigger as he approached us until the boatman made a sure stroke with the gaff. He and I heaved together and the skate was aboard, gouging a lump out of the thwart with his thorny tail.

We tried to fish on, but were so excited that within half an hour we packed up and set course for Looe. As we approached the harbour mouth we saw a number of people looking at our catch as we stood triumphantly in the stern. Then, just as we passed the pier head, my hat blew off into the sea!

The only scales big enough to weight the fish were the coal scales, on which, the skate was found to weigh 156lb., nearly vindicating my estimate of 1½cwt.

So much for the skate, and I fear that there is nothing much to say about my father's 51-lb. conger caught from the same boat the next year. The boatman caught a mackerel weighing 4lb. 10oz., a British record, but unfortunately it was on a hand line and so not eligible for competition.

The only other exciting catch on rod and line was a crayfish of 8lb. which I caught on 30th August 1939.

S.-LT. S. C. YARDE, R.N.V.R.

It sometimes happens to us to recognise an old friend in the habit of a fisherman – perhaps afar in a boat disguised in sou'wester and oilskins, or on a distant shore by some lonely loch side.

And here, by the wild waters of the Western Ocean we came across an old friend who has given us many a pleasant hour in bygone years – no less a person indeed than the versatile cleric who writes under the name of George A. Birmingham.

In addition to his literary ability he must be credited with a high degree of courage in entrusting himself to one of those curraghs or coracles which the Irish fishermen make for themselves from odds and ends of lathe and canvas.

Night Fishing in a Curragh

KNOWING my fondness for the sea, he arranged with some local fishermen to take me out for the night in one of their curraghs. The curragh is a long, narrow, canvas-built boat. So long as she is kept on the sea and away from rocks she is safe if skilfully managed. She will ride dry in any sea and float like a feather over the foaming tops of breaking waves. But, of course, being made of canvas, the merest touch of a rock would rip the bottom out of her.

My host and I arrived at Porteen, 'the little haven,' for that is what the name means. It was seven o'clock, and the surging of the waters was already eloquent with that peculiar sadness which comes upon the sea in the evening, especially with an ebbing tide. This is one of the most noticeable emotions of the sea. Even one of the old Hebrew prophets, who knew little of the sea, though he knew all things else, observed it. 'There is sorrow upon the sea, so that it cannot rest.' I have no doubt that when he spoke he was looking on the waves in their mood of evening melancholy.

193

Four men stood waiting for me beside their curragh, the most primitive kind of boat there is in the world. In just such waterproof baskets the first of our race must have ventured, centuries before history began, upon the sea. Now, in the twentieth century, the curragh survives, practically unchanged and unimproved; what is more strange, for certain kinds of work unimprovable. It is still the best boat there is in surf round sandy shores.

The men looked at each other when they saw me, and I felt rather than saw, a half-smile in their glances. I came among them a stranger with a reputation. My host was responsible for that. He had, I gather, represented me as a boatman of skill and daring. These Achill islanders had made up their minds to test my nerve. They would take me, and they did take me into places which would have brought disaster upon any other kind of boat, places which they rightly calculated, which would be strange and fearful to me. We launched the curragh and embarked. We headed towards the distant Kim Bay, where we meant to fish. We pulled five oars. To me it seemed strange that the odd oar should be put out on to the windward side of the boat. But the curragh is a curious craft. You manage her by an inversion of all the ordinary rules of seamanship. We crept along as close as possible to the shore, fringed with black, jagged rocks, so close that we sometimes floated in the foamy backwash of the breaking waves. 'If you touched that fellow,' I said, pointing to a savage-looking tooth of rock, 'there'd be a rip in the bottom of the curragh in half a second.'

'It would be easy mended,' said one of the rowers. 'We'd put a bit of paper over it and melt the tar on top of it with a lighted match.'

I dare say this is true, but I am not over anxious to test it. I do not so hunger for strange experiences as to want to tempt fate with no more than a sheet of paper between me and the Atlantic Ocean. We passed through a passage between two grim masses of rock, a passage which an active man could have leaped across. The waves surged into either end of it, broke up against rocks, drew back to meet other advancing waves, buffeted each other into steep, rugged crests. The whole surface was a mass of seething, swirling foam. Once by stretching out my hand I could have touched a flat limpet-covered shelf of rock, flecked with the spume of rushing water. Our four rowers steadied the curragh, swept her round, swept her forwards. No words passed among them. Each man acted for himself but all seemed moved by some common instinct, by an incredible inborn skill.

Afterwards we skirted high cliffs. The cormorants perched above our heads, peered down at us with their narrow, cruel eyes. Circling gulls and terns shrieked at us. The waves swung us up upon their very crests and then crashed noisily against the cliffs within a few feet of us. We passed by caves, and from them came the hollow roar of the great surges which lashed sides and stony roofs somewhere far out of sight in fearful darkness. Once we paused and pushed our way, stern first, into a cave. Heavy drops of water from the roof suddenly fell on us. The sea crashed behind us, roared in front of us. We shouted together and beat our oars against the gunwale of the curragh. We succeeded at last in frightening from their nests a flock of pigeons. They went flapping wildly over our heads, and we yelled again to speed their terrified flight. We came at last to our bay, the very last in all this desolate coast. Achill Head, facing the Atlantic, casts behind it a sheltering arm round Kim Bay. High cliffs rise on either side of the bay, and its shoreward end is the steep green slope of the towering mountain of Croaghaun. It was getting dark then, and the rollers broke sullenly on the sandy beach. We landed on the rocks at the westward side of the bay, and then the work of the evening began. The net which lay hidden in the forlorn ruin of a hut, was carried down and piled in the stern of the curragh. Then, two men aboard of her, the boat put out, pushing her way through a smother of surf and breaking waves. Sometimes she reared like a wild horse, standing for an instant on her stern with her curved bow pointing to the sky. The rower, his oars outstretched in the air, waited calmly, balanced on his seat, until she fell forward and he could grip the water again. Then the curragh shot out, till the next breaker caught her and she reared once more. All the while a man in the stern was paying out the rope of which we, who stood on shore, held the end. Then, hand over hand, he flung the net into the sea and we dimly discerned the curved line of its floating corks. The boat made a wide circle and dropped two hundred and fifty yards of net, weighted and floated as she went. She returned to the shore fifty yards or so away from where we stood. Then came the slow work of hauling. We pulled at our end of the rope, dragging the net slowly shorewards foot by foot with heavy toil. We gripped the rope, passed it over our shoulders and step by step with bent backs dragged our way up the beach. At a certain point every man dropped the rope, ran down until he stood ankle deep in the water, gripped again, and again began the slow ascent. As the net itself came home, we edged gradually nearer our fellow labourers who hauled on the other rope. At first we saw them dimly, black figures patched against a grey background, sloped in their pulling so that, not seeing the rope on which they leaned, it was impossible to imagine why they should not fall. At last we came together and the net itself was in our hands.

Standing in shallow water we pulled it in hand over hand. We saw the splashing of the fish in the bag of it. We gathered it in and stood with our booty flapping against our feet and legs; white trout, sole, turbot, plaice, codling, gurnet, scores of coalfish, skates, dogfish, one great salmon, a twenty-pounder, and numberless crabs. It was a great haul. We flung them into a sack, filled it, and fetched another sack. We took all that were worth taking, groping with our hands for the brown-backed sole and turbot which we could not see. The skate and dogfish were left on the beach. The crabs we smashed, trampling them with our boots, because it is almost impossible to disentangle their claws from the meshes of the net.

'Look, there,' cried one of the men suddenly. 'Isn't it we who have the luck to-night?'

Twenty yards from the shore floated a dim black shape, monstrous in the gloom. It disappeared, appeared, again, a rounded smooth thing, horribly suggestive of danger.

'What is it?' I asked.

'A shark,' he said. 'A basking shark. I mind the time when one of them got into the net. We were out after him, beating at his head with the oars, but he got the net torn in spite of us, and, what's more, he very nearly had the curragh upset. They're terribly dangerous, them basking sharks.'

The row home was the most wonderful part of the whole expedition. It was dark as it ever is, far north here, in the month of June. The water was phosphorescent when the oars splashed into it. The bases of the cliffs where the waves broke shone with tiny sparks, lit and quenched in millions every second, flashing and extinct while the eye caught their light. The broken water looked at moments like a sheet of strange white fire. Far up above us, lost in utter gloom, were the summits of the cliffs. They overhung us, and there came, to me at least, a sense of awe from their dark immensity and from the melancholy rise and fall of the sea's roar as it beat against them. We shot through the narrow passage between the rocks again, and I felt, as the shining water surged and foamed round us, felt, I think for the first time in my life, the terror of the sea. It was two o'clock in the morning or thereabouts, when we landed, and we discussed, I remember, the faint light in the sky, wondering whether it was the last legacy of yesterday's sun, or the first promise of the day that was before us.

G. A. BIRMINGHAM, *Pleasant Places*

FISHERMEN'S HAUNTS

The Waters of Comfort

THERE are no more refreshing places in Hampshire, one might almost say, England, than the green, level valleys of the Test and Itchen, that wind, alternately widening and narrowing, through the downland country to Southampton Water. Twin rivers they may be called, flowing at no great distance apart through the same kind of country, and closely alike in their general features; land and water intermixed – greenest water meadows and crystal currents that divide and sub-divide and join again, and again separate, forming many a miniature island and long slip of wet meadow with streams on either side.

At all times refreshing to the sight and pleasant to dwell by, they are best:

'When it is summer and the green is deep.'

Greens of darkest bulrushes, tipped with bright brown panicles, growing in masses where the water is wide and shallowest; of grey-green graceful reeds, and of tallest reed mace with dark velvety brown spikes; behind them all, bushes and trees silvery leafed willow and poplar, and dark alder, and old thorns and brambles in tangled masses; and always in the foreground lighter and brighter

197

This Quiet Hour

sedges, glaucous green flags, mixed with great hemp agrimony, with flesh-coloured, white-powdered flowers, and big leafed comfrey, and scores of other water and moisture-loving plants.

Through this vegetation, this infinite variety of refreshing greens and graceful forms, flow the rapid rivers crystal-clear and cold from the white chalk, a most beautiful water, with floating water grass in it – the fascinating *Poa fluviatilis*, which, rooted in the pebbly bed, looks like green loosened wind-blown hair, swaying and trembling in the ever crinkling swift current.

They are not long rivers – the Test and Itchen – but long enough for men with unfevered blood in their veins to find sweet and peaceful homes on their margins. I think I know quite a dozen villages on the former stream, and fifteen or sixteen on the latter, in any one of which I could spend long years of perfect contentment.

W. H. HUDSON, *Hampshire Days*

A Strange Happening on the Beaulieu River

THE Beaulieu River is tidal, and at the full of the tide in its widest part beside the village its appearance is of a small inland lake, grown round with oaks – old trees – that stretch their horizontal branches far out and wet their lower leaves in the salt water. The village itself that has this setting with its ancient water-mill, its palace of the Montagus and the Abbey of Beaulieu, a grey-ivied ruin, has a distinction above all Hampshire villages, and is unlike all others in its austere beauty and atmosphere of old-world seclusion and quietude. Above all is that quality which the mind imparts – the expression due to romantic and historical association.

One very still, warm summer afternoon, I stood on the margin looking across the sheet of glassy water at a heron on the farther side, standing knee-deep in the shallow water patiently watching for a fish, his grey figure showing distinctly against a background of bright green sedges. Between me and the heron scores of swallows and martins were hawking for flies, gliding hither and thither a little above the glassy surface, and occasionally dropping down to dip and wet their under plumage in the water. And all at once, fifty yards out from the margin, there was a great splash, as if a big stone had been flung out into the lake; and then two or three moments later out from the falling spray and rocking water rose a swallow struggling laboriously up, its plumage drenched, and flew slowly away. A big pike had dashed at and tried to seize it at the moment of dipping in the water, and the swallow had escaped as if by a miracle. I turned round to see if any person was near, who might by chance have witnessed so strange a thing, in order to speak to him about it. There was no person within sight, but if on turning round my eyes had encountered the form of a Cistercian monk, returning from his day's labour in the fields, in his dirty black and white robe, his implements on his shoulder, his face and hands begrimed with dust and sweat, the apparition on that day, in the mood I was in, would not have greatly surprised me.

W. H. HUDSON, *Hampshire Days*

Blagdon

THERE is not a lovelier sight (*pace* Ramsbury and Hurstbourne Priors in buttercup time) in England than Blagdon from the Butcombe end at sundown, with the tiny town straggling up the steep hillside like a Bavarian village, the red roofs of the houses peeping out of the thick orchards (with never a Methodist Chapel to shock the artist's eye) and the evening sunlight setting the windows of the old church aglow and flushing with purple pink the glassy surface of the lake. There is a stillness here that belongs to no other valley. You can hear the 'plop' of the big trout far out, half a mile away. You can talk to your friend across the water without ever raising your voice, and hear the scream of his reel in the blackness, and Blagdon is about seven miles round, and he may be half the length of the lake from you.

But the dominant impression in my mind is of the lovely colour of the evening light upon the valley as you face it looking east. It has a crimson velvet glow which hangs like an Aurora on the meadows and makes the shores and the scolloped hills burn with fires. It is Devonshire clay here, and the whole landscape warms pink and deepens to purple black as the sun sinks lower.

I know, too, that there was once a witch in the valley, and that they drowned her when they let the water in; and one night as I grope my way home in the dark I shall stumble on Hansel and Gretel asleep on the grass in a mist of white angels, with the myriad million stars of the milky way and the golden lights of Blagdon shining on their heads and winking in the watery glass at their feet.

H. PLUNKETT GREENE, *Where The Bright Waters Meet*

Blagdon

THE lake, as most people know, is one of the reservoirs which supply the needs of the great City of Bristol, but though the work of men's hands it has as much beauty as any place of nature's making. At one end there is a great stone dam, and there is some suggestion of prose about the buildings behind it, but turn your back on them and you have nothing but poetry. On the right lies Blagdon village, scattered delightfully over twin spurs of Blackdown, a fortunate village which seems to have grown naturally in the most becoming manner, not too crowded nor yet too widespread, a village whose very existence is an answer to those who cavil at the English nation for not being blessed with artistic sense. I have known rises from four-pounders missed because the angler was so busy admiring Blagdon Village, with its grey church tower and wealth of fruit blossom, and one cannot praise it more highly than by that confession. On the left lie thickly wooded slopes with a picturesque farm or two nestling among the trees. In front is the lake almost as far as one can see, perhaps three-quarters of a mile wide at the Blagdon end and gradually narrowing till one comes to the mouth of the river Yeo, which runs in past Ubley Mill, grey stone among the trees, where are the stock ponds and hatchery.

All round the lake are hills, Blackdown, the highest point of the Mendips being one of them. Its thousand odd feet show very impressively when thunder threatens and affords a superb spectacle when the lightning plays upon their summit. To agitated human beings at that time the ascent to the village and shelter is formidable. I shall never forget the race that Lorenzo and I raced one Sunday afternoon, or the breathlessness of our entry just before the deluge.

The lake itself is more than commonly attractive apart from its surroundings. It is no mere ordinary sheet of water with a deep portion in the middle, shallow portion at the sides and other features of 'expectedness' if I may so term it. A chart showing all the variations and inequalities in its depth and bottom would be an interesting but complicated thing. Winding tortuously through the middle of the lake is the old river-bed of the Yeo and criss-crossed everywhere are ditches, dykes, a submerged lane or so, with occasional little pools and pot-holes marking the spots once occupied by duck-ponds or depressions in the fields. One result of this is that anywhere one is likely to come upon an unexpected bit of deep water subtly disposed even in a shallow corner, and, of course, in such a place one expects to find a big trout lurking secure, but willing if one can but put a fly before him. Another result is that the bank angler is tempted to take plenty of exercise, for beyond every bend he hopes for some of that variety which is so calculated to lure him on. There is something particularly tempting about the Blagdon ditches, dark blue or olive ribbons stretching out across the yellow or brown of the shallows.

H. T. SHERINGHAM, An Angler's Hours

The Pageant of the Seasons

HAMPSHIRE combines both plains and rivers, and her downs and her trout streams can be seen in combination. The fisherman's season begins on 1st of April. If the spring be such as that of 1924 there is very little change from winter. The broad meadows are still grey. The woods are bare of leaves. The row of beech trees at the top of the chalk cliff does not show a tinge of green, and you have to look close to see the buds on the hawthorn trees at its base. The reeds and sedges bordering the river, bleached by the winter rains, have a faded appearance, and the water, by contrast, looks dark and gloomy. The river runs full and fast and weedless, swirling down all its broad expanse. There are no flowers, for the kingcup, which ought to be in bloom everywhere, hardly shows its glossy leaves as yet, and even the blackthorn does not yet whiten the hedges. Nor have the spring birds arrived. True, snipe are drumming; lapwings, in search of nesting sites, are wheeling and crying; redshanks, wariest of birds are so silent that they may have started laying, and pairs of sandpipers are resting on their way north, but there are no sedge or reed warblers and neither chiff-chaff nor willow wren are to be heard. However, by every hatch or hedge is a couple of those birds which are almost, I think my favourites – grey wagtails. Why they are called grey I cannot imagine. Apart from their backs, which are bluish rather than grey, it is the brilliant sulphur yellow of their underparts which gives them their character, and anything less like so sober a word as grey cannot be imagined when you see these bright and glowing creatures either poised in the air or tripping delicately over a weed patch. A bird of the north and the west, yet they breed freely in Hampshire, and there were certainly six pairs at Mottisfont. And there are not many days on which you do not see the flashing blue of the kingfisher. As the year runs on, and evenings grow longer and lighter and the sun gains in power, the valley wakes up. The first abundant flower of the Test is the kingcup. No plant possesses a better sense of arrangement and its patches of gold are spread over the flat meadows more skilfully than the cunning gardener could have planted them, with a luxuriant wastefulness as though to tell everyone that spring has really come. The grass, too, of these meadows begins to look less grey, and the band of horses finds somewhat more to eat. And, when once the movement starts everything comes with a rush. The willows grow green, and the fine black poplars which stud the valley show their bluish leaves. Weeds of all colours choke the river, and sedges begin to shoot up. This time, mid- or late April is one of the most attractive of the year. Trees are bursting into leaf, all their leaves are different in colour, and you do not get that somewhat heavy monotony which a wooded country presents in summer. And there is an air of expectancy and new birth over the landscape. The full glory of flowering bushes and trees has not come yet and the climax has not been reached: but, as it is always better to anticipate than to possess, no season makes a deeper appeal to the imagination. It is a time of leaf more than of flower. The different tones of the different trees are seen at once and together. And, remember that the green of leaves is never seen so well as by water, particularly by running water, for light is reflected at all angles off the glancing surface, making them delicate and translucent. Already, too, the spring birds will have come. The chiff-chaff's double call tells you that winter has really gone, the falling cadence of the willow wren strikes on the ear like dropping water, while the grasshopper warbler is trilling that endearing and reel-like note of his which ought to make him the patron bird of anglers.

The next stage is when the flowering trees come out. Hawthorns love the chalk, and never do better than in Hampshire, gardens are gay with laburnum and lilac, and chestnuts blossom in the woods. In the meadows the kingcup is dying, but its place is taken by cowslips and dark orchids. There is no more beautiful combination of colour, and the yellow and the purple make an admirable contrast. And one by one the summer birds arrive. Yellow wagtails, yellow as canaries, trot on the bank; reeds and sedges are full of warblers; blackcaps are singing and flycatchers busy on the fence posts. The climax of the year has come, bringing the wild rose, the yellow iris and the mayfly. The iris is another great Hampshire flower, and is everywhere in masses, arranged as though nature had gardened it. And the river now has its summer appearance. Patches of the white cups of the water crowfoot lie on the surface, many a hooked trout takes refuge in one of those thick jungles which fishermen call celery beds, the water grows crystalline, its surface flecked with windblown petals and pollen of the grass, trout come suddenly into sight, iron blues sail down in droves, and islands of dead weed form round the piers of bridges. The grass in the hay fields is growing long, large daisies appear in it, moths fly at night, and the hedges are starred with wild roses. The evening rise begins, red sedge flies blunder on to the surface, and you can fish till ten o'clock. Then June passes, birds have hatched their young, and family parties of linnets and goldfinches splash themselves at the shallow edge of the gravelly ford. As the year runs on, and the hay is cut, the valley loses individuality. It remains beautiful, but less distinctive. There are no flowering trees, and the only bush is the guelder rose, not enough by itself, though graceful. I never see its ivory flowers without thinking of chalk streams. There is a pause in nature, until the late summer flowers come. And they do come, in quantities, and at no time are the banks so gay. Clusters of mimulus with its melted gold, thick spires of purple loosestrife, the homely comfrey, the tall columns of mullein make a brilliant garden: ditches are full of meadow-sweet and the air is heavy with its scent, patches of yellow ragwort cover the bottom of the wood and willow herb is so thick that it looks like a pink mist. Some of these flowers last all through the hot days of July and August, until the turn of the year. Then we slip into autumn, catch perhaps a few fish in September, linger as long as we can, and finally say goodbye to the valley until next April.

But, before you go, do not forget to pay a tribute to the loveliest of all Test flowers, the loveliest and the rarest, the balsam. It is unmistakable with its olive-dark leaves and its red and orange blossoms, looking remote and exotic, more in keeping with an equatorial forest than our keen and strenuous air. It is not in full bloom till September. It is a wayward creature, because in some years it disappears entirely and in others it is difficult to find. But when it is plentiful it is one of the great sights afforded by English flowers. There are few places in these islands where it grows at all, and there can be still fewer where it blossoms so luxuriantly as on the Test.

J. W. HILLS, *A Summer on the Test*

The Myth

Where the bulrushes grow ranker
  (Oh, the long green spears a-gleam!)
There the punt shall rock at anchor
  In the stream;
By the weir's cool curve of thunder,
By the stones where wagtails plunder
  Foolish daddy-long-leg flies,
And the strings of rainbow bubbles in a rhapsody arise!

Hours may pass and go fleeting,
  You shall head them not, but stay
Lost to them and all the sweeting
  Of the may;
For beneath the swelling current
Where the midge-cloud hangs sussurant,
  And the sweeping swallows go,
Lives a most prodigous monster, lurking learnedly and
  slow!

No! I've never really seen him
  But the boatman tells a tale
Of a something (must 'a been 'im)
  Like a whale,
On the shelving shallow showing
'Where them kingcups is a-growing'
  Only just the other night,
And the frightened fry went leaping from the presence
  left and right!

But a crafty old cumudgeon
  He must be, for ne'er a fin
Does he move for any gudgeon
  That you spin;
With a wink he maybe watches
'Neath the willow-roots dark notches
  As you toil with aching wrist,
But the landing nets no nearer, nor the deft taxidermist!

But the skies are smiling bluely
  There is a shade along the shore,
And the chestnut's litten newly
  Lamps a score;
Drop the rod then and be thankful
For the sights that fill the bank full –
  Verdant reeds and ancient stems
And the broad paternal bigness and the peace of Father
  Thames!

  PATRICK CHALMERS, *Green Days and Blue Days*

Weir Pools

IT has something to do with the liveliness of the falling water, I suspect, that the weir pool is so beloved of anglers. The open reaches can be, and often are, so dull when fish are out of humour or of doubtful numbers. After watching an undisturbed float or casting a futile spinning-bait or fly for a number of hours, one is apt to lose heart about the business, and regard the unchanged yet ever changing expanse of water with a jaundiced eye. Why on earth should fish in such monotonous surroundings ever bite, or run or rise? Why, indeed, should fish be there at all? Why should a man be Boeotian enough to try and catch them, making of the practice of angling a mere iteration of purposeless manual exercises? At this point one would be quite likely to pack up and go home were it not for the sudden remembrance of the weir pool. Why, yes, of course, there is exactly what one wants – foam, turmoil, eddies, old piles, little commotions on the distance like feeding fish, shoals of minnows close to the camp sheathing, and all the variety that can charm a soul oppressed by too much sameness. So one shoulders the creel and goes thither at once. Being come to the weir pool, does one get sport? Here I confess I am minded to answer cautiously, after the fashion of those beyond the Border. Such a statement as 'Whiles' about expresses the facts. If the fish are not feeding elsewhere, there is not likely to be great slaughter at the weir pool; conversely, if there is great slaughter at the weir pool, a small sum might be safely wagered that they are feeding with considerable heartiness in other places, which would seem to destroy the foundations of one's faith in the foam, turmoil, eddies, and the rest of it. But the cautious answer does not, after all, quite cover the question, because it takes no account of the occasional fish, of which, my experience has been, the normal weir pool is more generous than the normal open reach. I believe one can generally get some proof of the existence of fish in a weir pool in the shape of bites or what not, even though elsewhere no signs have been vouchsafed.

I remember once exploring a little brook, narrow, sluggish, and sinuous, which had the reputation of holding quite large trout. It was somewhat heavily bushed and possessed some likely pools and corners, into most of which I insinuated a March brown in the orthodox wet fly manner. But never a fish did I move or see, except one small one that fled off a bit of gravelly shallow, and I began to think that the brook's reputation was fallacious and my informant something worse. At last, however, I came to a mill, no longer worked, but still dividing the stream into two channels. One of these began with a six-foot fall, over which a mere trickle of water splashed on to a large flat stone, and so into a little pool, perhaps twenty feet long and fifteen feet wide. The water was not more than three feet deep at the most, and the bottom was covered practically everywhere with a dense growth of silkweed, which showed how little stream had passed through that summer. Still, such as it was, the place was a weir pool, and caused hope to revive slightly. The best spot was, of course, where the trickle came over the stone, and made a slight disturbance in the pool; and there, sure enough, a good fish rose as soon as the fly fell. After a brisk fight, complicated by silkweed it came to the net, and proved to be nearly two pounds. The pool also yielded a small trout of a few ounces which was returned, and, after an interval of rest, a third of over a pound, thus making something like a good day out of what had seemed a certain blank.

At the time I thought it probable that there were hardly any trout in the other parts of the brook, and that the few survivors of rustic attack had taken up their quarters in the most favoured spots, such as the weir pools and mill ponds, a thing I had noticed in another very similar brook; but on subsequent visits I found there was a fair head of fish after all, catching a few and seeing others. Therefore I am inclined to ascribe the success to the merits of the weir pool as such. And other instances of a similar kind might be adduced as, for instance, a nice little dish of quarter-pound trout taken during a time of great dearth in Wales when the main river was yielding practically nothing. But an insignificant tributary burn was found with several little falls at short intervals and from each little pool came one or two little trout, but none from any other part of the stream. Weir pools, strictly speaking, they were not, but the incident has some bearing on the subject. Then again one might dwell on the chalk stream, and the frequency with which one finds a fish rising in a weir pool or a hatch hole when nothing is stirring elsewhere. Frequently has a well-oiled fly cast at a venture on the rough water fetched up a decent fish and helped a meagre basket, to say nothing of the alder or March brown which in times of stress has achieved like result without aid of oil. The wet fly in the hatch hole is – but perhaps I had better indicate it only, and so pass on.

Are trout which live in turbulent waters possessed of better appetite than those of the still places, or is it merely that the angler's lure is better disguised? . . . If a man is keen and confident he loses no chances, neglects no likely spots, and does not think it too much

207

trouble to change his method of lure if things are not going briskly. . . . Even in the foam of the fall fish can acquire a surprising knowledge of hooks, dressings, and gut; but for a weir pool to be no more productive than any other given part of the river it must, I should say, have been considerably harder fished. The Thames weir pools are hard enough fished, in all conscience, yet they give a surprising amount of sport to their many devotees. Nor can one wonder, apart from that, that they are favourite spots, for they have their own magic. The great river thundering over all barriers to the sea, the thought of those mighty trout, barbel, chub, and perch which surely inhabit the mysterious depths, the play of sunlight in the foam, the faint sweet scent of water-weeds, nowhere so noticeable as near the fall, all these are reasons enough why one should love to ply the angle here above all places. The open reaches are lovely and desirable at their proper times, but to the weir pool one always returns at the last.

H. T. SHERINGHAM, An Open Creel

The Valley of Enchantment

THERE are many places in England that a man remembers when he is tired and worn and old, or when he is hammering out a living in some tropic country or campaigning under foreign skies.

But he who has once lived awhile beside a Hampshire chalk stream, he will have the most tender and lovable memories, and, remembering, something will clutch at him, at his very heart's core, and he will feel like a man a-thirst in a heated and weary land.

For he will be thinking of a certain Hampshire valley where there is a village, a hidden village with a diminutive church which has a steeple-spire, almost like a toy in a child's model 'lay-out.'

He will see his own house among the limes – with the green lawn and orchard, which goes down to the river, in the early glow of a June evening.

There are swifts curving in a hazy golden light, rushing in a screeching band about the lichened tiles of the garage roof (they nest there, under the eaves.)

The air is richly fragrant with the scents of lush hedges, trees, and mowing grass, newly arrayed in their fresh summer dress. The snowy hawthorns – ah! those Hampshire hawthorns! – are almost past their best, but other blossoms deck the hedges and the meadows, the first dog rose bud will soon be breaking.

And as he makes his way through the orchard (where the white delicate froth of the 'gix' reaches to his knees) he hears the bubbling call of cuckoos from the willow thicket by the river, and the drowsy purr of turtle doves.

Then he is out of the dappled shade of the old apple trees, his shadow long across the grass of the water meadows. It is not possible to see very far in this gossamer-gold light for the valley is filled with a magic gauzy atmosphere, and over the luxuriant wet meadow, studded with innumerable flowers – milkmaids, clover, buttercups, creamy froth of meadowsweet, and uncounted variety of grasses – the mayflies are a-dancing, though soon every insect will be down.

There are no meadows anywhere in the world like these lush Test water-meadows, Elysium fields indeed; it seems a sacrilege to walk upon them! And so – the river is reached. Here is the most beautiful thing of all. So clear and clean, one can imagine such a stream has a Divine origin it is so spotless and pure, with its blurred white bed, and its impenetrable fairy subaqueous forests of 'celery' and poa grass, the exquisite islands of water-crowfoot, each a picture in itself.

The tiniest smut or black whirling particle is visible at once as it is borne along with the sweet current and eddies.

Wild iris and every variety of sedge and reed fence it in and there, in mid-stream, fixed like jewelled fish in transparent colourless amber, two trout are poised, one in the rear of the other. Occasionally one will give a very slight sideways lurch and his tail flutters, otherwise you would never believe they were alive.

So crystal-clear is that water you can see the little coloured cloudy spots on their gill covers and the reflection of the white chalk river-bed upon their stomachs.

It is the climax, this sight of unearthly fish, exquisitely jewelled beings in a jewelled setting.

On the faint soft wind which puffs once, so warm and so full of fragrance on the cheek, there comes the sleepy murmur of the weir by the mill, and the milkmaid flowers droop over the 'carriers.' Here indeed, as Hudson wrote, might a man with 'unfevered blood in his veins' find contentment and peace everlasting.

So the exile – remembering – takes hope that some time he will see that green valley again, and the heat and the burden of the day is lessened.

'BB', *Fisherman's Folly*

A Summer Night

THE June evening is almost over. The rosy light fades from the oaks, and from the willows the voices of the doves are ceasing; out of the nettles that hide the angler's lair comes one talking to himself. It seems natural in this light with the bats wheeling capriciously in the air. We follow him and his wicker basket along the footpath separating the wood and weed from plantations of young fruit trees, newly fenced with tall tarred stakes.

His walk, and ours, emerges into a lane, and he goes into a large white house with a quince tree by its gate – outpost to a few thatched cottages, an alehouse, a workshop, and a duck pond with the ducks asleep on the shore. We envy him the wide diamond window where he will be sitting a little later to enjoy the look and presence of the night.

The time is happy and serene, the darkness not that forbidding shroud which falls so often when there is no moon, but sweetly awake, luminous; the far-stealing dawn seems already to be glancing on the horizon of rounded hills and rising orchards. At times from the woods by the river, or woods by rivers of another world, a sigh passes through the element, and dimly answered by our trees for a brief moment is lessening away towards the horizon. We may fancy in such a night that it is the spirit of the wild cherries among the woods by the river, communing with their kindred sheltered here about the hamlet. The small, child-like complaint of birds awakened by fear is still again; and to us the hawthorn thickets round cattle-waterings far away at the end of the pastures are made as clear as though seen at noonday by the eclogues of nightingales.

Then comes your little suspecting owl to alight on the gate and at last discovers us. The pheasant's clamour, the fox's bark, do not disturb this world of dewy tranquillity. The whistle of the trains on the main line comes transformed into a voice of reverie, the rushing wheels only send us a murmur like the songs of the little waterfall below this gloom of fragrant interweaving boughs.

EDMUND BLUNDEN, *The Face of England*

INDEX OF AUTHORS

ACKNOWLEDGEMENTS

The Editor wishes to thank the following authors and publishers who contributed to this book and have allowed him to include extracts from the following works: to George A. Birmingham and William Heinemann Ltd, *Pleasant Places*; to Mr. Ernest Phillips and Allen & Unwin Ltd, *Float Fishing*; to Sampson Low, *Waterside Sketches* by 'Red Spinner'; to J.M. Dent Ltd for the extracts by W.H. Hudson from *Hampshire Days* and *Far Away and Long Ago*; to Arthur Ransome, Jonathan Cape Ltd and the *Manchester Guardian* for essays from *Rod and Line*; to Mr. Negley Farson and Country Life Ltd, *Going Fishing*; to Mr. Skues and A & C Black Ltd, *Nymph Fishing for Trout*; to Mr. Edmund Blunden and Longman Green & Co Ltd, *The Face of England*; to Mr. Percy Lubbock and Jonathan Cape Ltd, *Earlham*; to Thomas Nelson & Son and Mr. A.R.B. Haldane, *The Path by the Water*; W. Earl Hodgson and A. & C. Black Ltd, *Salmon Fishing*; to Major Kenneth Dawson and Country Life Ltd, *Modern Salmon and Trout Fishing*; to H.D. Turing and Herbert Jenkins Ltd., *Trout Fishing* and to Herbert Jenkins Ltd for the extract from Francis Francis' *A Book on Angling*; to Mr. Eric Taverner and Seely Service, *Salmon River*; to Mr. Macdonald Robertson and Herbert Jenkins Ltd, *In Scotland with a Fishing Rod*; to Richard Walker and McGibbon & Kee, *Still Water Angling*.

He would also like to thank all those anglers who have contributed their own experiences of battles with big fish, both game and coarse fish: Mr. Albert Buckley; the Reverend Alston; Mr. D. Bateman; Mr. H. Evans; Mr. J. Webb; Sir Harold Gillies; Mr. Frank Barber; Mr. W.E.B. Smith; Lt. G.C. Yarde; Sq.-Ldr. H.C. Norton; Mr. Victor James; Mr. Neville Bostock. Thanks are also due to Mrs. Muriel Cameron for obtaining the story of the Chef of Beauly Castle; to Mr. Derek Barber for the "Bishop Browne" story; to Dr Starkie for his recipe; to Mr. John Thompson and Mr. Alexander Barclay for their contributions.

This book does not pretend to be a complete Anthology, and a host of famous angling authors have had to be omitted through lack of space. But as far as possible, I have cut out much of the 'technical' side of fishing, and have given only stories of actual incidents which should be of interest to fishermen.

THE EDITOR